Religious Diversity in the UK

Religious Diversity in the UK

Contours and Issues

Paul Weller

continuum

Continuum

Continuum International Publishing Group
The Tower Building
11 York Road
London SE1 7NX
www.continuumbooks.com

80 Maiden Lane
Suite 704
New York NY 10038

British Library Cataloguing-in-Publication Data
A catalogue record for this book is available from the British Library.

ISBN: HB: 0-8264-9897-3
        9780826498977
        PB: 0-8264-9898-1
        9780826498984

Library of Congress Cataloging-in-Publication Data

Weller, Paul, 1956–
    Religious diversity in the UK : contours and issues / Paul Weller.
        p. cm.
    Includes bibliographical references and index.
    ISBN-13: 978-0-8264-9897-7 (HB)
    ISBN-10: 0-8264-8782-3 (HB)
    ISBN-13: 978-0-8264-9898-4 (pbk.)
    ISBN-10: 0-8264-8783-1 (pbk.)
    1. Great Britain–Religion. I. Title.
    BL980.G7W45 2008
    200.941'090511–dc22

                                2007037288

Typeset by Fakenham Photosetting Limited, Fakenham, Norfolk
Printed and bound in Great Britain by Athenaeum Press Ltd, Gateshead, Tyne and Wear

Dedication

This book has three dedications:

First of all, it is dedicated to the university students and other adult learners whom, during my professional life, I have had the privilege of working with in both formal and informal settings.

Secondly, it is dedicated to Dr. John Hey who, during his years of full-time work at the University of Derby was a committed and inspirational teacher and highly respected colleague and whom, during his retirement, I am privileged still to be able to call a friend.

Finally, it is dedicated to the Sociology team at the University of Derby, who have taken the initiative in offering an undergraduate module on 'Religion and Society' which I hope, in time, will form the basis for the further development of provision in this critically important area of study.

Contents

Acknowledgements

1 General Acknowledgements

The figure of 'The Preacher' in the biblical Book of *Ecclesiastes* (1 v. 9) declared: 'What has been will be again, what has been done will be done again; there is nothing new under the sun.' In writing for publication, authors are always conscious of a debt of gratitude to those who have published before them and which should be acknowledged, not only when intellectual property rights and copyright law require formal permissions, but also out of professional gratitude.

Therefore, as follows, the permission of relevant publishers and copyright holders to draw upon some previously published work for this volume is gratefully acknowledged while acknowledgement is also offered, as appropriate, where use has been made of co-authored materials. In addition, where the text of the present volume incorporates material that has been presented by the author in public, but has not yet been published, details are given of the event at which the original paper was presented.

At the same time, in no case should any co-author, publisher or commissioner of research be held responsible for any errors of fact or emphasis in the present text. These remain the responsibility of the author alone, as are any views that may be expressed by the author. Every attempt has been made to identify and contact the owner(s) of any copyright material appearing in this book. In the event of any appearing without due acknowledgement, such oversight will gladly be corrected in any reprints or future editions.

2 Acknowledgements and Permissions

Chapter 1 of the present volume includes numerical data on religious affiliation taken from the results of the 2001 decennial Census sourced from National Statistics (www.statistics.gov.uk). This is presented in absolute numbers in tabular form, and is used as a basis for related percentage calculations and textual discussion developed by the author. The chapter also uses data from *Census Table 275: Religion (Most Detailed Categories)*. In both instances, the original Census data is Crown copyright. Crown copyright material is reproduced with the permission of the Controller of HMSO.

Estimates of 'community membership' for the year 2000 and 'Church membership' for 2001, as well as some data on 'Christian-related' groups are quoted from P. Brierley, ed., *UK Christian Handbook: Religious Trends 4, 2003/4* (London: Christian Research). This is also presented in absolute numbers in tabular form and, again, the percentage calculations and the textual discussions are the author's.

A proportion of the text of chapter 1 draws upon material originally published in a chapter entitled 'The Changing Religious Landscape' that appeared in P. Weller (2005), *Time for a Change: Reconfiguring Religion, State and Society* (London, T. & T. Clark, pp. 69–124). Thanks are therefore extended to T. & T. Clark for their agreement to draw upon that work for use also in this volume. In this volume, this material has been reworked and updated also by reference to and use of material drawn from the 'Religious Landscape of the UK' chapter of P. Weller, ed. (2007), *Religions in the UK: Directory, 2007–10* (Derby: University of Derby and Multi-Faith Centre at the University of Derby, pp. 21–89).

The *Religions in the UK* directory is a general work of reference on the principal world religious traditions with significant populations in the UK, and the directory's accompanying CD-ROM contains contact and other details of religious organizations and places of worship in the UK. The present edition of the directory is the product of a longstanding project that builds on previous editions in which The Inter Faith Network for the UK and the University of Derby (1993 and 1997) and The Inter Faith Network for the UK and the Multi-Faith Centre at the University of Derby (2001) were project partners before the Inter Faith Network transferred its intellectual property to the Multi-Faith Centre in 2006, whose permission as current publishers and copyright holders of the directory, together with the University, should therefore be acknowledged.

Demographic and socio-economic data and discussion that was first published in a co-authored report by J. Beckford, R. Gale, D. Owen, C. Peach, and P. Weller (2006), *Review of the Evidence Base on Faith Communities* (London: Office of the Deputy Prime Minister, http://www.communities.gov.uk) has also been drawn upon and reworked in summary form into chapter 1, together with some direct quotations and the inclusion of a number of figures.

Acknowledgements are therefore due to the copyright holder of that report – the University of Warwick – and to the co-authors of the report, Professor James Beckford, Dr. Richard Gale, Dr. David Owen and Professor Ceri Peach. Special acknowledgement is made of Professor Peach's and Dr. Owen's work as the main originators and drafters of the relevant chapter ('Overview of the Hindu, Muslim and Sikh Populations of England', Beckford, et al., 2006: 10–37) in the original report. That report's chapter on 'Planning and Faith Communities' (Beckford, et al., 2006: 52–61) – of which Dr. Richard Gale was the main originator and drafter – is also drawn upon in summary form, together with some direct quotations, in chapter 2 of the present volume.

In addition, chapter 2 draws on materials relating to planning issues and places of worship, including some direct quotations, from the co-authored report P. Weller, A. Feldman and K. Purdam, et al. (2001), *Religious Discrimination in*

England and Wales, (London: Home Office, Research, Development and Statistics Directorate) originally found in that report's chapter on 'Housing and Planning' (Weller, et al., 2001: 63–78). That report was the product of a research project (1999–2001) of which the present author was Project Director. The report's other principal co-authors – Dr. Kingsley Purdam and Dr. Alice Feldman – were, respectively, Project Research Officer and Project Field Officer. Others in the research team included Professor Marie Parker-Jenkins (Associate Project Director), Mr. Ahmed Andrews, Ms. Anna Doswell, Professor John Hinnells, Mrs. Sima Parmar and Mrs. Michele Wolfe, and at various stages in the project: Mrs. Karen Rowlingson, Dr. Martin O'Brien and Ms. Lynne Kinnerley. Contributions to the project final report were also made by: Ahmed Andrews, Anna Doswell, John Hinnells, Marie Parker-Jenkins, Sima Parmar and Michele Wolfe.

Chapter 2 also draws upon materials relating to places of worship in the 'Religious Landscape of the UK' chapter of *Religions in the UK*, as well as on sections that deal with worship and places of worship in the chapters that introduce each of the religions covered in that directory. Those original chapters were developed in dialogue with consultants who have standing from within the religious groups concerned, together with academic experts. The names of these consultants, as well as those for the directory's 'Religious Landscape' chapter, are recorded in the 'Acknowledgements' chapter of *Religions in the UK* (Weller, ed., 2007: 329–38). The 'Religious Landscape' chapter is also drawn upon and reworked to contribute to parts of chapters 3, 4 and 6 of the present volume.

Chapter 3's discussion of *The Satanic Verses* controversy and the blasphemy laws draws on work in the author's unpublished doctoral thesis, P. Weller (1996), *The Salman Rushdie Controversy, Religious Plurality and Established Religion in England* (Leeds: University of Leeds). It also draws on material in a paper on 'Whose Justice From Which Perspective? Sex, Blasphemy, Religion and Law: The Satanic Verses Controversy in Retrospect' which was given to a seminar series on 'The Idea of Justice – In Literature, Religion and Law', at the Oxford Centre for Christianity and Culture, Regent's Park College, University of Oxford, 26 October 2004. Material on incitement to religious hatred draws on an unpublished paper by the author on 'Incitement to Religious Hatred: What Is It All About?', presented to the Faiths Regeneration Project, Leicester Faiths Regeneration Network Event, at Leicester Cathedral Centre, 20 March 2006.

Chapter 4's discussion of the representation of organized religion in the second chamber of the Westminster Parliament draws on a paper that was presented as P. Weller (2000), 'Written Submission to the Royal Commission on Reform of the House of Lords with special reference to the Role of Organized Religion in The Second Chamber', and published in *A House for the Future*, an accompanying CD to the report of The Royal Commission on Reform of the House of Lords, *A House for the Future: A Summary*, Cm 4534

(London: Royal Commission on Reform of the House of Lords), which is Crown copyright.

Chapter 4 also draws on a report of a research project undertaken in the city of Derby by P. Weller and M. Wolfe (2004), *Involving Religions: A Project Report on Religious Group Participation, Interfaith Infrastructure and Capacity-Building in Derby* (Derby: School of Education, Health and Sciences, University of Derby), acknowledgements for which are therefore due to Michele Wolfe as co-author.

Chapter 5's discussion of religion and higher education draws on unpublished papers on 'The Religious Landscape of Higher Education', given by the author to the Conference of Methodist Chaplains in Higher Education on *Chaplaincy at the End of the Age*, at St. Francis Hall, the University of Birmingham, Birmingham, 8–10 January 1997; and on 'Religious Understanding in a Modern University: An Exploration of Faith', delivered on 28 November 2005 at the Lecture Theatre Building on the Wivenhoe Park Campus as part of the *40th Anniversary Celebrations of the Foundation of the University of Essex*.

Finally, chapter 6 includes some materials that draw from various places in the previously mentioned report on *Religious Discrimination in England and Wales*, as well as from P. Weller and K. Purdam, et al., (2000), *Religious Discrimination in England and Wales: An Interim Report* (Derby: University of Derby).

3 Other Acknowledgements

Thanks and acknowledgements are also recorded to Rebecca Vaughan-Williams, Commissioning Editor for Religious Studies at the Continuum International Publishing Group for commissioning the volume, and for her enthusiasm about the project. Such thanks and acknowledgement are also extended to Tom Crick, Editorial Assistant: Humanities, for his help and support in the range of practical issues that need attention between the initial conception, the writing, and the final production of a book.

Days (and nights), hours and weeks in the study are involved in putting together a book of this kind. Therefore a final word of recognition and thanks is, as always, due to my wife, Margret Preisler-Weller; our son, David Weller; and our daughters, Lisa Weller and Katrina Weller, for their patience with my academic obsessions. The book is concerned with the contexts of their present lives and with issues of a kind that will surely continue to impact upon their lives in the future.

Introduction

1 Religious Diversity in the UK, the EU and the Wider Europe

'Three Dimensional' Religious Diversity: Issues and Possibilities

The primary focus of this book is on the religious diversity that is to be found in the contemporary religious landscape of the United Kingdom and the issues that arise from this diversity. In *Time for a Change: Reconfiguring Religion, State and Society* (Weller, 2005: 73), the author has summarized these issues in the following way:

> ... the contemporary religious landscape of the UK should be seen as exhibiting contours that are 'Christian, secular and religiously plural'. Thus, the contemporary socio-religious reality of England and the UK might be described as 'three-dimensional' in contrast with a more 'one-dimensional' Christian inheritance or the 'two-dimensional' religious-secular modifications made to that self-understanding during the course of the nineteenth and early twentieth centuries.

In the same publication it was noted that: 'Such a "three-dimensional" socio-religious reality is necessarily much more complex than a "one-dimensional" or a "two-dimensional" one' (Weller, 2005: 117) and that within that contemporary 'three-dimensional' landscape, 'a range of new points of intersection are developing between Christianity, religious diversity and secularity' (Weller, 2005: 116).

It is these points of intersection and the issues and debates that arise from them that form the focus of the present volume. Since these issues touch on so many aspects of private, family, civil society and public life, understanding of them is an increasingly necessary part of any rounded personal and vocational education and training.

Because of this, the present volume is written as a textbook. It is not, however, the kind of textbook in which one can look up all the answers. Rather, it is intended especially (although not exclusively) to support students in formal higher education by giving them access to some relevant information, encouraging them to ask some of the right questions, and then through further reading, tasks and discussions, to undertake their own explorations with the support of tutors. At the same time, it can also be used in more informal adult education settings by groups of people who are concerned to engage with a range of what are key social and religious issues in contemporary society.

The socio-geographical focus of the book, and therefore of the contexts and critical incidents with which it is concerned, is that of the UK. But it should also be noted that, within the UK, the political and legal contexts for these debates are becoming more distinctively national, regional and local while, at one and the same time, they are also increasingly being influenced by developments, initiatives, laws and conventions at European Union, wider European and international levels.

Religious Diversity and the Four Nations in the UK

The Scottish Parliament has been reconstituted and deals with some matters of devolved governance in relation to the Scottish Executive, the devolved government for Scotland, including significant aspects of law and social policy. A new National Assembly for Wales and the Welsh Assembly Government have been created, together with (as part of the peace process following the Good Friday/Belfast Agreement of 1998) the restoration of a Northern Ireland Assembly and the devolved government of the Northern Ireland Executive. There is no English Parliament, but within the English regions there are Regional Assemblies and Regional Development Agencies that, informed by national and local political and economic priorities, play a role in strategic and economic planning.

Thus, while the focus of the present publication is on issues to do with religion and plurality across the UK considered as a whole, these matters are increasingly taking on more national, regional and local forms as the structures for governance devolve to more national, regional and local levels. With increasing devolution, the issues with which this book is concerned are shaped by the variety of histories and contemporary profiles with regard to religious and cultural diversity that can be found in England, Wales, Scotland and Northern Ireland.

Constraints of space mean that it is not possible to deal with these differences in any great detail, although an attempt is made to take some account of this diversity, rather than to write only for an 'assumed' UK audience. But in using this volume especially in Northern Ireland, Scotland and Wales it will be necessary for groups of learners and their facilitators, in ways appropriate to their own specific national context, to contextualize and adapt the materials, learning outcomes and tasks presented.

Religious Diversity in the UK within the European Union and Wider Europe

Alongside the internal political devolution that is taking place in the UK, the issues with which this volume is concerned need to be considered in the context of the increasing social, legal and political significance of the European Union (EU), and especially so as the agenda of the EU widens from economic integration to include also social and political dimensions. This will be especially the case following the establishment, in 2007, of a Fundamental Rights Agency to take forward the EU's work in these areas on the basis of the extension of its competence to take appropriate action against discrimination on the basis of 'racial or ethnic origin, religion or belief, disability, age or sexual orientation'.

Debates over the eventually rejected EU Constitutional Treaty included a heated discussion about whether the Preamble to the constitution should contain any explicit reference to Christianity. This debate has also been connected with the question of whether it might be possible, at some point in the future, for Turkey – as a country in which Muslims numerically predominate – to become a full member of the EU.

Developments in the EU also need to be seen within the setting of the geographical, political and legal architecture of the wider Europe as a western outcrop of what extends geographically, politically, economically, culturally and religiously, into a much bigger Eurasian landmass. In this wider Europe, and over a number of decades, the Council of Europe has, within the framework of the *European Convention on Human Rights and Fundamental Freedoms*, carried out consistent work in the area of freedom of religion and belief.

Such work has become especially important in the context of the development of the post-Soviet states and societies of Central and Eastern Europe. There is also, of course, the important role of the European Court of Human Rights in terms of jurisprudence based on the *European Convention on Human Rights and Fundamental Freedoms*. Through its incorporation in domestic law via the *Human Rights Act*, 1998, the articles of the Convention now frame all legislative developments and policies of 'public bodies' in the UK by reference to the principle of equal treatment between 'religions' and 'belief'. Thus while space limitations mean that the emphasis is on examples and issues as these emerge specifically in the UK setting, at key points some cognizance will be taken of these wider EU, European and international contexts. It should therefore be possible for users of the book to build further upon this by reference to additional critical incidents and resources relevant to those wider contexts.

2 The Structure of the Book

This Volume and the Religions in the UK: Directory

As noted in the Acknowledgements of the present volume, in appropriate places this book draws upon a range of materials originally published in *Religions in the UK: Directory 2007–10*, edited by the author of the present volume. That directory aimed to be descriptive of the religious diversity of the UK. By contrast, while some material in this book also seeks to describe and inform, rather than seeking to present a relatively 'flat' descriptive summary, the main aim of the present volume is to facilitate critical exploration of the issues arising from that religious diversity.

There can thus be some benefit in using this book in tandem with *Religions in the UK* and its accompanying CD-ROM. For example, since it is not possible in this volume to set out detailed information concerning the beliefs, practices and organizations of the religions as they exist in the UK, the reader can find this in compact and accessible form in the *Religions in the UK Directory*. Access to the directory's accompanying CD-ROM that contains contact and other details of religious organizations and places of worship would be helpful in some of the learning tasks set out in chapter 2 of the present volume. Nevertheless, the present book has been written in such a way that it is possible to read and use it on its own.

The book proceeds by reference to a number of key issues and examples of 'critical incidents' that highlight a range of wider issues that are at stake and which each of the chapters aims to explore. Each chapter thus includes some learning outcomes that can be associated with consideration of the materials that are presented, together with a series of study activities and questions that are designed to help learners to reflect on, and to engage with, the issues that are highlighted. A 'Chronology of Key Religious Diversity-Related Events in the Past Two Decades' is also presented, providing a 'timeline' for critical incidents and developments that frames the issues explored in the main body of the book.

The Chapters of the Book

Following this introduction, chapter 1 offers a basic overview of the UK's religious diversity, drawing on census and other statistical information, alongside demographic and socio-economic data, and discussed by reference to religion and ethnicity. It also provides a general introduction to the key religious communities, their histories and patterns of presence in the UK.

Chapter 2 begins from the recognition that places of worship are a literal and physical part of the changing religious landscape. In addition, it is often the case that programmes of formal and informal learning involve organized visits to places of worship, sometimes including at least some encounter with the varied forms of religious practice that take place within them. Observation and reflection on places of worship and what goes on within them offers one important means of access to the fundamental beliefs and cultural traditions that are reflected in them. But in visiting the buildings and observing the activities that take place there there is a need for an appropriate etiquette, guidance for which is provided in this chapter.

Because of their symbolic meanings and the practical impact they have on the neighbourhoods in which they are located, places of worship can also become sites of contestation around issues concerned with planning approval. These planning issues in turn relate to wider issues concerning the development of, and limits to, the expression of religious plurality in the public sphere.

Chapter 3 explores themes in religion and governance, in the first instance through looking at the variety of structures and patterns that shape the relationships between religion(s), state and society in the UK, and in each of its countries. It then explores debates around the place of Anglican Bishops in the House of Lords and the possible alternatives to this, in the context of discussions about reform of the Second Chamber of Parliament. This is then set in the context of a recognition that, over the past decade, government at all levels has increasingly sought to bring religious groups into partnership initiatives, as key players in 'civil' society. It therefore examines the role of religious groups in relation to the notion of 'social capital'. By reference to a case study of local developments in the author's home city of Derby, this chapter also highlights the challenges attendant upon trying to identify appropriate forms for religious representation in public life. Finally, it encourages reflection on seven key theses around the relationship between religion, state and society that have been developed by the author out of a quarter of a century of academic and practical engagement with issues of religious diversity in public life.

Chapter 4 explores some of the key tensions in contemporary society around the plurality of religious beliefs and of non-religious perspectives, which have given rise to fundamental debates about the tensions that can exist between incitement to religious hatred, respect for religious beliefs and practice, and freedom of expression. These issues are explored with reference to well-known controversies such as those surrounding the publication of the book, *The Satanic Verses* (Rushdie, 1988) as well as, more recently, the play Behzti, and Jerry Springer the Opera. Also explored are debates around the appropriateness or otherwise of the current blasphemy laws and new legislation in the area of incitement to religious hatred.

Chapter 5 highlights the key relationships between religion and education, with particular reference at the level of schools to debates around the desirability or otherwise of so-called 'faith schools'. It also looks at emergent issues connected with religious groups in higher education institutions, including the activities of groups such as Hizbut-Tahrir, and tensions between Christian Unions and Student Unions.

Chapter 6 examines the emergence of religion as a distinctive 'strand' in equal opportunities policy and practice as it stands at the intersection between religion, human rights, discrimination and the law. This is explored in the context of growing debates around the future of multiculturalism in the light of the 7/7 bomb attack on the London transport system. This is explored also in relation to issues around a perceived 'separatism' on the part of some groups, which became focused on the symbolically charged question of whether or not it is appropriate for Muslim women to wear full body and face covering in public.

In order to promote further study, each chapter contains a bibliography presented in the form of a concluding section on 'Resources for Further Learning'.

3 A Note on Terminology

The collective descriptors of 'Buddhist', 'Christian', 'Hindu', 'Jewish', 'Muslim', 'Sikh' and others, appear in this volume from this point onwards without being qualified by the inverted commas used above. This reflects general practice in public policy discussion and debate about religion(s) in the UK.

Use of these categories reflects the way that the decennial Census of population deals with religion and it is also embodied in the descriptions and structures of many University courses on religion(s), notwithstanding the fact that scholars of religion are highly aware that the apparent clarity and simplicity of these categories can mask a substantial range of diversities and issues. Ultimately, though, it should be acknowledged that these categories are abstractions of a much more highly complex religious, ethnic and cultural landscape, the nature of which it is important to keep in mind even while continuing to use these terms as convenient 'shorthand'.

Resources for Further Learning

Weller, P. (2007), *Religions in the UK: Directory, 2007–10*. Derby: University of Derby and Multi-Faith Centre at the University of Derby.

(Copies of the directory/CD-ROM can be ordered from: The Multi-Faith Centre at the University of Derby, Kedleston Road, Derby, DE22 1GB – see further details in the panel at the end of this book.)

Chronology of Key Religious Diversity-Related Events in the Past Two Decades

Publication of Salman Rushdie's *The Satanic Verses*	1988 (26 September)
Public burning of a copy of *The Satanic Verses* in Bradford	1989 (14 January)
Fatwa against Rushdie by the Ayatollah Khomeini	1989 (14 February)
Passing of the *Human Rights Act*	1998 (1 January)
Good Friday/Belfast Agreement in Northern Ireland	1998 (10 April)
Coming into force of *Human Rights Act*	2000 (1 January)
Bradford 'Riots'	2001 (7 July)
9/11 Attacks on World Trade Center and Pentagon, USA	2001 (11 September)
Employment Equality (Religion or Belief) Regulations, 2003	2003 (2 December)
The play *Behzti* opens at the Birmingham Repertory Theatre	2004 (9 December)
Broadcast on BBC2 of *Jerry Springer: The Opera*	2005 (8 January)
7/7 Attacks on the London Transport System	2005 (7 July)
Equality Act, 2006	2006 (16 February)
Religious and Racial Hatred Act, 2006	2006 (16 February)
Formal Inception of Commission for Equality and Human Rights	2007 (1 October)

Religious Diversity and the Contours of the UK Religious Landscape

Learning Outcomes for Chapter 1

After studying this chapter, and referring to a range of its associated
Resources for Further Learning, you should be able to:

(i) *describe* the ways in which it might be appropriate to see the UK as
'Christian', as 'secular' and 'religiously plural' by reference to
(a) selected population groups
(b) statistical information
(c) key historical developments

(ii) *describe* key features of Christianity and at least one other religion
covered in the chapter in relation to the way in which it has developed
in the UK

(iii) *discuss* what statistical data on religions in the UK does and does not
tell us, by reference to the Census and selected other data sources and
examples

(iv) *discuss* the nature of 'the secular' in the religious landscape of the UK
by reference to statistical and other material

(v) *evaluate* the relationship between religion, ethnicity and migration in
relation to the main contours of the contemporary religious landscape
of the UK

1 Inheritance and Change

The rapid pace of global and national change that took place in the latter half of
the twentieth century means that the contours of the religious landscape of the
United Kingdom are today, in many ways, very different than was the case only
fifty years ago (Badham, ed. 1989; Wolffe, ed., 1993; Davie, 1994; Parsons, ed.,

1993, 1994; Gilley and Sheils, eds, 1994; Avis, ed., 2003). Today, that landscape is perhaps best described as 'Christian, secular and religiously plural' (Weller, 2005: 73).

The Christian inheritance remains the predominant religious tradition. But now, as also in many other European countries, Muslims form the largest religious group after Christians. In the UK there are also relatively large populations of Hindus, Sikhs and Jews, together with smaller numbers of Buddhists, Baháʼís, Jains, Zoroastrians and other groups. At the same time, while the nature, degree and impact of the processes referred to as 'secularization' are contested, significant numbers of people no longer identify with a particular religious tradition, community or group, and the relationship between religion(s) and public life has changed (Gilbert, 1980, 1994).

At the same time, religions in the UK continue to exhibit a considerable degree of vigour and significant numbers of people continue an active involvement in the corporate religious life. There are also significant numbers of people whose belief and practice can be described as 'folk religion' (Bailey, 1983, 1989), 'implicit religion', or 'residual Christianity'. Such people may turn to an active involvement in Christian religious life only, or mainly, at times of crisis or personal significance such as birth, marriage and death, or at festivals, such as Christmas. This can be part of a phenomenon that the sociologist of religion, Grace Davie (1990a), calls 'believing without belonging' which, for people of Christian background, can be manifested in what one of Davie's interviewees referred to as belief in 'an ordinary God' (Davie, 1990b).

Finally, there are individuals and groups who acknowledge their connection with a particular religious tradition but who find themselves in conflict with its official representatives over one or other single issue or across a whole range of ways of understanding the significance of that tradition. In individual instances this may or may not be linked with what the present author elsewhere calls 'belonging without believing' (Weller, 2005: 9) in which, while there may be disagreement with a range of beliefs and practices of a group, there can remain a strong sense of personal identification with the group.

Alongside those who have either a direct or indirect relationship with the major world religions, there are also those who follow other forms of religious life. Among these are groups often popularly referred to as 'sects' or 'cults' but which, in academic usage, have normally come to be described as 'NRMs' or 'New Religious Movements', as well as those who understand themselves as Pagans.

Another area of religious life, often described as 'New Age' spirituality (York, 1995), is characterized by a concern for personal growth and draws upon spiritual practices and traditions from a variety of sources, as can also be the case with those who follow esoteric teachings and traditions (Hanegraaff, 1996).

Finally, there are those who identify more generally with a concern for 'spirituality' (Heelas and Woodhead, et al., 2005) or a 'wholistic' approach to life

(Bloom, 2004) but not with a particular historic religious tradition, and/or those who unexpectedly find themselves having experiences that can be described as 'religious' or 'spiritual' in nature (Hay, 1982, 1990).

2 Counting Religion

Study Activity 1

After consulting the National Statistics Online Neighbourhood statistics at http:// neighbourhood.statistics.gov.uk/dissemination (search by postcode for ward and local authority data on 'religion', found within 'People and Society: Income and Lifestyles' data):

(i)   *discover* the local statistical profile for religion and belief for:

    (a) the local authority in which you live

    (b) the ward in which you live

(ii) *discuss* your local authority data for religion in comparison with:

    (a) your ward data for religion

    (b) UK data for religion

(iii) *discuss* (i) above in relation to a selection of other selected Census data (e.g., on ethnicity)

(iv) *evaluate* the significance of the data identified in (i) above and discussed in (ii) and (iii) above for:

    (a) your local authority

    (b) any religious group with which you may identify, or for your being of 'no religion'

The Census

With the exception of Northern Ireland (where a religion question had been asked in the Census since the inception of the Northern Ireland state), until the 2001 Census there had been no generally comparable data available on the size of the various religious groups in the UK (Barley, Field, Kosmin and Nielsen, 1987). In England, the only previous official Census relating to religion was conducted in 1851 and that focused on participation in public worship.

When considering the questions to be included in the 2001 decennial Census, the Office for National Statistics consulted both data users and religious communities on the desirability of including a question on religious identity. In the light of the outcomes of this consultation a question on religious affiliation was included in the 2001 Census for England and Wales. The necessary amending legislation to permit this was passed by the Westminster Parliament. The Scottish Parliament also passed the relevant legislation for a religion question to be included in the Census in Scotland.

As a result, in the 2001 Census, questions on religious identity were included on a voluntary basis in each of the four nations of the UK, with a range of differing pre-set options for response according to the country concerned. For Census respondents in Scotland, the questions were, 'What religion, religious denomination or body do you belong to?' and 'What religion, religious body or denomination were you brought up in?', and the sub-categories of 'Church of Scotland', 'Roman Catholic' and 'Other Christian, please write in' were also offered to Christian respondents.

In Northern Ireland, for the question, 'What religion, religious denomination or body do you belong to?' the pre-set responses offered were: 'Roman Catholic', 'Presbyterian Church in Ireland', 'Church of Ireland', 'Methodist Church in Ireland', and the general alternative, 'Other Christian, please write in'.

By contrast, for England and Wales, to the question 'What is your religion?' the only pre-set response offered to Christian respondents was that of 'Christian (including Church of England, Catholic, Protestant and all other Christian denominations)'. Hence no Census data is available that relates to Christian denominations in England and Wales or on a UK basis.

It should also be noted that it may be that use of the notion of 'belonging' in its Scottish and Northern Irish forms encouraged respondents to interpret the question in a 'harder-edged' way than the 'What is your religion?' question asked in England and Wales. Therefore, although one can often find UK figures quoted in relation to the religion questions in the Census, the differences in questions asked and responses offered mean that data relating to different parts of the UK may not be entirely comparable.

There remain, then, questions about the precise meaning of the Census results on religion (Weller, 2004a). But in terms of broad identification with a religion, as can be seen in Table 1, it would seem that religion remains a factor of at least some significance in the self-understanding of around three-quarters of the population of the UK (45,162,895 people or 76.8% of the population). Among these, Christians are by far the largest group, followed by Muslims; then Hindus and Sikhs; then Jews; then Buddhists; and then Jains, Bahá'ís and Zoroastrians.

Other Data

However other datasets – and in particular the British Social Attitudes Survey and the European Values Survey (Halman, 2001) – appear to give a different picture, indicating much lower numbers of people affirming religious belief than might be inferred from the results of the Census. Aspects of this will be explored further in the later section of this chapter on 'Humanism, Atheism, Religion and Belief'.

Table 1: Religion Responses in the 2001 Census by Country of the UK

Religion	England	Scotland	Wales	Northern Ireland	UK Total	UK %
Buddhist	139,046	6,830	5,407	533	151,816	0.3%
Christian	35,251,244	3,294,545	2,087,242	1,446,386	42,079,417	71.6%
Hindu	546,982	5,564	5,439	825	558,810	1.0%
Jewish	257,671	6,448	2,256	365	266,740	0.5%
Muslim	1,524,887	42,557	21,739	1,943	1,591,126	2.7%
Sikh	327,343	6,572	2,015	219	336,149	0.6%
Other Religion	143,811	26,974	6,909	1,143	178,837	0.3%
Total	38,190,984	3,389,490	2,131,007	1,451,414	45,162,895	76.8%
No religion	7,171,332	1,394,460	537,935	*	9,103,727	15.5%
Not stated	3,776,515	278,061	234,143	*	4,288,719	7.3%
No religion/ not stated	10,947,847	1,672,521	772,078	233,853	13,626,299	23.2%

*In Northern Ireland, separate statistics for those of 'No religion' and 'not stated' are not available.

Table reproduced from *Inter Faith Update,* 21, 3, the newsletter of the Inter Faith Network for the United Kingdom. Due to rounding, percentages may not total 100%.

At this point, though, it is important to underline that the Census questions were to do with religious affiliation, in the sense of broad identification with a religion, and that they did not ask about either religious belief or religious practice.

In the European Values Survey respondents were asked about how important religion is in their life. Of respondents in Great Britain 12.6% said 'very important' and 24.8% said 'quite important', while 33.0% said 'not important' and 29.7% said 'not at all' (Halman, 2001: 33). In the 2001 Home Office Citizenship Survey, from a list of fifteen things, respondents were asked to identify which they would say was important if using these words to describe themselves. Across all groups, ranking the items in order of frequency, 'religion' was ranked 9th. However, there was considerable variation of response between different ethnic groups. Thus, among 'Asians' religion was ranked as high as second, while for 'whites' it was as low as tenth (O'Beirne, 2004:18–19).

In this context, critics such as Voas (2003) and Voas and Bruce (2004) suggest that the relatively high Christian results of the Census might say more about how respondents perceive the challenge of religious plurality to a broad Christian cultural inheritance than about their own positive identification with Christianity. At the same time, even Voas and Bruce acknowledge that Christianity has a signif-icance that goes beyond the actual numbers of those who identify with it. Thus, as a result of its historical position Christianity is extensively woven into much of the fabric of the historical, artistic, cultural, legal and other aspects of the heritage of the UK and its constituent parts in ways that will be explored in the later chapters of this volume.

3 Geographical, Ethnic, Demographic and Socio-Economic Profiles

---

Study Activity 2

After reading section 2 and section 3 of the chapter:

(i) *describe* what key statistical information about the religious diversity of the UK tells us and does not tell us

(ii) *discuss*, in the light of 2001 Census data on religion and ethnicity, key aspects in the diversity of the contemporary religious landscape of the UK

(iii) *evaluate* the relationship between migration and religion in the diversity of the contemporary religious landscape of the UK

Geography of Religions in the UK

Of the four nations that comprise the UK, England has both the broadest and most numerous variety of religious traditions and communities (Thomas, 1998). In this, 6.0% of the total population and 7.7% of the population indicating identification with any religion at all identify with a religion other than Christianity. Among these, Muslims form the largest religious minority followed by Hindus, and then by Sikhs, Jews, 'Other Religions' and Buddhists.

In Scotland, as in England, Muslims make up the largest religious minority. But in Scotland this was followed by those using the write-in option for 'Other Religions', and then by Buddhists, Jews, Sikhs and Hindus. For Wales, as in all other countries in the UK, Muslims form the largest religious minority. As in Scotland, this is followed by 'Other Religions', then by Hindus, Buddhists, Jews and Sikhs.

In Northern Ireland, forms of religious believing and belonging that are other than Christian often seem to be relatively invisible. But while both the absolute and relative size of these groups is much smaller than in the rest of the UK, religious diversity does exist (Ryan, 1996). As in other parts of the UK, Muslims constitute the largest religious minority and, as in Wales and Scotland, Muslims are followed by those of 'Other Religions', and then by Hindus, Buddhists, Jews and Sikhs.

In addition to differences between the countries of the UK, because of the differing patterns of migration and settlement, some geographical areas within each country are characterized by a more pronounced religious diversity, including parts of the country in which there was some early settlement by small groups of traders, seamen and others (Visram, 1986; Beckerlegge, 1997; Fisher, Lahiri and Thandi, 2007). In each nation, the greatest diversity of religions is to be found in cities, metropolitan boroughs and some towns. Seaports such as Liverpool, Cardiff and London generally have longer-established communities because trade led to the local settlement of seafarers.

In addition, many old industrial towns and cities of the English Midlands and North, such as Leicester and Bradford, have communities of South Asian origin that were established as a result of migration from particular areas of Commonwealth countries in response to the labour shortages in British industry following the Second World War (Ballard, ed., 1994; Chryssides, 1994; Vertovec, 1991; Knott, 1996; Coward, Hinnells and Williams, 2000; Jacobsen and Kumar, eds, 2004). In the English regions the minority religious presence is at its greatest in the West Midlands, the North West, Yorkshire and the Humber and the East Midlands, and the main concentrations are found in the areas of greatest general population density, including London, the West Midlands, the Leicester-Nottingham area, and the conurbations of the Pennines.

The cosmopolitan nature of London means that religious as well as ethnic and linguistic diversity is at its widest there (Peach, 2006), with only three-fifths of London's population recording their religion as Christian. For all the other religions the greatest concentration of their regional populations is to be found in London, with the exception of the Sikhs, whose share of the regional population is at its greatest in the West Midlands. Table 2, for England, shows the local authorities inside and outside of London that have the greatest percentage share of Census respondents identifying with various religions, while Table 3 shows this for Wales. As will be noted, in Wales, the concentrations of minority religious populations relative to the majority populations are much smaller, apart from Cardiff.

Table 2: Main Concentrations of 2001 Census Respondents by Religion in English Local Authority Areas

Religion	Local Authority Areas in London	Percentage of the Population	Local Authority Areas Outside of London	Percentage of the Population
Buddhist	Westminster + Camden	13.0%	Ribble Valley	11.0%
Christian	Havering	76.1%	St. Helen's	86.9%
Hindu	Harrow	19.6%	Leicester	14.7%
Jewish	Barnet	14.8%	Bury	4.9%
Muslim	Tower Hamlets	36.4%	Blackburn & Darwen	19.4%
Sikh	Hounslow	8.6%	Slough	9.1%

Source: Census, April 2001. National Statistics website: www.statistics.gov.uk. Crown copyright, 2004.

Table 3: Main Concentrations of 2001 Census Respondents by Religion in Welsh Local Authority Areas

Religion	Welsh Local Authority Areas	Percentage of the Population
Buddhist	Ceredigion/Ceredigion	0.4%
Christian	Isle of Anglesey/Ynys Môn	79.4%
Hindu	Cardiff/Caerdydd	0.8%
Jewish	Cardiff/Caerdydd	0.3%
Muslim	Cardiff/Caerdydd	3.7%
Sikh	Cardiff/Caerdydd	0.3%

Source: Census, April 2001. National Statistics website: www.statistics.gov.uk. Crown copyright, 2004.

In particular local areas in the UK, members of religious communities may also share in particular ethnic, cultural and linguistic backgrounds. Thus, in a specific local area, the bulk of those adhering to a religion may be Muslims from Pakistan or, in others, Muslims from Bangladesh, from particular regions in Bangladesh, or even from specific villages within these regions. However, there are also significant variations of tradition, organization, ethnicity and language. For example, in Preston the Muslim population is largely Gujarati, as are the local Hindus.

Religion, Ethnicity and Language

Religion is an important marker of identity for significant numbers of individuals and groups. For some it is the most important. Other aspects of identity are represented by ethnicity and language. These are often linked with religious identity because of the history of when and where religious traditions developed (Barot, ed., 1993). Thus, for example, the majority of people in the UK with Pakistani antecedents are also Muslim, and nearly all Sikhs have some antecedents in the Punjab.

The relationship between broad religious and ethnic self-identification as found in the 2001 Census results for England and Wales is set out in percentage terms in Table 4. It should be noted that interpreting these data, other than in very broad terms, is not straightforward. Thus, while the majority of Muslims in the UK have ancestral origins in the Indo-Pakistani subcontinent (coming to Britain either directly or via earlier migrations to East Africa and the Caribbean), the remainder have ethnic and national origins in countries such as Cyprus, Malaysia, Turkey, Iran and the Arab world, together with the growing numbers of indigenous Britons who have embraced Islam.

Table 4 shows that, for England and Wales, 11.6% of those identified as 'Muslim' are also identified as 'white'; 4.2% of the 'Muslim' population is 'mixed';

73.7% of the 'Muslim' population is 'Asian'; 6.9% of the 'Muslim' population is 'Black' or 'Black British'; and 3.7% of the 'Muslim' population is 'Chinese or Other Ethnic Group'. However, while the number of 'white' adherents to Islam is increasing, some of the 11.6% of 'Muslims' recorded as 'white' are likely to include Middle Eastern respondents who opted for the descriptor of 'white' in preference to any of the other pre-set categories for response.

At the same time, there are regional differences within this diversity. This is because, while in northern England and the West Midlands Muslims are predominantly 'Asian' (and mostly of Pakistani and Bangladeshi ancestral origins), in north London boroughs the 'white' Muslim population (including Turks and Turkish Cypriots) outnumbers 'Asian' Muslims, while 'Black' or 'Black British' Africans also form a substantial part of the Muslim population in some London boroughs.

The Christian population includes, among others, people of African, African-Caribbean, Chinese, Korean, East and Central European and South Asian backgrounds. Buddhists in the UK are also of very diverse ethnic and national origins. Other groups are less diverse. Most Bahá'ís in the UK are of indigenous British ethnic origin and the majority are converts from other religions or former agnostics or atheists. There are, though, also Bahá'ís whose family roots are in Iran, most of whom have arrived since the Iranian Revolution. The vast majority of Sikhs are of Punjabi ethnic background, while Jains are of South Asian ancestral origin, including Gujaratis, Rajasthanis and Punjabis.

Hindus in the UK have ancestral origins as Gujaratis and Punjabis, and also from other parts of India such as Uttar Pradesh, West Bengal, and the southern Indian states, as well as in countries such as Sri Lanka. Thus the Hindu population is composed of many ethnic and linguistic groups, the most common of which are Gujarati, Punjabi, Bengali and Tamil.

The contemporary Zoroastrian community includes both Parsees (originally from India) and Irani Zardushtis or, simply, Iranis (originally from Iran). The majority of Zoroastrians in the UK are of Parsi origin, though in more recent years an Irani presence has also developed as a result of refugee movements arising from the Iranian revolution.

When looked at in terms of ethnicity by religion, as can be seen from Table 5, in England and Wales the overwhelming majority of those who are recorded as being of 'Asian' origins are also recorded as 'Muslim', 'Hindu' or 'Sikh'. Muslims of Bangladeshi origin are, in fact, the most homogeneous religio-ethnic grouping in the UK, with nearly all having their ancestral origins in the Sylhet District of the north-east of what is today Bangladesh.

The Pakistani population of the UK is also almost entirely Muslim and has origins mainly in the Punjab and the north of Pakistan including, especially, Pathans and other groups from the Afghan border districts, while there are also

Table 4: Percentage of Religion By Ethnic Group in England and Wales Among 2001 Census Respondents

Ethnic Group	Christian	Buddhist	Hindu	Jewish	Muslim	Sikh	Other	No religion	Not Stated	All People	Base
White	96.3	38.8	1.3	96.8	11.6	2.1	78.4	94.5	90.9	91.3	47,520,866
Mixed	0.9	3.2	1.0	1.2	4.2	0.8	2.5	2.0	1.9	1.3	661,034
Asian	0.3	9.6	96.6	0.7	73.7	96.2	13.7	0.4	3.1	4.4	2,273,737
Black or Black British	2.2	1.0	0.5	0.4	6.9	0.2	3.3	1.1	3.1	2.2	1,139,577
Chinese or Other Ethnic Group	0.3	47.3	0.6	0.9	3.7	0.7	2.0	2.0	1.0	0.9	446,702
All People					Due to rounding, figures may not total 100%						52,041,916

Source: Census, April 2001. National Statistics website: www.statistics.gov.uk. Crown copyright, 2004. Percentages calculated by the present author.

people from more diverse areas such as Mirpur. Nevertheless, it should also be noted that as many as 4.1% of all those recorded as 'Asians' are also recorded as 'Christians'. Finally, only 1.4% of all 'Asians' indicate 'no religion' as compared with a relatively very high 33.7% of 'Chinese and Other Ethnic Group' respondents, 15.3% of the 'white' population (as compared with 15.5% of the population as a whole).

It should also be noted that shared language can be an important factor in the relationship between religion and ethnicity. For example, other than English, Punjabi is the common language among most Sikhs. In Wales there are local Christian communities for whom Welsh is the first language of both worship and everyday life and this is also true of Gaelic for smaller numbers of Christians in Scotland.

Demography

There are considerable contrasts in age and gender structure between the various religious groups. Based on 2001 Census data (it needing to be recognized that, since then, over half a decade has passed), in Table 6 it can be seen that, on average, the oldest populations are the Jewish and Christian ones, while the Muslim population is the youngest religious group by a long way.

The overall shape of the Muslim population is typical of a population experiencing rapid increase. This reflects both a relatively high birth rate and also continuing immigration to the UK. Thus, in England, a third of the Muslim

Table 5: Percentage of Ethnic Group By Religion of Respondents in England and Wales in the 2001 Census

Religious Group	White	Mixed	Asian	Black or Black British	Chinese or Other Ethnic Group
Christian	75.7	52.5	4.1	71.1	27.2
Buddhist	0.1	0.7	0.6	0.1	15.3
Hindu	*0.02	0.9	23.5	0.3	0.7
Jewish	0.5	0.5	0.1	0.1	0.5
Muslim	0.4	9.7	50.1	9.3	12.8
Sikh	*0.01	0.4	13.9	0.1	0.5
Other	0.3	0.6	0.9	0.4	0.7
No Religion	15.3	23.3	1.4	7.6	33.7
Not Stated	7.7	11.5	5.5	11.1	8.6
All People	100	100	100	100	100

*In this table, in two instances, percentages are shown to two decimal points because, with rounding up to a single decimal point, the differences between the relatively small proportions of ethnic groups in some religions would otherwise be invisible.

Source: Census, April 2001. National Statistics website: www.statistics.gov.uk. Crown copyright, 2004. Percentages calculated by the present author.

Table 6: Demographic Summary of Religious Groups in England in the 2001 Census

	Males per 1000 females	Mean age (years)	Mean age of males	Mean age of females	Percent born in the UK
ALL PEOPLE	949	38.60	37.3	39.8	90.8
Christian	878	41.22	39.7	42.5	93.6
Buddhist	988	36.35	35.9	36.5	45.3
Hindu	1017	33.26	33.1	33.3	37.5
Jewish	922	42.81	41.3	44.2	83.2
Muslim	1067	25.99	26.3	25.6	46.4
Sikh	999	31.37	31.0	31.6	56.0
Any other religion	924	39.53	39.3	39.8	80.0
No religion	1295	30.08	31.1	28.4	93.4
Not stated	1024	36.84	35.0	38.7	90.8

Source: 2001 Census of Population, Table S149, as presented in the report by J. Beckford, R. Gale, D. Owen, C. Peach, and P. Weller (2006: 25).

population is aged fifteen or under compared with the England average of 20%, while only 5% are aged sixty or over as compared with the general average for England of 20%. The population shapes for Christians, Hindus, Muslims and Sikhs can be visually seen in Figures 1a–d.

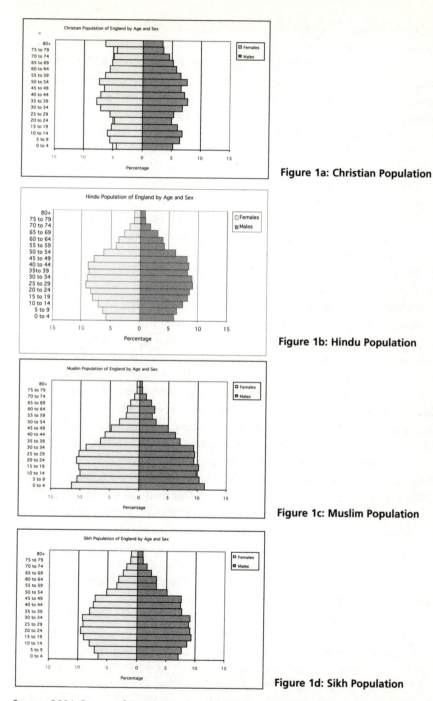

Figure 1a: Christian Population

Figure 1b: Hindu Population

Figure 1c: Muslim Population

Figure 1d: Sikh Population

Source: 2001 Census of Population, Standard Table 149, as presented in the report by J. Beckford, R. Gale, D. Owen, C. Peach, and P. Weller (2006: 33).

Socio-Economic, Educational and Occupational Profiles

As well as demographic differences, there are also significant differences in socio-economic profiles between groups of people understood with reference to religion. For those in work and those seeking to gain access to it, employment is an area of central significance to their individual lives and to those of their families, relating closely to personal esteem as well as economic opportunity. For the wider society, employment provides a means by which the skills, talents and enterprise of individuals can contribute towards the creation of financial and cultural wealth. It is therefore an arena in which it is very important that individuals and groups are not denied fair opportunities on grounds that are unrelated to their ability to do the job.

In terms of participation, the report by Beckford, Gale, Owen, Peach and Weller (2006: 16–20) shows that Muslims are significantly less involved in the formal labour force than are other groups considered in terms of religion. While in England, the overall average participation rate for those aged twenty-five or above was 67%, for Muslims it was 50% as compared with a 70% and 71% participation rate, respectively, for Sikhs and Hindus. The Muslim figures for economic participation are very largely due to the low female participation rate in the formal economy. Only 29% of Muslim women aged twenty-five and over were economically active, which is half the overall average (59%) for women in England, while the economic activity rates for Hindus and Sikhs were just above the average at 62%. Alongside the data for 'economic activity', nearly 18% of Muslims aged sixteen to twenty-four were unemployed and nearly 14% of those aged twenty-five and above. By contrast, the unemployment rates for Hindus aged sixteen to twenty-four and twenty-five and over were, respectively, 7% and 5%.

In terms of occupational profile, among males aged twenty-five and above in England, at 42% Muslims have the lowest proportion of men in the four white-collar major groups of the year 2000 Standard Occupational Classification (SOC) – in other words among managers and senior officials, professionals, associate professionals and technical occupations and administrative and secretarial occupations. This compares with an overall England average of 50%, and 63% among Hindu males and 80% among Jewish males. By contrast 34% of Muslim men in England work in semi-skilled and unskilled occupations as compared with 18% among Hindus and 31% among Sikh men.

Muslims have an above average family size and the concentration of Muslim households in flats or terraced homes leads to a higher than average degree of overcrowding. The higher the percentage of children brought up in overcrowded conditions, the poorer the living conditions of a community and the worse their children's life chances. 40% of Muslim children, 20% of Sikh and 30% of Hindu children in England live in overcrowded homes, compared with an all-England

Table 7: Percentage of males aged 16–74 in work by occupation, England 2001

SOC 2000 major group	ALL PEOPLE	Christian	Buddhist	Hindu	Jewish	Muslim	Sikh	Any other religion	No religion	Religion not stated
1. Managers and Senior Officials	18.5	18.7	19.3	21.5	31.6	16.0	19.2	18.3	17.9	16.9
2. Professional Occupations	12.2	10.7	20.2	22.4	25.2	12.4	12.5	19.0	15.6	13.4
3. Associate Professional and Technical Occupations	13.5	13.0	17.3	11.1	17.8	8.1	9.2	18.6	15.7	13.9
4. Administrative and Secretarial Occupations	5.4	5.2	5.7	7.9	5.7	6.0	5.8	7.4	5.7	5.8
5. Skilled Trades Occupations	19.5	20.7	15.5	9.1	4.8	12.6	13.1	11.9	17.6	18.6
6. Personal Service Occupations	2.0	2.1	3.2	1.4	1.9	1.9	1.1	3.3	1.9	2.1
7. Sales and Customer Service Occupations	4.1	3.7	4.0	8.8	4.0	9.3	7.8	4.4	4.2	4.3
8. Process; Plant and Machine Operatives	13.1	13.8	5.5	8.7	5.5	17.4	18.3	7.8	10.7	12.7
9. Elementary Occupations	11.9	12.1	9.2	9.0	3.5	16.3	12.9	9.1	10.8	12.3
All in work	12,791,618	8,766,810	39,689	149,851	63,908	279,194	80,140	41,745	2,467,126	903,155

Source: 2001 Census of Population, Table S154, as presented in J. Beckford, R. Gale, D. Owen, C. Peach, and P. Weller (2006: 27).

Table 8: Percentage of females aged 16–74 in work by occupation, England 2001

SOC 2000 major group	ALL PEOPLE	Christian	Buddhist	Hindu	Jewish	Muslim	Sikh	Any other religion	No religion	Religion not stated
1. Managers and Senior Officials	11.1	10.9	12.5	11.7	17.1	9.4	11.3	11.7	12.1	11.1
2. Professional Occupations	10.0	9.2	15.5	13.8	20.0	12.5	8.9	14.9	13.1	10.8
3. Associate Professional and Technical Occupations	14.2	13.6	20.6	11.8	19.9	11.8	10.7	21.0	17.0	14.3
4. Administrative and Secretarial Occupations	22.7	23.3	14.4	22.3	23.7	19.9	19.5	20.9	20.0	22.5
5. Skilled Trades Occupations	2.4	2.4	5.7	1.5	1.2	1.8	2.2	2.4	2.3	2.5
6. Personal Service Occupations	12.7	13.4	8.1	5.6	6.8	12.0	6.5	10.2	10.7	11.6
7. Sales and Customer Service Occupations	11.9	11.9	8.8	15.6	7.6	17.4	14.6	9.3	11.4	11.9
8. Process; Plant and Machine Operatives	3.1	3.0	2.7	7.7	0.6	4.7	12.0	2.0	2.7	3.2
9. Elementary Occupations	11.9	12.2	11.7	10.1	3.0	10.7	14.3	7.7	10.6	12.0
All in work	10,836,136	8,179,911	31,581	116,495	51,807	122,809	66,755	39,395	1,558,496	668,887

Source: 2001 Census of Population, Table S154, as presented in J. Beckford, R. Gale, D. Owen, C. Peach, and P. Weller (2006: 28).

average of 10%. Patterns of disadvantage are also reflected in educational attainment as seen by religious group. Thus, among people aged 16–64, 41% of Muslims have no educational qualifications, as compared with less than 30% for all other religious groups.

The degree to which these socio-economic differences are specifically rooted in discrimination and disadvantage on the basis of religious identity, or else pertain to pre-existing socio-economic factors shared by people in a particular group, is a matter of some debate (V. Robinson, 1990 and Lindley, 2002). It could, for example, be that the relatively better socio-economic position of the Hindu and the Sikh populations, as compared to Muslims, owes as much to the position of the forebears of these groups prior to their migration to the UK as to what has occurred since their arrival. A significant part of both Hindu and Sikh populations had origins among those who fled from East Africa, where they had generally formed a professionalized middle class. In contrast, many among the original Muslim migrants came from a rural peasant background.

At the same time, there are many who argue that Muslims experience specific discrimination and disadvantage on the basis of religion which some have gone so far as to describe by reference to the explanatory concept of 'Islamophobia' (Runnymede Trust, 1997). Conclusions from the research conducted in the Religious Discrimination in England and Wales Research Project (Weller, Feldman and Purdam, et. al., 2001: vii) do identify that:

> A consistently higher level of unfair treatment was reported by Muslim organisations than by most other religious groups, both in terms of the proportion of the respondents indicating that unfair treatment was experienced, and by the proportion indicating that these experiences were frequent rather than occasional.

And this is a pattern that indicators from the 2001 census also reveal in consistently highlighting the relative vulnerability of Muslims as compared with people from other religious groups. At the same time, examination of the demographic and socio-economic profiles of the diverse religious groups of the UK is a reminder that, while religious identity, believing and belonging are of great importance, there are also other factors that play an important role, and that what the actual inter-relationship between these factors is in particular examples can be complex.

4 Religions in the UK: Profiles

Christianity in the UK: A Profile

Christianity is the largest and longest established of the world religious traditions in the UK. In its various forms, it has shaped the past and present life of these

Study Activity 3

After reading section 4 of the chapter in relation to Christianity, and then in relation also to one other religion:

(i) *describe* some of the diversities of those religions in the UK

(ii) *discuss* the relationship between key features of that diversity

(iii) *evaluate*, in a preliminary way, the place of those religions within the overall religious landscape of the UK

islands, helping to mould legal structures, public institutions, and the social and intellectual tradition. It was introduced into Britain from continental Europe when some of its Celtic inhabitants were converted during the early centuries of the Common Era.

Following the arrival, in 597 CE, of Augustine, an emissary of Pope Gregory the Great of Rome, the Catholic form of Christianity gradually displaced the Celtic form, although in Wales and Ireland this continued independently for some centuries. Western Christianity became consolidated under the jurisdiction of the Pope, and Christians in the different parts of these islands remained part of what was known as the Catholic (meaning universal) tradition.

However, arising from the new learning of the Renaissance coupled with the translation of the scriptures into vernacular languages, popular and theological discontent developed in relation to a range of practices and teachings that had developed within the Catholic Church during the late Middle Ages. This eventually led to the fracture of Western Christendom known generally to history as the 'Protestant Reformation'. The development of Christianity from the time of the Reformation down to the present is taken up below in individual sub-sections on Christianity in England, Wales, Scotland and Northern Ireland.

Christianity is not only of historical importance to the development of the UK, but it remains a significant dimension of contemporary UK life. As already noted, in response to the Census questions on religion, 71.6% of the population as a whole or 92.3% of the population identifying itself with any specific religion at all, identified itself in some way as 'Christian'. For the UK as a whole and for each country within it, Table 9 shows the numbers of respondents identifying themselves as 'Christian' – as an absolute number; as a proportion of the population as a whole; and as a proportion of respondents who identify with any specific religion at all.

As has already been noted, while the forms of the Census question on religious affiliation used in Scotland and in Northern Ireland asked about both denominational background and current affiliation, the form of the question

Table 9: Census Respondents Identifying as 'Christian' by Country of the UK in 2001

Country	Total Numbers of Christians	Percentage of Total Population	Percentage of Population Identifying with any Specific Religion at all
England	35,251,244	71.7%	92.3%
Scotland	3,294,545	65.1%	97.2%
Wales	2,087,242	71.9%	98.0%
Northern Ireland	1,446,386	85.8%	99.7%
United Kingdom	42,079,417	71.6%	93.2%

Source: Census, April 2001. National Statistics website: www.statistics.gov.uk. Crown copyright, 2004. Percentages calculated by the present author.

as asked in England and Wales did not. However, the organization Christian Research provides broad estimates for 'community membership' of the Trinitarian Christian denominations. Its *UK Christian Handbook: Religious Trends, No. 4, 2003/2004* provides data for the year 2000 as set out in Table 10.

'Community membership' is a way of understanding the relationship of individuals, families and groups to a religion that has broader rather than narrower meanings and implications. Arguably, it most closely aligns with the kind of information about religion that is found in the Census data. But, when taking the more restrictive notion of 'Church membership', and based on Christian Research estimates for the year 2001, the proportions of 'Church membership' in the UK are set out in Table 11.

Table 10: Estimates of Christian 'Community Membership' by Denominational Tradition in the UK in 2000

Denomination	'Community by Denomination'	Percentages of 'Community by Denomination'
Anglican	28,300,000	67.5%
Baptist	500,000	1.2%
Catholic	5,800,000	13.8%
Independent	400,000	1.0%
Methodist	1,300,000	3.1%
New Churches	400,000	1.0%
Orthodox	500,000	1.2%
Pentecostal	400,000	1.0%
Presbyterian	2,900,000	6.9%
All Other Churches	1,400,000	3.3%
Total	41,000,000	100.0%

Source: From figures in P. Brierley, ed., 2003, Table 2.2.3, p. 2.2. Percentages calculated by the present author.

As illustrative of the relationship between the two kinds of data it is instructive to look at the proportion seen as 'Anglicans' under both definitions. Considered in terms of 'community membership', just over two-thirds of Christians identify in some way with Anglican Christianity. But taking the more restrictive notion of 'Church membership' (defined by Christian Research for this purpose as including those aged fifteen or over), and based on estimates for the year 2001, the relative positions of the traditions in the UK are quite different. In this, the proportion of all Anglicans is just below that of Catholic 'Church membership' and considerably below that of the combined 'Church membership' of the other Christian Free Church, Orthodox and Presbyterian traditions.

The position of Christianity in the UK and in its various denominational traditions needs to be set within an appreciation of the implications of the UK being a multi-national state. Not only do different parts of the UK have different religious profiles, but there is also a range of arrangements for defining the relationships between religious bodies, the state and society, as set out in chapter 3.

Such national diversity, and the issues that flow from it have, in recent years, grown in significance since the New Labour Government's implementation of devolution in Scotland, Wales and Northern Ireland. But even before these latest developments, Tom Nairn's book on *The Break-Up of Britain* could start with a chapter (Nairn, 1997: 11–91) entitled 'The Twilight of the British State'. Insofar, then, as the varied Christian traditions are themselves reflections of the national diversity (Jenkins, 1975) that can be found in the three nations of England, Wales

Table 11: Estimates of 'Church Membership' by Denominational Tradition in the UK in 2001

Denomination	'Church membership'	Percentages of Total 'Church membership'
Anglican	1,668,025	28.3%
Baptist	215,062	3.6%
Catholic	1,745,652	29.6%
Independent	187,497	3.2%
Methodist	343,696	5.8%
New Churches	136,054	2.3%
Orthodox	255,308	4.3%
Pentecostal	253,722	4.3%
Presbyterian	958,268	16.2%
Other Churches	139,983	2.4%
Total	5,903,267	100.0%

Source: From figures in P. Brierley, ed., 2003, Tables 2.22.2 – 2.23.7, pp. 2.22–2.23.
Percentages calculated by the present author.

and Scotland, as well as among people of the province of Northern Ireland, it is important to look at Christianity in each country in turn.

Christianity in England: A Profile

In England, the Reformation led to the establishment of what is now called the Church of England through the 1534 *Act of Supremacy* of King Henry VIII, who initially styled himself Head of the Church. This title was later modified under Queen Elizabeth I to Supreme Governor. Thus the Church in England became independent of the jurisdiction of Rome, but closely identified with the monarchy. In the following years, Christians who maintained allegiance to the Roman Catholic Church were persecuted under King Edward VI (1549–53), while under the Catholic Queen Mary (1553–58) Protestants were, in turn, persecuted. Under Queen Elizabeth I, the position was again reversed. The Church of England preserved many of the characteristics of Catholic Christianity, but also embraced a number of Protestant features leading to its traditional understanding of itself as both 'Catholic' and 'Reformed'.

During the English Civil War, with the victory of the Parliamentary forces Presbyterian Christianity became strong throughout Britain and Ireland. But other Protestant movements emerged, including Congregationalists and Baptists, whose origins lay in the conviction that the Christian Church consists of committed believers. After the political and religious upheaval of the English Civil War and the Restoration of the Monarchy, the 1662 *Act of Uniformity* led to over one thousand clergy being ejected from their parishes in England due to their refusal to accept compulsory use of the *Book of Common Prayer*. This strengthened the Presbyterian, Independent, Congregationalist and Baptist movements who were joined by many formerly Anglican clergy who did not wish to conform to these requirements.

Following a period during which the post-Civil War and Restoration settlement continued to privilege the Church of England and to marginalize Nonconformists and Roman Catholics, towards the end of the nineteenth century, the Free Churches came to occupy a prominent place in public and religious life. More recently, during the latter part of the twentieth century and the beginning of the twenty-first, Roman Catholic Christianity has re-emerged, strengthened by successive migrations of Roman Catholic Christians from around the globe, including from Africa and Latin America, as well as from Poland when the latter's accession to the EU brought with it unrestricted travel and settlement rights.

In England, the 2001 Census showed that 71.7% of the population, and 92.3% of the population of England identifying itself with any specific religion at all, identified in some sense as 'Christian'. However, as has already been noted in connection with the 'Christian' responses to the Census in England it may be that the form of question asked means that the answers given reflect more of what Voas (2003: 98) suggests may be 'a cultural background rather than a current affiliation'. At the same time, it is likely that some form of identification with Christianity may well be felt by larger sections of the population than is immediately apparent. Thus the sociologist of religion Grace Davie argues that one needs to take account of the phenomenon of 'believing without belonging' (Davie, 1990a) in the 'ordinary God' (Davie, 1990b) of folk Christianity.

Christianity in Scotland: A Profile

It was in Scotland that the Reformation tradition of Calvinism had its greatest impact. In 1560 the Church of Scotland was reformed along Calvinist principles, with a Presbyterian form of Church government based upon a collective local church leadership of both clergy and non-clerical elders, known as the presbytery.

Following the 1603 accession of James Stuart to the English Crown as James I of England, attempts were made to introduce into Scotland a model of church government based on bishops, and the minority who supported an episcopalian model formed the Scottish Episcopal Church. Following the union of the Westminster and Scottish Parliaments in 1707 there has been both a shared monarch and political system. However, Scotland has in many ways remained distinct. This has especially been the case in terms of its systems of law and education and has also applied in matters of religion (Brown, 1987).

The Church of Scotland (popularly known as 'The Kirk') is the established form of religion in Scotland, and has generally been understood by Scottish Presbyterians as a 'National Church'. While Scotland has also had a substantial presence of both Episcopalian and Roman Catholic Christians, Catholicism has often been identified with Irishness and Episcopalianism with Englishness. Even as late as the mid-1980s it could still be written that 'To be a Scot is to be a Presbyterian, even though that designation may say more of cultural identity than religious persuasion' (Bisset, 1986: 3). Against this background, sectarianism has played a role in Scottish life. Indeed, it was in part a recognition of the need to tackle sectarian issues that led to the form of the Census question on religion in Scotland asking, like that in Northern Ireland, about familial inheritance as well as current identification with particular Christian traditions.

Table 12 gives the breakdown by denomination of those identifying as 'Christian' in Scotland, in the 2001 Census. Overall, the 2001 Census showed that, in Scotland, 65.1% of the population, and 97.2% of the population identifying itself with any specific religion at all identified themselves, in some sense, as 'Christian'. Given the popular wisdom that Christianity is stronger and taken more seriously in Scotland than in England, this is a perhaps surprisingly lower proportion of the population responding as 'Christian' than in England. However, it should be noted that, as previously suggested, it is possible that this difference derives from the differences in the form of the Census questions on religion.

Table 12: Census Results by Religious Denomination for Those Identifying as 'Christian' in Scotland

Religious Denomination	Total Numbers	Percentage of Scotland Population	Percentage of Population of Scotland Identifying as 'Christian'
Presbyterian	2,146,251	42.4%	65.1%
Roman Catholic	803,732	15.9%	24.4%
'Other Christian'	344,562	6.8%	10.5%
Total	3,294,545	*	100%

Other Religions and Philosophies are 1.9% of the population. Those of 'no religion' are 27.5% and 'not stated' are 5.5% of the population.

Source: Census, April 2001. National Statistics website: www.statistics.gov.uk. Crown copyright, 2004. Percentages calculated by the present author.

Christianity in Wales: A Profile

In Wales, the Church also shared the Reformation history of England in terms of the impact of the 1534 *Act of Supremacy* of King Henry VIII becoming, as in England, independent of the jurisdiction of Rome, but being closely identified with the monarchy. During the sixteenth and early seventeenth centuries the Bible and the *Book of Common Prayer* (containing prescribed orders of worship of the Church of England) were translated into Welsh and were accepted into common use among Christians in Wales.

Today, a substantial proportion of the congregations of the Free Churches conduct their worship and congregational life in the Welsh language, including the Union of Welsh Independents; the majority of congregations in the Baptist Union of Wales and the Presbyterian Church of Wales; all churches within the Cymru District of the Methodist Church; and some Anglican churches and several Unitarian chapels.

In the 2001 Census results for Wales 71.9% of the population of Wales, and 98% of the population of Wales identifying itself with any specific religion at all, is recorded as, in some sense, identifying itself as 'Christian'. As has already been noted, the Census question as asked in Wales did not differentiate between denominational traditions of Christianity. In terms of religion, following the 1920 disestablishment of the Church in Wales there has been no established form of religion in Wales and no single predominant religious tradition that has acted as a focus for national identity (Rhys, n.d.).

Until the recent creation of the Welsh Assembly, Wales had very little modern constitutional distinctiveness, but it has had a vigorous ancient culture and language, the latter having been revived during the 1960s through the campaigns of *Cymdeithas yr Iaith Gymraeg* (the Welsh Language Society). At the same time, the Nonconformist Churches have played a significant role in Wales' social, political and cultural life (Jones, 1992) and were often at the forefront of nineteenth and early twentieth-century agitation for disestablishment in Wales. As noted above, they have also played a major role in preserving and promoting the use of the Welsh language, while since disestablishment, the Church in Wales has become more attuned to nationalist feeling.

Christianity in Northern Ireland: A Profile

In Northern Ireland, as in Wales, there is no officially established form of religion, with the Episcopalian Church of Ireland having been disestablished in 1871. Furthermore, the 1920 *Governance of Ireland Act* specifically proscribed the establishment of any particular religion or religious tradition, although the Presbyterian tradition is now the largest Protestant Christian tradition in Northern Ireland (Richardson, 1999).

In Northern Ireland, the 2001 Census showed that 85.8% of the population and 99.7% of the population identifying with any specific religion at all, identify in some sense as 'Christian'. But the form of the 2001 Census question on religion as asked in Northern Ireland (as also in Scotland) also asked about both original and current identification with particular Christian traditions. From this, and as shown in Table 13, the largest single Christian tradition in Northern Ireland is the Roman Catholic, while the Presbyterian tradition forms the largest Protestant grouping.

Table 13: Census Results by Religious Denomination for those Identifying as 'Christian' in Northern Ireland

Religious Denomination	Total Numbers	Percentage of Northern Ireland Population	Percentage of Population of Northern Ireland Identifying as 'Christian'
Catholic	678,462	40.3%	46.9%
Presbyterian	348,742	20.7%	24.1%
Church of Ireland	257,788	15.3%	17.8%
Methodist Church in Ireland	59,173	3.5%	4.1%
Other Christian	102,221	6.1%	7.1%
Total	1,446,386	*	100%

Other Religions and Philosophies are 0.3% of the population. Those of 'no religion'/'not stated' (in Northern Ireland these categories are not differentiated) are 13.9% of the population.

Source: Census, April 2001. National Statistics website: www.statistics.gov.uk. Crown copyright, 2004. Percentages calculated by the present author.

Christianity in the UK: Ethnic and Religious Diversity

Alongside the traditions of Christianity that emerged according to the specific national histories of England, Wales, Scotland and Ireland there is a now a much wider diversity of Christian forms of both 'believing' and 'belonging'. In part this has come about through ethnic diversification in the wider population through the migration, settlement and development of new Christian communities further diversifying the profile of Christianity in England even beyond its already relatively (as compared with many other European countries) pluralistic Christian inheritance of Anglican, Presbyterian, Roman Catholic and Free Church traditions.

Considered in terms of ethnicity, as Table 4 shows, in England and Wales 96.3% of 'Christian' respondents are 'white', 2.2% are 'Black or Black British', 0.9% are 'mixed', 0.3% are 'Asian' and 0.3% are of 'Chinese or Other Ethnic Group'. As set out in Table 5, 75.7% of all those recorded as 'white' are recorded as 'Christian', along with 71.1% of 'Black or Black British', 52.5% of 'mixed', 27.3% of 'Chinese or Other Ethnic Group' and 4.1% of 'Asian' people.

A significant proportion of migrants from African, and especially those from West-African, countries brought with them forms of indigenous Christian life that were developed in African Independent Churches (ter Haar, 1998), such as those of the Cherubim and Seraphim traditions (Omoyajawo, 1982). In their home countries, many Caribbean Christian migrants were members of one of the traditional Christian denominations. Following their experience of racism within these churches in England (Wilkinson, 1993) many black Christians formed independent congregations where they could practise Christianity in ways that could draw upon the integrity of their own Christian experience and leadership (Gerloff, 1992).

The Orthodox Christian population remains numerically small, although in the earlier part of the century it was strengthened by Russian emigrés following the Bolshevik Revolution in Russia and by economic migration from Greece and refugee migration from Cyprus. In more recent times, it has grown further through the arrival of refugees from the Balkans. Migration and refugee movements from Africa and Latin America have also added to the size of the Roman Catholic Christian community.

But for reasons other than from migration, Christianity has undergone other significant transformations in which new forms of Christian life and organization have emerged either outside of, or overlapping with, the more traditional Christian churches. This has, for example, occurred in the development of the so-called 'Restorationist' or 'New Church' movements (Walker, 1985). These seek to recover a more authentic form of Christian life than they feel has been transmitted by the traditional churches, with such congregations increasingly being organized in wider groupings and networks.

Christianity in the UK: Related/Disputed Groups

Finally, it should be noted that there are also traditions and groups that have an historical relationship with the wider Christian tradition, but the precise natures of these are often disputed, resulting as they do from conflicting and often mutually exclusive self-understandings. These include the Church of Jesus Christ of Latter-day Saints, popularly known as the 'Mormons'. This understands itself to be a true, restored, Christian church for the latter days, while for Trinitarian Christians this is problematic due to Mormons' rejection of the doctrine of the Trinity.

Where respondents from these disputed groups did not use the category 'Christian', but wrote the name of their group in under the write-in 'religion other' option, a statistical breakdown (for England and Wales only) is available from the Office for National Statistics, the results of which are set out in Table 14. At the same time, it should be noted that Christian Research (Brierley, ed., 2003) provides higher 2001 estimates for some of these groups. These figures are therefore also included in Table 14 for the purposes of comparison with the Census data. Even allowing for the possibility of an overestimate by Christian Research, the discrepancies with the data from the Census write-in responses would seem to indicate that significant numbers of respondents from these groups may well have simply ticked the box 'Christian' rather using the write-in option for 'other religion'.

Islam in the UK: A Profile

The earliest Muslim presence in the UK was of individuals who, during the expansion of the British Empire, arrived as servants, *ayahs*, visitors or settlers. Significant localized communities began to emerge during the nineteenth century when Muslim seafarers and traders from the Middle East and the Indian subcontinent began to settle around major seaports.

Some of the seamen later moved inland after failing to secure employment in the ports or on the ships and the pattern of settlement thus widened. After the First World War there was further settlement by Muslims demobilized from military service in the Imperial Army. But the size of the Muslim population increased significantly with the arrival in the 1950s and 1960s of workers from the Indo-Pakistani subcontinent who had been recruited for employment in the mills and factories. As a direct result of the implementation of Africanization policies in the newly independent African states, the early 1970s saw the arrival from Kenya and Uganda of a large number of Muslims of Asian ethnic origins.

Table 14: Census Respondents of 'Christian-Related/Contested' Groups

Tradition	Numbers in England in Census Table 275	Numbers in England according to Religious Trends, 2004	Numbers in Wales in Census Table 275	Numbers in Wales according to Religious Trends, 2004
British Israelites	30	-	-	-
Church of Jesus Christ of Latter-day Saints/Mormons	11,673	148,310	1,049	8,510
Christadelphians	2,123	16,350	245	1,000
Christian Scientists	556	6,000	22	150
Christian Spiritualists *	1,246	-	215	-
Jehovah's Witnesses	65,453	109,288	5,198	7,430
Unitarians **	3,604	4,350	383	1,000

* As distinct from those who responded as 'Spiritualists'.

** As distinct from those who responded as 'Unitarian Universalists'.

Both the above were coded by the Office for National Statistics as 'other religions'.

Sources: Census, April 2001. *Table M275 Religion (Most Detailed Categories)*. Crown copyright, 2004; and Brierley, ed., 2003, p. 10.2, tables 10.2.3, 10.2.6, 10.3.4 and p. 10.4, Table 10.4.6.

More recently, Muslim refugees have arrived from countries such as Somalia and Bosnia.

Muslims are today the largest and most diverse religious minority in the UK (see Badawi, 1981; Joly and Nielsen, 1985; Wahhab, 1989; Nielsen, 1992: 39–59; and Raza, 1992). Table 15 shows, by country of the UK, the numbers of people in the 2001 Census identifying themselves as, in some sense, 'Muslims'.

In England, as a proportion of the total population in local authority areas, the 2001 Census shows that the greatest concentration of respondents identifying as Muslims is to be found in the London Boroughs of Tower Hamlets (36.4%) and Newham (24.3%); Blackburn and Darwen (19.4%); Bradford (16.1%); and the London Borough of Waltham Forest (15.1%).

As seen in Table 4, 73.7% of the 'Muslim' population in England and Wales are recorded as 'Asian', 11.6% as 'white', 6.9% as 'Black or Black British', 4.2% as 'mixed' and 3.7% as 'Chinese or Other Ethnic Group'. As set out in Table 5, this means that 50.1% of all those recorded as 'Asians' are recorded as 'Muslim', as are 12.8% of 'Chinese or Other Ethnic Group', 9.7% of 'mixed', 9.3% of 'Black or Black British' and 0.4% of 'white' people.

Table 15: Census Respondents Indicating Themselves as 'Muslim' by Country of the UK

Country	Total Numbers of Muslims	Percentages of the Total Population of Each Country	Percentages of the Population of Each Country Identifying with any Specific Religion at all
England	1,524,887	3.1%	4.0%
Scotland	42,557	0.8%	1.3%
Wales	21,739	0.8%	1.0%
Northern Ireland	1,943	0.1%	0.1%
United Kingdom	1,591,126	2.7%	3.5%

Source: Census, April 2001. National Statistics website: www.statistics.gov.uk. Crown copyright, 2004. Percentages calculated by the present author.

The largest group of Muslims in the UK have ancestral origins in the Indo-Pakistani subcontinent, coming to Britain either directly or via earlier migrations to East Africa and the Caribbean. The majority of the remaining Muslim populations have ethnic and national origins in countries such as Cyprus, Malaysia, Turkey, Iran and the Arab world. There are also growing numbers of indigenous Britons who have embraced Islam.

The Muslim population of the UK has religious as well as ethnic diversity with Sunni and the Shi'a Muslim traditions being present, and Sunnis being the majority here as globally. The Shi'a tradition emerged when, following the death of the Prophet Muhammad, there was a serious dispute within the Muslim community concerning the location of authority. The word Sunni comes from 'one who adheres to the *sunna*', the *sunna* being one of the four sources of Islamic law and relating to the actions and sayings of the Prophet Muhammad. The word Shi'a comes from an Arabic word that literally means follower or associate. Shi'ite comes from *shiat 'Ali* (the follower of 'Ali).

Within the Sunni Muslim tradition there are a number of what might be called 'tendencies' or 'movements' (Robinson, 1988; Andrews, 1994). In the UK, the majority of these groupings are of South Asian origin (Hardy, 1972) such as the Barelwis, Deobandis, the Tablighi Jamaat and the Ahl-e-Hadith, each of which has its own emphases, networks, structures and organizations (Raza, 1992; Geaves, 1996).

Shi'a Muslims believe that a succession (the descendants of Ali and Fatima, the Prophet's youngest daughter) of individual Imams (spiritual leaders) was instituted from within Muhammad's family in order to continue to give guidance to the community. Along with other Muslims, they believe that the process of revelation was completed with Muhammad. However, they also believe that there are Imams or *Hujjah* (Proofs of God) who are specially selected by God to interpret the Qur'an, and that these leaders can provide authoritative contemporary guidance to believers.

Shi'a Muslims all agree that Ali was the first Imam, but a minority known as 'Seveners', among whom are Ismailis, accept the leadership of the first six Imams. There are also Nizari Ismailis who are more generally known as Agha Khanis and accept the Aga Khan as their living Imam. The majority of Shi'a globally and in the UK are known as 'Twelvers' (or 'Ithna Asherites).

The mystical dimension of Islam found in both the Sunni and Shi'a traditions is known as *Tasawwuf* (Sufism). While committed to the practical aspects of the *Shar'iah*, Sufism emphasizes Islam's inner or esoteric aspects. Members of Sufi Orders engage in meditation, chanting the names of God, and ritual dancing. Global Sufi Orders include the Naqshbandi, the Qadiri, the Chishti and the Suhrawardi, and active Sufi groups can be found throughout the UK.

Hinduism in the UK: A Profile

Small numbers of Hindus have visited and worked in the UK for centuries. But it was not until the 1950s and 1960s that significant numbers settled here and the contours of an organized community began to emerge (Bowen, ed., 1981; Burghart, ed., 1987; Thomas, 1993b; Knott, 2000; and Weller, 2004b).

Some arrived directly from India, but between 1965 and 1972 others came from countries of previous migration (such as Kenya, Tanzania, Uganda, Zambia and Malawi) when the Africanization policies of the newly independent states resulted in ethnic Asians becoming economic migrants and/or refugees. Hindu migrants also came from Fiji, as well as from Trinidad and other Caribbean islands (Vertovec, 1994). Table 16 shows the numbers of people in the 2001 Census who identified themselves as in some sense 'Hindus'.

As seen in Table 4, 96.6% of those recorded as 'Hindus' are also recorded as being of 'Asian' ethnic origin, 1.3% are 'white', 10.0% are 'mixed'; 0.6% are

Table 16: Census Respondents Identifying Themselves as 'Hindu' by Country in the UK

Country	Total Numbers of Hindus	Percentages of the Total Population of Each Country	Percentages of the Population of Each Country Identifying with any Specific Religion at all
England	546,982	1.1%	1.4%
Scotland	5,564	0.1%	0.2%
Wales	5,439	0.2%	0.3%
Northern Ireland	825	0.1%	0.1%
United Kingdom	558,810	1.2%	1.0%

Source: Census, April 2001. National Statistics website: www.statistics.gov.uk. Crown copyright, 2004. Percentages calculated by the present author.

'Chinese or Other Ethnic Group' and 0.5% are 'Black or Black British'. As set out in Table 5 this means that 23.5% of all those recorded as 'Asians' are also recorded as Hindu, as well as 0.9% of 'mixed', 0.7% of 'Chinese or Other Ethnic Group', 0.3% of 'Black or Black British' and 0.02% of those recorded as 'white'.

Across the UK, the majority of Hindus are of Gujarati background and a minority Punjabi, while others have ancestral origins in Uttar Pradesh, West Bengal, and the Southern states, along with Tamils from Sri Lanka and Hindus from the Caribbean. Within the Hindu population as a whole, but especially among Gujaratis, caste or *jati* groups have important functions ranging from social networking to voluntary welfare support. Although in the UK these do not necessarily correlate with the social, economic or occupational status of individuals and families they do remain significant social, cultural and economic networks within many aspects of internal Hindu community life. Due to differential patterns of settlement, jati groups can be found concentrated in specific localities including, for example, a concentration of Mochis in Leeds and Lohanas in Leicester and North London.

Sampradaya or spiritual traditions also often have a linkage with a regional base in India. These include Swaminarayan Hindus (Williams, 1984 and Dwyer, 1994) who, in the UK, are predominantly of Gujarati origin, and the Pushtimarg or Vallabha *sampradaya* whose members are largely Lohana by *jati*. There are also members of ISKCON, The International Society for Krishna Consciousness (Carey, 1983 and Knott, 1986), the Arya Samaj and the Ramakrishna Mission, as well as a large number of Hindu-related traditions and movements, including TM (Transcendental Meditation) and the Divine Life Society.

Sikhism in the UK: A Profile

In 1854, Prince Dalip Singh, the son of Maharaja Ranjit Singh, arrived in the UK as a fifteen-year-old exile, and was one of the first Sikhs to reside here. He acquired the Elveden Estate in Norfolk, which is now often visited by Sikhs keen to mark their early connections with the UK. Many Sikhs served in the British Indian armies in the First and Second World Wars and a number of ex-servicemen migrated to Britain, particularly after the Second World War.

Some Sikhs settled in the UK between the 1920s and the 1940s. But the vast majority of Sikh migrants arrived in the 1950s and 1960s (Cole, 1989; Thomas, 1993a; Ballard, 2000; Weller, 2004b). Many came directly to the UK from the Punjab although, like many Hindus and Muslims, a significant minority came from East Africa and other former British colonies to which members of their families had initially migrated (Bhachu, 1985). The current UK Sikh population is the largest outside the Indian subcontinent. Table 17 shows the numbers of people in the 2001 Census who identified themselves as in some sense 'Sikh'.

Table 17: Census Respondents Indicating Themselves as 'Sikh' by Country in the UK

Country	Total Numbers of Sikhs	Percentages of the Total Population of Each Country	Percentages of the Population of Each Country Who Identify with any Specific Religion at all
England	327,343	0.7%	0.9%
Scotland	6,572	0.1%	0.2%
Wales	2,015	0.1%	0.1%
Northern Ireland	219	0.01%	0.02%
United Kingdom	336,149	0.6%	0.7%

Sikh percentages for N. Ireland are shown to two decimal points otherwise, if rounded up to a single decimal point, the very small numbers identified as Sikhs would be invisible.

Source: Census, April 2001. National Statistics website: www.statistics.gov.uk. Crown copyright, 2004. Percentages calculated by the present author.

As a proportion of the population in local authority areas, the 2001 Census shows that, in England, the greatest concentration of respondents identifying themselves as Sikhs is to be found in Slough (9.1%); in the London Boroughs of Hounslow (8.6%) and Ealing (8.5%); and in Wolverhampton (7.6%) and Sandwell (6.9%).

As can be seen in Table 4, 96.2% of those recorded as 'Sikh' are also recorded as being of 'Asian' origin, 2.1% are 'white', 0.8% are 'mixed', 0.7% are 'Chinese or Other Ethnic Group' and 0.2% are 'Black or Black British'. As set out in Table 5, this means that 13.9% of all those recorded as 'Asians' are also recorded as 'Sikh', as are 0.5% of 'Chinese and Other Ethnic Groups', 0.4% of 'mixed', 0.1% of 'Black or Black British' and 0.01% of 'whites'. Most Sikhs are of Punjabi ethnic origin. A very few Sikhs in the UK are indigenous converts.

Sikh religious teachings emphasize that there should be no distinctions between people and reject the concept of caste (or *Zaat*). Although this therefore has no religious significance for Sikhs, social groups do continue to play a role in the life of the community. Thus Bhatras were historically itinerant traders, many of whom settled in British ports before the Second World War, with some of the earliest gurdwaras being founded by them. Ramgarhia is the preferred designation of Sikhs who have ancestral roots in the occupations of carpentry, bricklaying and masonry. They are known after their distinguished eighteenth-century leader, Jassa Singh, who renamed himself after the Ramgarh Fort in Amritsar that had, in turn, been named after Guru Ram Das.

At the end of the nineteenth century, the British encouraged groups of Ramgarhias to move to East Africa in order to assist in the development of the transport network from where, in the 1960s, many migrated to the UK or arrived as refugees as a result of Africanization policies of the newly independent East African states.

Sikhs do not acknowledge a diversity of doctrinal schools. However, there are groups with origins in the revivalist movements that have emerged throughout Sikh history. These movements were generally founded by individuals who, on the basis of their reputation for spiritual guidance and teaching, have often been given the honorific titles of Sant, Bhai or Baba and who may have particular significance and influence within specific gurdwaras and Sikh organizations in the UK.

Judaism in the UK: A Profile

Jewish people have had historical roots in England that go back for many centuries (Campbell, 1994). However, they suffered sporadic outbreaks of persecution until Edward I expelled them in 1290. Following the English Civil War and during the period of the Commonwealth, Menasseh ben Israel of Amsterdam successfully campaigned for the re-admission of Jews to England.

After the death of six million European Jews in the killing fields and the death camps of continental Europe during the Second World War, the community in the UK is now one of the largest in Europe (Lerman, 1989). At the same time, it is a population that is in decline, with the results of the 2001 Census confirming what had previously been indicated by internal community surveys. Table 18 shows the numbers of people in the 2001 Census identifying themselves as in some sense 'Jews'.

As a proportion of the total population in local authority areas, the 2001 Census shows that, in England, the greatest concentration of respondents identifying themselves as Jews is to be found in the London Borough of Barnet (14.8%);

Table 18: Census Respondents Identifying Themselves as 'Jews' by Country of the UK

Country	Total Numbers of Jews	Percentage of Total Population	Percentage of Population Who Identify with any Specific Religion at all
England	257,671	0.5%	0.7%
Scotland	6,448	0.1%	0.2%
Wales	2,256	0.1%	0.1%
Northern Ireland	365	0.02%	0.03%
United Kingdom	266,740	0.5%	0.6%

Percentages for Jews in N. Ireland are shown to two decimal points otherwise, when rounding up to a single decimal point, the relatively small numbers identified would be invisible.

Source: Census, April 2001. National Statistics website: www.statistics.gov.uk. Crown copyright, 2004. Percentages are calculated by the present author.

Hertsmere (11.3%); and the London Boroughs of Harrow (6.3%), Redbridge (6.2%) and Camden (5.6%). Outside of the Greater London area, the largest provincial Jewish population is found in Bury.

In terms of ethnicity, as can be seen in Table 4, 96.8% of those recorded as 'Jews' are also recorded as 'white', 1.2% as 'mixed', 0.9% as 'Chinese or Other Ethnic Group', 0.7% as 'Asian' and 0.4% as 'Black or Black British'. As set out in Table 5, this means 0.5% of all those recorded as being 'white', 'mixed' and as 'Chinese or Other Ethnic Group' are also recorded as being 'Jews', as are 0.1% of all those recorded as 'Black or Black British' and of those recorded as 'Asians'.

Historically, the Jewish community in the UK was predominantly Sephardi, which refers to those Jews who originated in Spain and Portugal. Today, however, the majority of Jews in the UK are Ashkenazi, and descendants of those groups whose origins can be traced to two major migrations from Central and Eastern Europe. The first migration was between 1881 and 1914 and took place in the context of restricted social and economic possibilities as well as escape from the outbreak of anti-Jewish pogroms within the Russian Empire. The second migration took place from 1933 onwards, and consisted of refugees from persecution in Germany and other Nazi-occupied European countries.

There are some differences of religious identity and practice between Sephardi and Ashkenazi, but in terms of religion the more significant differences are now to be found between Orthodox and Progressive (including the Reform and Liberal movements) Judaism. There are a number of Orthodox groupings, the largest of which is the United Synagogue, established in 1870, with the spiritual leader of many Orthodox Jews being the Chief Rabbi of the Hebrew Congregations of the Commonwealth. There are also Hasidic groups, the best known of which in the UK is part of a global movement called the Lubavich.

With regard to Progressive Judaism, the first Reform synagogue, the West London Synagogue, was opened in 1840 while the Liberal movement began in 1902 with the founding of the Jewish Religious Union. The Liberal movement was originally more radically different from the Orthodox than were Reform Jews. Today, in practice, the Liberal and Reform movements have largely converged.

Buddhism in the UK: A Profile

In the late nineteenth century, western scholars translated an increasing number of Buddhist texts and, in this context, some also developed an interest in Buddhism as a philosophy, a way of life and a religion (Almond, 1988). Among these was Edwin Arnold, whose account of the life and teaching of the Buddha in the best-selling book, *The Light of Asia*, was first published in 1879. In 1881 T.W. Rhys founded the Pali Text Society to foster developments of this kind.

In 1899, Gordon Douglas, the first English person to be ordained as a Buddhist monk, took his vows in Colombo, Sri Lanka and became Bhikkhu Asoka. In 1898 another Englishman, Alan Bennett, went to study Buddhism in Sri Lanka. In 1901, whilst in Burma, he was ordained as a monk, taking the name Ananda Metteyya. In 1907, a Buddhist Society of Great Britain and Ireland was formed to receive a Buddhist mission led by him, and that eventually arrived in 1908.

However, the Society was not firmly established and, in 1924, Christmas Humphreys incorporated its remnants in the foundation of the Buddhist Centre of the Theosophical Society. In 1926, this became the Buddhist Lodge of the Theosophical Society, while in 1943 it became a new and independent organization known as The Buddhist Society. In 1926, Humphreys had welcomed the Sinhalese Anagarika Dharmapala (who had previously visited Britain in 1893, 1896, and 1904) on a mission. This led to the foundation of a branch, in London, of the Maha Bodhi Society. In 1928 this was followed by the foundation of the first monastery for Sinhalese monks.

Throughout the twentieth century, individuals and small groups of migrants with Buddhist beliefs arrived from Sri Lanka, Thailand and Burma. Indian (mostly Ambedkarite) Buddhists and the Hong Kong Chinese came mainly with the New Commonwealth migrations of the 1950s and 1960s. The number of Buddhists in the UK has been further expanded by refugees, including those following the Dalai Lama's 1959 flight from Tibet; then by Vietnamese Buddhist refugees, who arrived in the late 1960s and early 1970s (Humphreys, 1968; Oliver, 1979; Batchelor, 1994). Table 19 shows the numbers of people in the 2001 Census identifying themselves as in some sense 'Buddhists'.

Table 19: Census Respondents Identifying as 'Buddhist' by Country in the UK

Country	Total Numbers of Buddhists	Percentage of Total Population	Percentage of Population Who Identify with Any Specific Religion at all
England	139,046	0.3%	0.4%
Scotland	6,830	0.1%	0.2%
Wales	5,407	0.2%	0.3%
Northern Ireland	533	0.03%	0.04%
United Kingdom	151,816	0.3%	0.3%

Percentages for Buddhists in Northern Ireland are shown to two decimal points otherwise, when rounding up to a single decimal point, the relatively small numbers identified as Buddhists would be invisible.

Source: Census, April 2001. National Statistics website: www.statistics.gov.uk. Crown copyright, 2004. Percentages calculated by the present author.

As a proportion of the population in local authority areas, the 2001 Census shows that in England the greatest proportion of respondents identifying themselves as Buddhist was found in the London Boroughs of Westminster (1.3%), Camden (1.3%), Kensington and Chelsea (1.1%) and Hackney (1.1%); and, outside London, in the Ribble Valley (1.1%).

In terms of ethnicity, Table 4 shows that 47.3% of Buddhists are also recorded as being of 'Chinese and Other Ethnic Groups', 38.8% are 'white', 9.6% are 'Asian', 3.2% are 'mixed' and 1.0% are 'Black or Black British'. As set out in Table 5, 15.3% of all those recorded as 'Chinese and Other Ethnic Groups' are also recorded as being 'Buddhist', as are 0.7% of 'mixed', 0.6% of 'Asians', 0.1% of 'Black and Black British' and 0.1% of people recorded as 'white'.

Buddhism has two main streams of teaching and practice, both of which are found in the UK. There is the so-called 'Southern Transmission' of Theravada Buddhism, meaning 'the way of the Elders', and also the 'Northern Transmission' of Mahayana Buddhism, meaning 'the great vehicle'. Theravada Buddhism includes groups that have Sri Lankan, Burmese, Thai and other national and ethnic backgrounds. It also includes Ambedkarites who are followers of Dr. Ambedkar, who led a movement for emancipation and conversion to Buddhism among low and 'scheduled' caste Indians.

Mahayana Buddhism includes Tibetan Buddhism which itself has a number of different traditions. The first Tibetan Buddhist centre in the west was founded at Johnstone House in Dumfriesshire, in Scotland in 1967 by Chogyam Trungpa, a former Abbot of the Surmang group of monasteries in Tibet and by Akong Rinpoche, the former Abbot of the Drolma Lhakhang Monastery. The Centre is known as Kagyu Samye Ling and it is representative of the Kagyupa tradition which, together with the Gelugpa, is the strongest of the Tibetan traditions in Britain. The former tends towards a more direct mystical experience, while the latter is more graduated in its approach and is typified by the Manjushri Institute, founded in 1976 by pupils of Lama Thubten Yeshe.

There are a number of Buddhist groups that have recognizably Japanese origins, including some Zen groups of the Rinzai and Soto schools. In its meditational practice Soto Zen emphasizes 'just sitting', sometimes also known as Serene Reflection Meditation, while in the Rinzai tradition meditation is accompanied by the use of *koans* or questions from Zen Masters that are designed to engender and test insight. There are also a number of Nichiren groups, including the Rissho Kosei-Kai (Society for Righteousness and Friendship) and the lay Buddhist movement Sokka Gakkai. There is also the Nipponzan Myohoji Order that has constructed the well-known Peace Pagodas in both London and Milton Keynes.

Finally, as Buddhism becomes more indigenized in the UK, a number of 'non-aligned' and specifically 'western Buddhist' groups have developed, the most well known of which is the Friends of the Western Buddhist Order that draws upon all the traditions of Eastern Buddhism, while maintaining a strong engagement with western culture.

Bahá'ís in the UK: A Profile

Bahá'ís have been present in the UK since 1898, when Miriam Thornburgh-Cropper, the first Bahá'í to live in London, started to attract others to the Faith, having been inspired by a visit to the Holy Land to meet 'Abdu'l-Bahá, the eldest son and successor of Bahá'u'lláh, the founder of the Bahá'í Faith. The Bahá'í Faith then grew through the 1911–13 visits to a number of cities in England and Scotland of 'Abdu'l-Bahá. Until 1939 most Bahá'í activity was centred in England, but after the Second World War the Bahá'í Faith was also established in Scotland, Wales and Ireland.

In the 2001 Census questions on religion, there was no pre-set box for Bahá'í respondents to use. However, if Bahá'í respondents ticked the category of 'Other religions – write in' then, on the basis of coded analyses of the 'write-ins', the Office for National Statistics' *Table M275 Religion (Most Detailed Categories)* shows that there were 4,374 Bahá'í respondents in England and 271 in Wales. Across the UK as a whole the Bahá'í Community itself estimates its membership as being between 5,500 and 6,000.

Most Bahá'ís in the UK are of indigenous ethnic origin and the majority are converts from other religions or are former agnostics or atheists. There are, though, also Bahá'ís whose family roots are in Iran, most of whom have arrived since the Iranian Revolution. Bahá'ís are not organized into any identifiably distinct traditions of interpretation or practice. Indeed, it is part of the Bahá'í self-understanding that their religion is unique among the world's religions in that, although at each stage in the development of the Bahá'í religion there have been those who have split off from the community, it has survived a century and a half without splitting into sects.

Jainism in the UK: A Profile

Most Jains in the UK migrated directly from India in the 1950s or else came in the 1960s and 1970s from the East African countries in which they or their forebears had previously settled, such as Kenya, Uganda and Tanzania. Jains have long been engaged in business and finance and in the UK they are well represented in the professions of accountancy, medicine and pharmacy.

In the 2001 Census questions on religion, there was no pre-set box for Jain respondents to use. If instead, Jain respondents ticked the category of 'Other religions – write in' then, on the basis of coded analyses of the 'write-ins' the Office for National Statistics' *Table M275 Religion (Most Detailed Categories)* shows that there were 15,067 Jain respondents in England and 65 in Wales. Many of the Jains in the UK live in and around the Greater London area and in Leicester. Jain communities are also found in Coventry, Luton, Manchester, Northampton and Wellingborough.

Many Jains can trace their historical and ethnic origins back to the Gujarat and Rajasthan areas of India while some Jain groupings have membership that is specific to particular castes. These include the Oshwal and Navnat who were originally Indian trading communities and are grouped in organizations such as the Navnat Vanik Association of the UK, representing Vaniks.

In religious terms, Jains have two main monastic traditions: the Shvetambara, meaning 'white-robed', and the Digambara, meaning 'sky-clad'. The majority of Jains globally, and in the UK, are Shvetambara. The two groups, which emerged in the third and fifth centuries CE, differ in some of their beliefs and practices but agree in their basic philosophy.

Zoroastrianism in the UK: A Profile

Navroji Rustom Maneck Sett was the first Zoroastrian, and possibly the first Indian, known to have visited the UK, arriving in 1723. The first Indian firm to open for business in Britain began in 1855, was run by a Parsi family and was called Cama and Company. The first three Asian Members of Parliament came from the small Parsi community. The first of these was the Liberal MP, Dadabhai Naoroji, elected in 1892; followed in 1895 by the Conservative MP, Sir Mancherjee Meherwanjee Bhownaggree; and then by Shapurji Dorabji Saklatvala for Labour in 1922, and for the Communist Party in 1929.

Other Parsis came from India in the 1950s, immediately following Indian independence and later, prior to the introduction in the 1960s of tighter immigration controls on migration, from New Commonwealth countries. There were also Indian-origin Parsis who came from Aden and from East Africa (mainly Zanzibar, Kenya and Uganda) in the 1960s and 1970s, after the introduction of Arabization and Africanization policies in these newly independent states.

In the 2001 Census questions on religion, there was no pre-set box for Zoroastrian respondents to use. Instead, if Zoroastrians ticked the category of 'Other religions – write in' then, on the basis of analyses of the coded 'write-ins' the Office for National Statistics' *Table M275 Religion (Most Detailed Categories)* shows that there were 3,355 Zoroastrians in England and 383 in Wales, while the Zoroastrian Trust Funds of Europe Incorporated estimates a population of over 5,000 Zoroastrians across the UK as a whole.

The contemporary Zoroastrian community includes both Indian and Iranian elements. In 936 CE, the Parsees or Parsis (Pars being a province of Iran) migrated from Persia to Sanjan in Gujarat, India and, over the next thousand years, were joined by many more. Those who remained in Persia were known as the Irani

Zardushtis or simply as Iranis. The majority of Zoroastrians in the UK are of Parsi origin, though in more recent years an Irani presence has also developed as a result of refugee movements following the downfall of the Pahlavi dynasty and the foundation of the Islamic Republic in 1979. The main differences amongst Zoroastrians arise from the differing ancestral histories of these two main groups and manifest themselves especially in relation to the Zoroastrian calendar and some festivals.

Paganism in the UK: A Profile

Contemporary Paganism understands itself as inheriting the indigenous religious tradition and practice of these islands. In some regions of the UK, the original Pagan traditions remained strong even after Christianity gained ascendancy. In more recent times, this inheritance has been redeveloped through the modern revivals and/or reinterpretations found among the neo-Pagan and deep ecology movements.

Paganism is a religious outlook that can broadly be characterized as nature-venerating. It recognizes many deities, both goddesses and gods. It is not a credal system but finds expression in many theologies and practices. Paganism is therefore not a single tradition, but consists of a loose network of people, sometimes working as individuals, and sometimes as part of groups across a variety of traditions (see Crowley, 1994, and Harvey and Hardman, 1996) that include the Craft (or Wicca), Druidry, Odinism (Asatru), Shamanism, Women's Traditions, and Men's Traditions.

There are significant differences between these groups, but all Pagans share in a sense of the organic vitality of the natural world and women's spirituality is respected in all traditions. Table 20 sets out the numbers of Census respondents to the 'Other' tick-box with 'write-in' responses for England and Wales that were coded to a group that is actually related to Paganism, while Table 21 gives figures obtained by the Scottish Pagan Federation as a 2001 Census Commissioned Table from the General Register Office for Scotland.

It should, however, be noted that the Scottish Pagan Federation advised Pagans to respond to the write-in option with 'Pagan'. It is therefore likely that these figures cannot be taken as a breakdown of the Scottish Pagan population by specific Pagan tradition. Nevertheless, taken together, the English and Welsh and Scottish figures are suggestive of there being around 42,890 Pagans in Great Britain.

New Religious Movements in the UK: A Profile

Then, there are also groupings of what the media often disparagingly refer to in an undifferentiated way as 'sects' or 'cults', but which are usually known in academic

Table 20: Census Respondents in England and Wales Coded to a Group Connected with Paganism

	Total Numbers in England	Total Numbers in Wales
Asatru	90	3
Celtic Pagan	460	48
Druidism	1,568	89
Pagan	28,943	1,714
Wicca	6,844	383
Totals of Pagan-Related *	37,905	2,237

* 368 respondents in England and 38 in Wales were recorded under 'Animism' which may also be seen as related to Paganism. In addition, there were 95 responses in England and 3 in Wales that were recorded as 'ancestor worship' that could either relate to (see Table 23 below) forms of religion connected with people of Chinese descent and/or to Pagan-related traditions. Finally, it should be noted that 265 respondents in England and 13 in Wales were recorded as 'Heathens' (which is a form of Pagan tradition as well as a more general linguistic descriptor for 'irreligiousness') whom the Office for National Statistics coded among the overall figure for those of 'no religion'.

Source: Census, April 2001. *Table M275 Religion (Most Detailed Categories)*. Crown copyright, 2004. This particular grouping and linking together of traditions within an overall Pagan-related Table and total is the author's.

Table 21: Census Respondents in Scotland Coded to a Group Connected with Paganism

Tradition	Total Numbers in Scotland
Animism	28
Celtic Pagan	15
Druidism	53
Heathen	12
Neo Pagan	13
Pagan	1,140
Pagan Other	133
Pagan Wiccan	27
Pagan Wicca	17
Pantheist	60
Shaman	19
Spiritual Pagan	10
Wiccan	248

It is also possible that the 12 Discordianism, 10 Gaian, and 14 Nature responses can also appropriately be understood as Pagan, inclusion of which would bring the overall Pagan total for Scotland to 1,966.

Source: 2001 Census Table from the General Register Office for Scotland, commissioned by the Scottish Pagan Federation.

discourse by the less prejudicial terminology of 'New Religious Movements' (Barker, 1982, 1990), often referred to by the abbreviation of 'NRMs'. Table 22 sets out the numbers of Census respondents whose responses were coded to such groups.

Unificationists have often popularly – and sometimes disparagingly – been referred to as 'Moonies', in reference to the founder of their movement, Revd. Sun Myung Moon (Chryssides, 1991). Today, the movement is more formally known by the name of Family Federation for World Peace and Unification. Scientology, founded by L. Ron Hubbard, is a movement that has had a considerable national and international profile, including debates over the extent to which it can be considered to be a religious organization.

Religions of People of Chinese Descent in the UK: A Profile

Many Chinese people may have chosen to tick the Census pre-set option of 'Buddhist'. However, the reality of Chinese religious life is often much more complex and multi-faceted than can be reflected in a single 'tick-box' response (Pan, 1998). Table 23 sets out responses coded to traditions that may be seen as being related to the religious life of people with Chinese descent (though it is likely that some small number of 'white', indigenous, followers of Taoism will be included in the figures for this).

Yet Other Religions in the UK: A Profile

There are, of course, a range of other religious and philosophical groupings that do not fit neatly into any of the categories of description above and which form

Table 22: Census Respondents Coded to a Group Often Seen as a 'New Religious Movement'

Group	Total Numbers in England	Total Numbers in Wales
Hare Krishna **	612	28
Scientology	1,757	24
Unification Church *	241	11

* Those using the write-in 'Unificationist' were coded by the Office for National Statistics to the overall 'Christian' data, but are listed here on the basis that they project a more 'independent' and 'universalist' role.

** Those using the write-in 'Hare Krishna' are likely to be related to the ISKCON, the International Society for Krishna Consciousness, which was once often seen as an NRM, but which in the UK now has a close relationship within the overall Hindu tradition and community.

Source: Census, April 2001. *Table M275 Religion (Most Detailed Categories)*. Crown copyright, 2004.

Table 23: Census Respondents Coded to Traditions That May be Seen as Being Related to the Religious Life of People of Chinese Descent

Tradition	Total Numbers in England	Total Numbers in Wales
Chinese Religions	141	7
Confucianist	80	3
Taoist	3,576	16
Tin Tao	4	0

As has previously been noted in Table 20, there were also 95 responses in England and 3 in Wales coded to 'Ancestor Worship' that could relate to Chinese forms of religiosity and/or to 'Ancestor Worship' in the context of Pagan-related traditions.

Source: Census, April 2001. *Table M275 Religion (Most Detailed Categories)*. Crown copyright, 2004.

a part of the overall religious diversity of the UK even though they cannot all be dealt with in any detail. These include religions that are important among specific ethnic groups, such as Rastafarianism among peoples of African-Caribbean descent, through to followers of various esoteric religions, holistic spiritualities and practitioners of various New Age approaches.

The latter may have more or less to do with religion, depending on the individuals involved. Thus, for example, the sociologist of religion, Steve Bruce (1995: 105), characterizes 'New Age' as 'a milieu in which people acquire and absorb a variety of beliefs and practices that they combine into their own pockets of culture and attend to with differing degrees of seriousness'.

5 Secularization, Humanism, Atheism, Religion and Belief

Study Activity 4

After reading section 5 of the chapter:

(i) *describe* some of the key meanings attributed to 'secularization'

(ii) *discuss* what statistical data may indicate in relation to the place of people of 'no religion' in the UK landscape of religion and belief

(iii) *evaluate*, in a preliminary way, some of the tensions likely to be involved in the governance of a society that is Christian, religiously plural and secular

---

Secularization: Its Nature and Extent

Having so far noted both the diversification and persistent importance of religious identity, communities and groups, this closing section of the chapter takes account of the degree to which the UK can appropriately be characterized as 'secular' as well as 'Christian' and 'religiously plural'. The development of secularity, the origins of which are to be found in the humanism of the Renaissance, has partly been a by-product of the Industrial Revolution and the urbanization of life that it brought. The sense grew that humanity was becoming increasingly insulated from the mysteries and unpredictabilities of natural life. The machine became the emblem of progress and its mechanical precision a symbolic ideal. With what seemed to be the increasing loss of mystery, it appeared that God was being banished (Berman, 1988). Nietzsche proclaimed the death of God.

The world seemed to have become explainable solely in terms of itself. Darwinism offered a new explanation of human beginnings; anthropology questioned the uniqueness of claims about religious revelation; and with Freud, psychoanalysis began to explain human mysteries in terms of sexuality. Technology began to shrink the world as air travel became ever faster, cheaper and more popular. Communication by satellite and the development of the mass media brought the whole world into the living rooms of ordinary people. The first cosmonaut, Yuri Gagarin of the Soviet Union, declared that when he had been in space he had seen no God.

By the 1960s, Christian theological and ecclesiological awareness of the challenges posed by secularity intensified. Some theologians, influenced by contemporary interpretations of Dietrich Bonhoeffer's (1971) ideas of 'religionless Christianity' sought to incorporate the 'secular' as part of the inner meaning of Christianity, as in Harvey Cox's (1965) famous book, *The Secular City*. However, for many other Christians the secular became seen as more of a threat.

While the concept of secularization has been commonplace in both academic and popular writing, the meanings associated with it, and the extent of the social reality that it attempts to describe and to interpret are both varied and contested (Martin, 1978; Dobbelaere, 1981, 1984; Bruce, 1992; Barker, Beckford and Dobbelaere, 1993). The sociologist of religion, Bryan Wilson (1969: 14) characterized secularization as 'the process whereby religious thinking, practice and institutions lose social significance', while Peter Berger (1967: 107) defined secularization as 'the process by which sectors of society and culture are removed from the domination of religious institutions and symbols.'

Although different, the definitions offered by Wilson and Berger share an analysis of the role that religion plays in the public sphere. Neither argument depends on any position concerning an absolute decline in religious belief and practice of a kind that, from the 1960s onwards, has often been popularly associated with the concept of secularization. Whatever position is taken in these debates, it is clear that the reality signified by the concept of secularization has brought something distinctively and significantly challenging to all religions.

Writing in the middle of the 1960s, when consciousness of the technological revolution was at its height, the scholar of comparative religion, A.C. Bouquet

(1958: 100) referred to Karl Jaspers' theory of 'the axial age' that gave rise to the historic world religions of today. He observed that, 'now, just as we Christians are beginning to know more about the religions of our neighbours, it looks as though all of us, whoever we are, are being faced with the arrival of a second axial age, the age of the scientific revolution, in which a far greater challenge to religion will have to be faced than ever before'.

People of 'No Religion' in the 2001 Census

In the 2001 Census, 9,103,727 people (or 15.5% of the population) across the UK stated that they are of 'no religion'. These are set out by country in Table 24.

Those classified by the Office for National Statistics as of 'no religion' included the phenomenon of 39,127 people in England and Wales (or 0.7% of the population) who identified themselves as 'Jedi' or 'Jedi Knights', after the key characters in the *Star Wars* series of films. This followed an internet campaign that occurred also in Australia, Canada and New Zealand to encourage people to respond to the Census question on religion in this way, and which led to 2.6% (6,480 people) of the population of Brighton and Hove in England declaring themselves in this way.

The 'no religion' headline figure also included 14,067 respondents in England and 842 in Wales who indicated 'agnostic'. In addition, it included 269 people who used the write-in option to give the description of 'Heathen' (which can be a form of Pagan religious identity as well as being taken in its more popular sense of meaning generally irreligious). In addition, it is also worth noting that census *Table M275 Religion (Most Detailed Categories)* – which gives the breakdown (for England and Wales only) of respondents who used the 'Other Religions – write in'

Table 24: Census Respondents Indicating 'No Religion' by Country of the UK

Country	Total Numbers of 'No religion'	Percentage of Total Population
England	7,171,332	14.6%
Scotland	1,394,460	27.6%
Wales	537,935	18.5%
Northern Ireland	*	*
United Kingdom	9,103,727	15.5%

* Note: For Northern Ireland, separate figures for 'No religion' and 'Not stated' are not available.

As already noted in Table 20 above, it particularly problematically included the coding of the write-in response of 'Heathen' to the overall data for 'no religon'.

Source: Census, April 2001. National Statistics website: *www.statistics.gov.uk* and *Table M275 Religion (Most Detailed Categories)*. Crown copyright, 2004. Percentages calculated by the present author.

response to the religion question – also includes some respondents from groups often associated as being of 'no religion' or, at least, of philosophical alternatives to religion. These are set out by country of the UK in Table 25.

Non-Respondents to the Religion Questions in the 2001 Census

Alongside those who, in response to the 2001 Census questions on religion stated that they were of 'No religion', there were, in addition, 4,288,719 people (or 7.3% of the population) who did not respond to the voluntary question. These are set out in Table 26. A significant number of these respondents may not identify with religion in general and/or any religion in particular. However, since the religion question was a voluntary one, there is a real difficulty in securely interpreting the significance of the respondents who did not state a religion. For example, some research (Weller and Andrews, 1998) has indicated that non-respondents to questions of this kind *may* include individuals with or without a strong religious identity but who, on principle, refuse to answer such questions believing religious identification to be a private matter. These may also have included individuals, religious or otherwise, who were concerned about the possible uses to which this data might be put.

'No Religion', 'Not Believing', 'Not Religious'

In contrast with the Census data, it should be noted that, in the British Social Attitudes survey for 2001 (Office for National Statistics, 2003: 226), as many as 41% of respondents said they belonged to 'no religion', while only just over half of the population (54%) of Great Britain indicated that they regarded themselves as being Christian (with 29% being Church of England/Anglican; 11% being Catholic, and 14% being of other Christian denominations) and only 4% regarded

Table 25: Census Respondents Coded to Stances Often Associated with Being as of 'No Religion'

Tradition	Total Numbers in England	Total Numbers in Wales
Free Thinker	571	15
Humanist	7,866	430
Internationalist	3	0
Rationalist	37	0
Realist	104	0
Secularist	11	0

Source: Census, April 2001. *Table M275 Religion (Most Detailed Categories)*. Crown copyright, 2004.

Table 26: Census Respondents Not Answering the Religion Question by Country of the UK

Country	Total Numbers of 'Not Stated'	Percentage of Total Population
England	3,776,515	7.7%
Scotland	278,061	5.5%
Wales	234,143	8.1%
Northern Ireland	*	*
United Kingdom	4,288,719	7.2%

*Note: For Northern Ireland, separate figures for 'No religion' and 'Not stated' are not available.

Source: Census, April 2001. National Statistics website: *www.statistics.gov.uk* and *Table M275 Religion (Most Detailed Categories)*. Crown copyright, 2004. Percentages calculated by the present author.

themselves as belonging to another religion. At the same time, it should be noted that, in contrast to the Census, the BSA survey is based on a very small sample.

In relation more to beliefs, the British Social Attitudes Survey, 1998 (Office for National Statistics, 2000: 219) had shown only 10% of respondents affirming that 'I don't believe in God'; while 15% took the position that, 'I don't know whether there is a God and I don't believe there is any way to find out'; 14% said, 'I find myself believing in God some of the time, but not at others', and 3% did not respond. 21% of respondents affirmed that, 'I know God exists and I have no doubt about it'; 23% said 'While I have doubts, I feel that I do believe in God' and 14% said, 'I don't believe in a personal God, but I do believe in a Higher Power of some kind'.

In the 1999–2000 European Values Survey (Halman, 2001), when asked a 'yes' or 'no' question about 'belief in God', 28.2% of respondents in Great Britain answered 'no' and 71.8% said 'yes'. When asked 'which of these statements comes closest to your beliefs', 31% said 'personal God', 40.1% said 'spirit or life force', 18.7% said 'don't know what to think' and 10.2% said there is 'no spirit, God or life force'. When the European Values Survey asked 'independently of whether you go to church or not' would you say you are 'a religious person', while only 5% of respondents in Great Britain said they were 'a convinced atheist', 53.4% said they were 'not a religious person', and 41.6% affirmed that they were 'a religious person'.

Atheism and secularism as systematized epistemologies and integrated ways of life were once sponsored by the states and political systems that were controlled by Marxist-Leninist ideology. But now, principled stances of atheism can be found only among relatively small numbers of people. Thus, the 2001 Home Office Citizenship Survey showed that 'only four per cent of those not affiliated to a faith community stated that not having a religious affiliation was important to their identity' (O'Beirne, 2004: 19).

6 The 'Three-Dimensional' Society: Religion(s) and 'the Secular'

The Diversity of 'the Secular'

The kind of secularity in which many of those who are non-religious are indifferent to religion rather than antagonistic towards it is very much a part of the plurality of the contemporary UK. At the same time, there are those who do not identify with any religion and who have deeply felt concerns about allowing a privileged or too prominent a role for religion in public life. In terms of organized campaigning, these concerns are expressed by the National Secular Society.

However, such concerns are also likely to be considerably more widespread than among 'signed up' secularists, especially following the 9/11 attacks in the USA and 7/7 in the UK and anxieties about religious extremism to which these gave rise. Similar concerns may be held by Humanists (among whom the British Humanist Association offers a value system, philosophical beliefs and rites of passage, while nevertheless seeing itself as non-religious) as well as by 'non-religious' members of the general public who may identify themselves explicitly as either Humanists (Fowler, 1999) or Secularists.

In the 1999–2000 European Values Survey, in response to the question of whether respondents agree or disagree with the statement that 'religious leaders should not influence government decisions', 20.3% of respondents from Great Britain indicated that they 'agree strongly' and 44.9% that they 'agree', while 19.1% said they 'neither agree nor disagree', with 12.1% saying they 'disagree' and 3.6% that they 'disagree strongly'.

Overall, then, the nature and extent of religious belief, belonging, participation in worship and secularization is not straightforward to portray in a statistical way since the results obtained from various surveys are highly dependent on the form in which the questions are asked. However, it remains clear that all three dimensions of the 'Christian', 'secular' (Bailey, ed., 2002) and 'religiously plural' (Badham, 1994) aspects of the contemporary socio-religious reality form a significant part of the religious landscape of contemporary England and the UK.

Balancing the 'Christian', the 'Secular' and the 'Religiously Plural'

Finding an appropriate balance in terms of inclusiveness, equity and participation for the intersecting interests and perspectives of diverse individuals and groups of religious and non-religious identity and conviction is likely to prove one of the major challenges of the coming decades in the UK. In the chapters that follow, these issues will be explored in relation to the areas of places of worship and planning; governance and civil society; education; hatred, respect and freedom of expression; discrimination and equal opportunities. This begins in the next chapter with an examination of religious diversity and places of worship.

Resources for Further Learning

Almond, P. (1988), *The British Discovery of Buddhism*. Cambridge: Cambridge University Press.

Andrews, A. (1994), 'The concept of sect and denomination in Islam'. *Religion Today*, 9, 2, 6–10.

Avis, P., ed. (2003), *Public Faith? The State of Religious Belief and Practice in Britain*. London: SPCK.

Badawi, Z. (1981), *Islam in Britain*. London: Ta Ha Publishers.

Badham, P. (1994), 'Religious Pluralism in Modern Britain', in S. Gilley and W. Sheils, eds, *A History of Religion in Britain: Practice and Belief from Pre-Roman Times to the Present*. Oxford: Blackwell, pp. 488–502.

Badham, P., ed. (1989), *Religion, State and Society in Modern Britain*. Lampeter: Edwin Mellen Press.

Bailey, E. (1983), 'The implicit religion of contemporary society: an orientation and plea for its study'. *Religion*, 2, 69–83.

Bailey, E. (1989), 'The Folk Religion of the English People', in P. Badham, ed., *Religion, State and Society in Modern Britain*. Lampeter: Edwin Mellen Press, pp. 145–58.

Bailey, E., ed. (2002), *The Secular Quest for Meaning in Life: Denton Papers in Implicit Religion*. Lampeter: Edwin Mellen.

Ballard, R. (2000), 'The Growth and Changing Character of the Sikh Presence in Britain', in H. Coward, J. Hinnells and R. Williams, eds, *The South Asian Religious Diaspora in Britain, Canada and the United States*. New York: State University of New York Press, pp. 127–44.

Ballard, R., ed. (1994), *Desh Pardesh: The South Asian Presence in Britain*. London: Hurst and Co.

Barker, E. (1982), *New Religious Movements: A Perspective for Understanding Society*. Lampeter: Edwin Mellen Press.

Barker, E. (1989), *New Religious Movements: A Practical Introduction*. London: HMSO.

Barker, E., Beckford J. and Dobbelaere, K., eds (1993), *Secularisation, Rationalism and Sectarianism*. Oxford: Oxford University Press.

Barley, C., Field, C., Kosmin, B. and Nielsen, J. (1987), *Religion: Reviews of United Kingdom Statistical Sources, Volume XX*. Oxford: Pergamon Press.

Barot, R., ed. (1993), *Religion and Ethnicity: Minorities and Social Change in the Metropolis*. Kampen: Kok Pharos.

Batchelor, S. (1994), *The Awakening of the West: The Encounter of Buddhism and Western Culture*. London: Aquarian Press.

Beckerlegge, G. (1997), 'The Followers of "Mohammed, Kalee and Dada Nanute": The Presence of Islam and South Asian Religions in Victorian Britain', in J. Wolffe, ed., *Religion in Victorian Britain, Volume 5, Culture and Empire*. Manchester: Manchester University Press, pp. 221–70.

Beckford, J., Gale, R., Owen, D., Peach, C., Weller, P. (2006), *Review of the Evidence Base on Faith Communities*. London: Office of the Deputy Prime Minister.

Bell, P. (1969), *Disestablishment in Ireland and Wales*. London: SPCK.

Berger, P. (1967), *The Social Reality of Religion: Elements of a Sociological Theory of Religion*. London: Faber and Faber.

Berman, D. (1988), *A History of Atheism in Britain: From Hobbes to Russell*. London: Croom Helm.

Bhachu, P. (1985), *Twice Migrants: East African Sikh Settlers in Britain*. London: Tavistock.

Bisset, P. (1986), *The Kirk and Her Scotland*. Edinburgh: Handsel.

Bloom, W. (2004), *SOULution: The Holistic Manifesto: How Today's Spirituality Changes Everything*. London: Hay House.

Bonhoeffer, D. (1971), *Letters and Papers From Prison* (enlarged edition). London: SCM Press.

Bouquet, A. (1958), *The Christian Faith and Non-Christian Religions*. London: James Nisbet and Co.

Bowen, D., ed. (1981), *Hinduism in England*. Bradford: Faculty of Contemporary Studies, Bradford College.

Brierley, P., ed. (2003), *UK Christian Handbook: Religious Trends 4, 2003/4*. London: Christian Research.

Brown, C. (1987), *A Social History of Religion in Scotland Since 1730*. London: Methuen.

Brown, C. (2001), *The Death of Christian Britain: Understanding Secularisation 1880–2001*. London: Routledge.

Brown, M. (2000), 'Religion and economic activity in the South Asian population'. *Ethnic and Racial Studies*, 23, 6, 1035–61.

Bruce, S. (1992), *Religion and Modernisation: Sociologists and Historians Debate the Secularisation Thesis*. Oxford: Oxford University Press.

Bruce, S. (1995), *Religion in Modern Britain*. Oxford: Oxford University Press.

Burghart, R., ed. (1987), *Hinduism in Great Britain: The Perpetuation of Religion in an Alien Cultural Milieu*. London: Tavistock.

Campbell, J. (1994), 'The Jewish community in Britain', in S. Gilley and W. Sheils, eds, *A History of Religion in Britain: Belief and Practice from Pre-Roman Times to the Present*. Oxford: Blackwell, pp. 427–48.

Carey, S. (1983), 'The Hare Krishna movement and Hindus in Britain'. *New Community*, 10, 3, 477–86.

Chryssides, G. (1991), *The Advent of Sun Myung Moon: The Origins, Beliefs and Practices of the Unification Church*. Macmillan: Basingstoke.

Chryssides, G. (1994), 'Britain's changing faiths: adaptation in a new environment', in G. Parsons, ed., *The Growth of Religious Diversity: Britain From 1945, Volume II. Issues*. London: Routledge, London, pp. 57–84.

Clark, C., Peach, C. and Vertovec, S., eds (1990), *South Asians Overseas: Migration and Ethnicity*. Cambridge: Cambridge University Press.

Cole, W. (1989), 'Sikhs in Britain', in P. Badham, ed., *Religion, State and Society in Modern Britain*. Lampeter: Edwin Mellen Press, pp. 259–76.

Coward, H., Hinnells, J. and Williams, R. (2000), *The South Asian Religious Diaspora in Britain, Canada and the United States*. Albany, State University of New York Press.

Cox, H. (1965), *The Secular City: Secularisation and Urbanisation in Theological Perspective*. London: SCM Press.

Crowley, V. (1994), *Phoenix From the Flame: Pagan Spirituality in the Western World*. London: Aquarian.

Davie, G. (1990a), 'Believing without belonging: is this the future of religion in Britain?'. *Social Compass*, 37, 455–69.

Davie, G. (1990b), 'An ordinary God: the paradox of religion in contemporary Britain'. *British Journal of Sociology*, 41, 3, 395–421.

Davie, G. (1994), *Religion in Britain Since 1945: Believing Without Belonging*. Oxford: Blackwell.

Dobbelaere, K. (1981), 'Secularisation: a multi-dimensional concept'. *Current Sociology*, 29, 2,1–216.

Dobbelaere, K. (1984), 'Secularisation theories and sociological paradigms: convergences and divergences'. *Social Compass*, 31, 199–219.

Dwyer, R. (1994), 'Caste, religion and sect in Gujarat: followers of Vallabhacharya and Swaminarayan', in R. Ballard, ed., *Desh Pardesh: The South Asian Presence in Britain*. London: Hurst and Co., pp. 165–90.

Fisher, Michael H., Lahiri, S. and Thandi, S. (2007), *A South-Asian History of Britain: Four Centuries of Peoples from the Indian Sub-Continent*. Oxford: Greenwood Publishing.

Fowler, J. (1999), *Humanism: Beliefs and Practices*. Brighton: Sussex Academic Press.

Geaves, R. (1996), *Sectarian Influences within Islam in Britain: with Reference to the Concepts of 'Ummah' and 'Community'*. (Community Religions Project Monograph Series). Leeds: University of Leeds Department of Theology and Religious Studies.

Gerloff, R. (1992), *A Plea for British Black Theologies: The Black Church Movement in Britain in its Transatlantic Cultural and Theological Interaction, Parts I & II* (2 volumes). Frankfurt am Main, Germany: Peter Lang.

Gilbert, A. (1980), *The Making of Post-Christian Britain: A History of the Secularization of Modern Society*. Essex: Longman.

Gilbert, A. (1994), 'Secularisation and the Future', in S. Gilley and W. Sheils, eds, *A History of Religion in Britain: Belief and Practice from Pre-Roman Times to the Present*. Oxford: Blackwell, pp. 503–21.

Gilley, S. and Sheils, W., eds (1994), *A History of Religion in Britain: Practice and Belief from Pre-Roman Times to the Present*. Oxford: Blackwell.

ter Haar, G. (1998), *Halfway to Paradise: African Christians in Europe*. Cardiff: Cardiff Academic Press.

Halman, L. (2001), *The European Values Study: A Third Wave. Sourcebook of 1999/2000 European Values Study Survey*. Tilburg: WORC Tilburg University.

Hanegraaff, W. (1996), *New Age Religion and Western Culture: Esotericism in the Mirror of Secular Thought*. Leiden: E.J. Brill.

Hardy, P. (1972), *The Muslims of British India*. Cambridge: Cambridge University Press.

Harvey, G. and Hardman, C. (1996), *Paganism Today*. London: Thorsons.

Hay, D. (1982), *Exploring Inner Space: Is God Still Possible in the Twentieth Century?* Harmondsworth; Pelican.

Hay, D. (1990), *Religious Experience Today: Studying the Facts*. London: Mowbray.

Heelas, P. and Woodhead, L., et al. (2005), *The Spiritual Revolution: Why Religion is Giving Way to Spirituality*. Oxford: Blackwell.

Hooker, R. and Sargant, J., eds (n.d.), *Belonging to Britain: Christian Perspectives on a Plural Society*. London: Council of Churches for Britain and Ireland.

Humphreys, C. (1968), *Sixty Years of Buddhism in England 1907–1967: A History and a Survey*. London: The Buddhist Society.

Jacobsen, K. and Kumar, P., eds (2004), *South Asians in the Diaspora: Histories and Religious Traditions*. Leiden: E.J. Brill.

Jenkins, D. (1975), *The British: Their Identity and Their Religion*. London: SCM Press.

Joly, D. and Nielsen, J. (1985), *Muslims in Britain: An Annotated Bibliography, 1960–1984*. Coventry: Centre for Research in Ethnic Relations, University of Warwick.

Jones, R. (1992), 'Religion, Nationality and State in Wales, 1840–1890', in D. Kerr, ed., *Religion, State and Ethnic Groups,* Aldershot: Dartmouth Publishing, pp. 261–76.

Knott, K. (1986), *My Sweet Lord: The Hare Krishna Movement*. Wellingborough: Aquarian Press.

Knott, K. (1996), 'The religions of South Asian communities in Britain', in J. Hinnells, ed., *The New Handbook of Living Religions*, Oxford: Blackwell, pp. 756–74.

Knott, K. (2000), 'Hinduism in Britain', in H. Coward, J. Hinnells and R. Williams, eds, *The South Asian Religious Diaspora in Britain, Canada and the United States*. New York: State University of New York Press, pp. 89–107.

Lerman, A. (1989), *The Jewish Communities of the World*. Basingstoke: Macmillan.

Lindley, J. (2002), 'Race or religion? The impact of religion on the employment and earnings of Britain's ethnic communities'. *Journal of Ethnic and Migration Studies*, 28, 3, 427–42.

Martin, D. (1978), *A General Theory of Secularisation*. Oxford: Blackwell.

Nairn, T. (1997), *The Break-Up of Britain: Crisis and Neo-Nationalism* (second edition). London: Verso.

Nielsen, J. (1992), *Muslims in Western Europe*. Edinburgh: Edinburgh University Press.

O'Beirne, M. (2004), *Religion in England and Wales: findings from the 2001 Home Office Citizenship Survey*, Home Office Research Study 274. London: Home Office.

Office for National Statistics (2000), *Social Trends 30: 2000 Edition*. London: The Stationery Office.

Office for National Statistics (2003), *Social Trends 33: 2003 Edition*. London: The Stationery Office.

Oliver, P. (1979), *Buddhism in Britain*. London: Rider and Company.

Omoyajowo, J. (1982), *Cherubim and Seraphim: The History of an African Independent Church*. New York: Nok Publishers International.

Pan, L. (1998), *The Encyclopaedia of the Chinese Overseas*. Richmond: Curzon Press.

Parsons, G., ed. (1993), *The Growth of Religious Diversity: Britain From 1945, Volume I: Traditions*. London: Routledge/Open University.

Parsons, G., ed. (1994), *The Growth of Religious Diversity: Britain From 1945, Volume II: Issues*. London: Routledge/Open University.

Peach, C. (2006), 'Islam, ethnicity and South Asian religions in the London 2001 census'. *Transactions of the Institute of British Geographers*, nos 31, 353–70.

Raza, S. (1992), *Islam in Britain: Past, Present and Future* (second edition). Leicester: Volcano Press.

Rhys, G. (n.d.), 'The Divine Economy and the Political Economy: the Theology of Welsh Nationalism', in R. Hooker and S. Sargant, eds, *Belonging to Britain: Christian Perspectives on a Plural Society*. London: Council of Churches for Britain and Ireland, pp. 55–74.

Richardson, N. (1999), *A Tapestry of Beliefs: Christian Traditions in Northern Ireland*. Belfast: Blankstaff Press.

Robinson, F. (1988), *Varieties of South Asian Islam*. (Centre for Research in Ethnic Relations, Research Paper, No. 8), Coventry: University of Warwick.

Robinson, V. (1990), 'Boom and gloom: the success and failure of South Asians in Britain', in C. Clarke, C. Peach and S. Vertovec, eds, *South Asians Overseas: Migration and Ethnicity*. Cambridge: Cambridge University Press, pp. 251–67.

Ryan, M. (1996), *Another Ireland: An Introduction to Ireland's Ethnic-Religious Minority Communities*. Belfast: Stranmillis University College.

Thomas, T. (1993a), 'Old allies, new neighbours: Sikhs in Britain', in G. Parsons, ed., *The Growth of Religious Diversity: Britain from 1945, Volume I: Traditions*. London: Routledge, pp. 205–41.

Thomas, T. (1993b), 'Hindu Dharma in dispersion', in G. Parsons, ed., *The Growth of Religious Diversity: Britain From 1945, Volume I: Traditions*. London: Routledge, pp. 205–41.

Thomas, T., ed. (1988), *The British: Their Religious Beliefs and Practices*. London: Routledge.

Vertovec, S. (1994), 'Caught in an ethnic quandary: Indo-Caribbean Hindus in London', in R. Ballard, ed., *Desh Pardesh: The South Asian Presence in Britain*. London: Hurst and Co., pp. 272–90.

Vertovec, S., ed. (1991), *Aspects of the South Asian Diaspora, Volume II, part 2: Papers on India*. Delhi: Oxford University Press.

Visram, R. (1986), *Ayahs, Lascars and Princes: The Story of Indians in Britain 1700–1947*. London: Pluto Press.

Voas, D. (2003), 'Is Britain a Christian country?', in P. Avis, ed., *Public Faith: The State of Religious Belief and Practice in Britain*. London: SPCK, pp. 92–105.

Voas, D. and Bruce, S. (2004), 'The 2001 Census and Christian identification in Britain'. *Journal of Contemporary Religion*, 19, 1, 23–28.

Wahhab, I. (1989), *Muslims in Britain: Profile of a Community*. London: Runnymede Trust.

Walker, A. (1985), *Restoring the Kingdom: The Radical Christianity of the House Church Movement*. London: Hodder and Stoughton.

Weller, P. (2004a), 'Identity, politics and the future(s) of religion in the UK: the case of the religion questions in the 2001 decennial Census'. *Journal of Contemporary Religion*, 19, 1, 3–21.

Weller, P. (2004b), 'Hindus and Sikhs: community development and religious discrimination in England and Wales', in K. Jacobsen and P. Kumar, eds, *South Asians in the Diaspora: Histories and Religious Traditions*. Leiden: Brill, pp. 454-97.

Weller, P. (2005), *Time for a Change: Reconfiguring Religion, State and Society*. London: T. & T. Clark.

Weller, P. and Andrews, A. (1998), ' "How Many of Them Are There?": Counting Religion: Religion, Statistics and the 2001 Census'. *World Faiths Encounter*, 21, November, 23–34.

Weller, P., Feldman, A. and Purdam, A., et al. (2001), *Religious Discrimination in England and Wales* (Home Office Research Study, No. 220). London: Research, Development and Statistics Directorate, The Home Office.

Wilkinson, J. (1993), *Church in Black and White: The Black Christian Tradition in 'Mainstream' Churches in England: A White Response and Testimony*. Edinburgh: Saint Andrew Press.

Williams, R. (1984), *A New Face of Hinduism: The Swaminarayan Religion*. Cambridge: Cambridge University Press.

Wilson, B. (1969), *Religion in Secular Society: A Sociological Comment*. Harmondsworth: Penguin.

Wolffe, J., ed. (1997), *Religion in Victorian Britain, Volume 5, Culture and Empire*. Manchester: Manchester University Press.

Wolffe, J., ed. (1993), *The Growth of Religious Diversity: Britain From 1945. A Reader*. Sevenoaks: Hodder and Stoughton.

York, M. (1995), *The Emerging Network: A Sociology of New Age and Neo-Pagan Movements*. London: Rowman and Littlewood.

Religious Diversity and Places of Worship

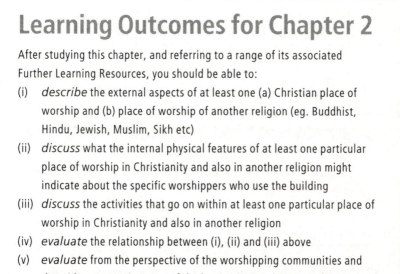

2

> ## Learning Outcomes for Chapter 2
>
> After studying this chapter, and referring to a range of its associated
> Further Learning Resources, you should be able to:
>
> (i)   *describe* the external aspects of at least one (a) Christian place of
> worship and (b) place of worship of another religion (eg. Buddhist,
> Hindu, Jewish, Muslim, Sikh etc)
> (ii) *discuss* what the internal physical features of at least one particular
> place of worship in Christianity and also in another religion might
> indicate about the specific worshippers who use the building
> (iii) *discuss* the activities that go on within at least one particular place of
> worship in Christianity and also in another religion
> (iv) *evaluate* the relationship between (i), (ii) and (iii) above
> (v) *evaluate* from the perspective of the worshipping communities and
> the wider community some of the key issues in relation to planning and
> places of worship

1 The Role of Places of Worship

Places of Worship in the Physical Landscape

Chapter 1 introduced key elements of the diversity of religion and belief found
in the UK. This chapter now turns to the presence and role of places of worship
within that landscape, understood both literally and figuratively.

The historical development and present diversity of the religious profile of the
UK is, in fact, both mirrored in, and given expression by, the religious architecture
of the country (Gale, 1999). One way in which the religious landscape has quite
literally changed is in terms of the presence and range of a variety of different
religious buildings (Weller, 1995). Church steeples and towers are a familiar part
of both the urban and rural landscape of the UK. Jewish synagogues have had

a long historical presence. Increasingly, too, Sikh *gurdwaras*, Hindu and Jain *mandirs*, Muslim mosques and Buddhist *viharas* are also becoming part of the skyline in a significant number of areas (Nasser, 2003; Peach and Gale, 2003).

The Role of Places of Worship

Study Activity 5

Before reading further in this chapter or visiting any place of worship as part of the activities associated with the learning in this chapter:

(i)   *describe* the interior and exterior of a place of worship, as appropriate, of either:

- a place of worship of a religion to which you yourself belong
- a place of worship that you have visited
- a place of worship of which you have seen photographs

(ii) *discuss* what the external and internal features described might indicate about the religion or tradition concerned

(iii) *discuss* what the external physical features you observed might indicate about the worshippers who use the building

(iv) *evaluate* the possible significance of the relationship between (i), (ii) and (iii) above

As well as being functional buildings for religious worship and meeting, places of worship also incorporate a physical reflection of the sources and goals of their religious traditions and signify the established presence and geographical belonging of these traditions of faith within both national and local society (Inter Faith Network for the UK, 1995).

Places of worship also often play a significant role within their local communities, with many places of worship offering part or all of their premises as a base and a resource for community activities. In recent years this aspect of religious buildings has become increasingly recognized by government and by other funding bodies (Finneron and Dinham, n.d.). At the same time, because of the way in which religious traditions and organizations can be experienced by parts of the wider community as exclusive to believers, and/or as discriminatory towards specific groups (such as women and gay people) the siting of services in places of worship is not without ambiguity and difficulty.

2 Registered and Recorded Places of Worship in England and Wales

---

Study Activity 6

Using a resource such as a local directory of religions, phone book, the *Religions in the UK* (2007) directory CD-ROM, or other similar available resources:

(i) *discover* how many places of worship of each religion there might be in the place where you live

(ii) *record* in photos* (if possible using a digital camera)

    (a) a Christian place of worship and one in another religion,

      or (in an area without many different religions):

    (b) a second Christian place of worship but of a different Christian tradition (eg. Anglican, Roman Catholic, Methodist, etc.)

(iii) *describe* the external physical features of at least one Christian place of worship and one of those of another religion that you photographed

(iv) *discuss* what the external physical features you observed might indicate about the religion or tradition concerned

(v) *discuss* what the external physical features you observed might indicate about the worshippers who use the building

(vi) *evaluate* the possible significance of the relationship between (iii), (iv) and (v) above

*Note: It may be both courteous and wise to consider making contact with the place(s) of worship that you aim to photograph, in order to explain what you are doing and why. This may also facilitate contacts for some other activities associated with this chapter, for example, visits to places of worship.

Certifying, Registering and Recording Places of Worship

An indication of numbers of places of worship in various religions in England and Wales (no parallel figures are kept for Scotland and Northern Ireland) can be derived from tables kept in the *Annual Register of Statistics of the Registrar General in the Office for National Statistics*. This is not published, but can be consulted, and contains annual cumulative totals relating to three kinds of buildings.

Buildings of all religious bodies are 'registered' as places of worship once the denomination in question has 'certified' them and the Registrar General has considered the recording of this certification. Before 'certification' of a place of worship can be recorded, the Registrar General needs to be satisfied that it is being used predominantly as a place of religious worship. This is done by submitting to the local Superintendent Registrar of Births, Marriages and Deaths two copies of a document signed by an owner, occupier, minister or member of a building's congregation, declaring an intention to use this building for the purposes of worship, and naming the religious tradition concerned. The Superintendent Registrar forwards this to the Registrar General who, if satisfied that the certified place is to be used 'wholly or predominantly' for worship by an identifiable and settled group will then, through the Superintendent Registrar, record the 'certification'.

Churches of the established Church of England and the Anglican Church in Wales do not need to apply to be 'certified', since they are automatically 'recorded'. The legislative framework for 'registration' is the *Places of Worship Registration Act*, 1855. 'Registration' is not compulsory, but has benefits. Provided that the worship held in the building is accessible to the general public, 'registration' can bring exemption from local taxation to both the place of worship itself and to buildings directly associated with that place of worship. Especially for the earlier years in which records were kept, the number of places of worship listed is likely to have reflected an under-reporting. Not all in the minority religions knew the procedures for 'certification' and, since many early places of worship were house-based, they were less likely to follow this procedure.

Trends in Places of Worship

The columns in Tables 27, 29 and 30 present the earliest cumulative figures held by the General Register Office in Southport, namely, those for 1972. They then give figures at five-yearly intervals between 1975 and 2000, ending with the latest figures available at the time of the publication of this volume, which are those for 2004. From these cumulative totals, it is possible to discern certain trends in the provision of places of worship. Thus from Table 27, it can be seen that the overall number of registered and recorded Christian churches has shown a pattern of decline over the period shown. Over the same period, Muslim mosques, Sikh gurdwaras, and places of worship of 'Other Bodies' have more or less consistently increased in number. This is also true of Jewish synagogues, perhaps surprisingly in view of the overall demographic decline of the Jewish population.

Most of the increased numbers of Muslim and Sikh places of worship is due to the opening of new buildings, while most of the decrease in the number of Christian churches is due to the closure of buildings. However, some of both is due to buildings that were formerly Christian places of worship becoming, instead, places of worship in other than Christian religions.

The total figures do, however, hide a number of other variations that are more clearly visible in Table 28. For example, with the exception of the Roman Catholic tradition having had a small increase over the same period, the main decline in the numbers of certified and recorded Christian places of worship has been among the Trinitarian Christian traditions. Until the most recent set of figures, the Unitarians had also reflected the pattern of decline found among the Anglican and traditional Free Churches. However, the Society of Friends has, since 1980, shown some slight upward movement bringing them, in 2004, back to the number of Meeting Houses recorded in 1972 and 1975. The number of places of worship for the Jehovah's Witnesses has grown significantly, making the overall trend among non-Trinitarian churches one of growth.

The 'Other Christian' category has also seen a significant expansion. This is likely to include churches of the Pentecostal and Independent movements, as well as the other burgeoning 'black-led' or 'black majority' churches. At the same time, it should be noted that there may be places of worship within the 'New Church' movement that may form an important part of the Christian scene in a given locality, but which are not likely to be 'certified'. This is because they are network-based, often meeting in private homes or hired public buildings rather than in specially constructed and/or specifically dedicated church buildings.

Table 29 illustrates regional variations in the distribution of 'recorded' and 'registered' places of worship, reflecting the broad geographical concentrations of people within minority religious traditions. Thus the 2004 figures of over 150 mosques in each of Yorkshire and Humberside, the North West and the West Midlands, reflect the main concentrations of Muslim settlement. The presence of 209 synagogues in the London area underlines the importance of London for the Jewish community, while the 63 and 34 synagogues in, respectively, the North West and the South East, demonstrate the clear provincial centres of the Anglo-Jewry. Finally, the 51 gurdwaras in the West Midlands testify to the large Sikh settlement in that area.

Table 27: Christian (Trinitarian, non-Trinitarian, and Christian 'other'), Jewish, Muslim, Sikh and 'Other' Places of Worship in England and Wales listed in the Classification of Denominations and Production of Annual Statistics on 30 June 2004 (with 2004 being the latest year for which data is available)

	1972	1975	1980	1985	1990	1995	2000	2004
Christian Churches	47,638	47,139	45,378	45,129	44,922	44,722	44,729	44,563
Jewish Synagogues	320	348	335	351	355	357	360	367
Muslim Mosques	79	90	193	314	452	535	621	708
Sikh Gurdwaras	40	59	90	129	149	174	182	190
Other (Eastern)	222	217	219	264	305	342	394	447

The Register does not give separate figures for Bahá'ís, Hindus, Jains and Zoroastrians whose places of worship are included in the overall category of 'Other Eastern'.

Table 28: Church of England and Church in Wales, other Christian Trinitarian, non-Trinitarian and 'other Christian' Places of Worship in England and Wales listed in the Classification of Denominations and Production of Annual Statistics on 30 June 2004 (with 2004 being the latest year for which data is available)

	1972	1975	1980	1985	1990	1995	2000	2004
Christian:	47,683	47,139	45,378	45,129	44,922	44,722	44,729	44,678
Trinitarian:								
Anglican	17,046	16,901	16,721	16,614	16,563	16,529	16,481	16,447
Roman Catholic	3,502	3,585	3,630	3,673	3,693	3,699	3,711	3,704
Traditional Free Church	21,059	20,237	18,655	18,117	17,668	17,235	17,125	16,841
Non-Trinitarian:								
Jehovah's Witnesses	652	723	759	809	872	907	921	929
Society of Friends	368	368	355	358	365	363	365	368
Unitarian	192	199	186	186	178	178	180	180
Other:								
'Other Christian'	4,864	5,126	5,072	5,372	5,583	5,811	5,946	6,094

What is presented above as 'Trinitarian' Christian figures are derived from the Register's categories of Baptist, Brethren, Methodists, Church in Wales, Church of England, Congregationalist, Methodist, Roman Catholic, Salvation Army and United Reformed Church. The 'non-Trinitarian' Christian figures are derived from the Register's categories of Jehovah's Witnesses, Society of Friends and Unitarians. 'Christian other' is used for all other Christian organizations.

3 Visiting Places of Worship

Study Activity 7

After preparing for (see appropriate sub-sections of the rest of section 3) and visiting (a) a Christian place of worship and (b) a place of worship of another religion:

(i) *describe* the internal physical features of the places of worship that you visited

(ii) *discuss*, in relation to the places of worship visited, what the internal physical features you observed might indicate about the religion concerned

(iii) *discuss*, in relation to the places of worship visited, what the internal physical features you observed might indicate about the particular worshippers who use the building

(iv) *evaluate* the possible significance of the relationship between (i), (ii) and (iii) above

Table 29: Places of Worship by Region in England and Wales listed in the Classification of Denominations and Production of Annual Statistics on 30 June 2004 (with 2004 being the latest year for which data is available)

	Trinitarian Christian	Non-Trinitarian Christian	Other Christian	Jewish Synagogues	Muslim Mosques	Sikh Gurdwaras	Other (Eastern) Religious Bodies
North East	2,162	74	275	10	17	6	10
Yorks and Humb*	3,309	165	511	15	173	25	33
North West	4,035	210	873	63	151	11	60
East Midlands	3,385	114	446	5	47	17	46
West Midlands	3,123	138	644	9	158	51	57
Eastern	4,724	135	525	6	10	14	31
London	2,493	125	936	209	112	33	113
South East	3,538	222	789	34	46	24	71
South West	5,066	179	587	10	7	6	22
Wales	5,157	115	508	6	17	3	4
TOTALS	36,994	1,477	6,094	367	738	190	447

* Yorkshire and Humberside is now the government office region of Yorkshire and the Humber, the county of Yorkshire and Humberside having been abolished while, from 2000 onwards, Essex was moved from alignment with the South East region to alignment with the Eastern region.

The Etiquette of Visiting

When planning a visit to a place of worship, the introductions to worship and places of worship in each of the religions covered in the remainder of this chapter should help to prepare visitors for how to behave and for what may be seen and experienced (see also Magida, 1996).

Usually people are delighted to show others their place of worship. They will, however, hope that the visitor observes certain basic rules of conduct. Therefore, before going to a place of worship it is important that visitors give some thought to how they might feel about such matters as joining in a service, or receiving food that has been offered to the deities of (an)other religion and/or has been blessed. It is quite possible to visit places of worship without this kind of participation as long as reservations are explained courteously in advance. The host religious group would not want visitors to feel ill at ease. Likewise, they would not wish to be made ill at ease themselves by negative or hostile criticisms of their ways of worship or of their religion.

Whether visiting alone, or as a group, it is important to follow the guidelines for clothing and behaviour so as not to cause offence. For groups, it is important not to talk or otherwise disturb any who may be praying. If any group members have special needs the hosts should be notified about this in advance so that they can prepare to help. For example, although the normal custom of the place of worship in question may be to sit on the floor or to stand for worship, chairs can often be provided for elderly, infirm or disabled visitors. It is wise to ask before taking any photographs as this is not always allowed.

Visiting Christian Churches

Most Christian places of worship are referred to as churches, but in some Protestant branches of Christianity, especially among the Free Churches, the word 'Church' is generally reserved for describing the people who make up the believing community. In these cases, in England and Wales (though not generally in Scotland or Ireland) the word 'chapel', instead of church, may be used to describe the building. At the same time, it should be noted that the word chapel is also used among Roman Catholics and Anglicans to denote a small church without a parish building or a small part of a larger building.

Some Nonconformist places of worship, such as those of the Quakers, are called meeting houses. These are not consecrated buildings, thus underlining the belief that it is the people who are the Church and the place where they meet for worship does not confer sanctity on the proceedings. For the same reason, and especially with regard to Quaker Meeting Houses, they are usually without religious decoration or symbols of any kind.

From the outside, Christian places of worship vary quite considerably in appearance. However, many older churches have a range of recognizable features, such as a tower or spire that makes them landmarks in both town and countryside. Very old buildings of this kind are, in England and Wales, generally now of the Anglican Christian tradition (although the origins of many pre-date the Reformation). By contrast, other Christian places of worship may have the external appearance of a simple square or rectangular hall. Many churches of all kinds have stained glass windows depicting scriptural characters, stories or events.

The main church building of Anglican, Roman Catholic and Orthodox dioceses is known as a Cathedral. Such buildings act as local and regional focal points since they are where the bishop has his *cathedra* or seat of authority. Church of England Cathedrals, in particular, are often seen as places where events of civic and social importance are held, as well as being significant parts of the architectural and spiritual heritage and can thus also be tourist attractions.

Although there is a wide variation of custom and practice with regard to clothes to be worn, when visiting a Christian church it is generally wise to dress tidily and avoid particularly revealing clothing. This is especially true in Orthodox as well as conservative Catholic and Protestant churches. When entering church, men traditionally remove their hats. It would therefore be courteous for any male visitors of other religious traditions, who normally keep their head covered for religious reasons, to explain this fact to their hosts. In some very conservative Christian churches women are expected to cover their heads.

Most churches have pews (benches with raised backs) or rows of seats, although in Orthodox churches people generally stand for worship. Christians will not generally expect visitors to bow or show other forms of special outward respect to the altar (or to any of the statues or icons that may be found respectively in Catholic or Orthodox churches). In some Orthodox and Eastern Catholic churches, women go on the left and men on the right.

Baptist or Methodist chapels may have an interior that is fairly bare of religious symbols except perhaps for a wooden cross on the wall. At the same time, an increasing number of Free Church chapels now have colourful banners hanging from their walls. In many Protestant buildings, attention is focused on the pulpit, which is the raised and enclosed platform from which the preacher addresses the congregation. Often it has a simple table in front of it from which the service of Holy Communion is led. But in some chapels the pulpit is no longer used, even if it remains in the building, and worship and prayers are led from a more portable reading desk known as a lectern.

Visitors are generally welcome to join in the prayers and hymns of the service if they wish. The Lord's Prayer (which is the prayer that Jesus is recorded in the Gospels as having taught his first disciples) is included in most Christian services of worship. During services, the congregation may kneel, stand or sit. Visitors who are not Christians usually sit and stand with the rest of the congregation and kneel if they feel comfortable doing so.

In Orthodox, Roman Catholic and Anglo-Catholic Anglican church buildings, worship services may be accompanied by the use of incense. Organs and often other musical instruments, sometimes including guitars, are used to accompany singing in Anglican, Protestant and Roman Catholic churches, but not in Orthodox churches. Choirs are to be found in most Christian traditions, but vary greatly in style between the traditional and formal Cathedral choirs and the more informal and contemporary Gospel choirs of the Pentecostal tradition.

All Christian denominations in the UK give an important place to preaching and to expounding the scriptures during worship. But among the Churches of the Reformation and those founded following the Evangelical Revival of the seventeenth and eighteenth centuries, preaching has traditionally been given greater prominence than the celebration of the sacrament of Holy Communion. Preaching is normally a special responsibility of ordained ministers, but most Churches in addition authorize appropriately trained and designated lay preachers to share in the leading of worship, including preaching. In the Roman Catholic Church, only bishops, priests and deacons may normally preach at Mass.

An Orthodox Christian church may have brightly coloured frescoes and many religious pictures called icons, the purpose of which is to bring the worshipper close to the spiritual realities that they depict in iconographic form. In Roman Catholic and Anglican churches one may also find statues of the Virgin Mary and perhaps also of saints. These are not intended to be objects of worship, but are rather intended to help worshippers to focus their devotion.

Instead of a simple table for Communion, an Orthodox church has an altar hidden from general view behind a screen known as an iconostasis. This is a screen covered in icons which has doors in the middle through which the priest passes to bring out the bread and wine to the congregation. In Roman Catholic and Anglican churches in the Catholic tradition the main focal point is the altar. Another focal point is the tabernacle, a secure container in which is placed the consecrated bread from the eucharist, the presence of which is indicated by a lightened lamp or candle.

Holy Communion is the most characteristic and central act of Christian worship, although some Christians, such as the Religious Society of Friends (the Quakers) and the Salvation Army, do not celebrate it. The Gospels record Communion as having been instituted by Jesus at what is known as the Last Supper when, before his crucifixion, he blessed and gave thanks over bread and wine, declaring it to be his body and his blood, and then shared this with his disciples.

Holy Communion is also known as the Eucharist; among Roman Catholics as the Mass; among the Orthodox churches as the Divine Liturgy; and among some Protestant churches as the Sacrament of the Lord's Supper, or the Breaking of Bread. Its content, interpretation and frequency vary considerably among Christians of different traditions. Roman Catholic and some Anglican churches celebrate the Mass daily, while others have one or more weekly celebrations. Some Protestant churches celebrate only monthly or quarterly.

The elements of the Eucharist also differ from church to church. Roman Catholics normally use a flat wafer of unleavened bread. This can also be found among Anglicans, although ordinary bread is used in a number of Anglican churches. Anglicans normally receive wine also, whereas among Roman Catholic churches, while some offer both bread and wine, others offer the bread only. Orthodox Christians receive a small piece of bread dipped in wine from a long spoon. In some Protestant churches pieces of bread are taken from a single loaf and each individual receives an individual cup of wine, which may be non-alcoholic. In most churches, though, wine is alcoholic and is drunk from a common cup.

In Roman Catholic, Orthodox and Anglican churches the congregation usually go up to the front of the church to receive communion, from either the priest or, in the Anglican and Roman Catholic churches, from a deacon or lay eucharistic minister who is authorized to assist in the distribution of the sacrament. In some Protestant churches the bread and wine are taken to the congregation by lay officers of the church or are passed from member to member.

Visitors attending a Holy Communion service who are not communicant Christians will not be expected to receive Communion (and in many churches, may not be allowed to do so). If bread and wine is passed around the seated congregation, non-communicant visitors would let the elements pass to the person next to them. Where people go up to the altar to receive Communion, visitors can simply remain in their seats unless non-communicants are also invited to come forward and receive a blessing from the priest.

It is quite acceptable to remain in one's place, but if a visitor opts to receive a blessing it is helpful to stand or kneel with head bowed and hands kept folded together or holding a book or service paper so that the priest can see a blessing is sought rather than Communion. It is important to be aware that the form of any blessing is likely to be specifically Christian, including invocation of the name of Jesus, or of God the Son.

Visiting Muslim Mosques

Within the Muslim community mosques are known by a number of terms, the most common being *masjid*. The English word mosque comes from the Arabic word *masjid*, meaning a place of prostration. *Jami'* is used to refer to the 'central mosque'. The earliest mosques in the UK were established in Liverpool and Woking around the end of the nineteenth century. At present many mosques are buildings that were formerly private residences, or even rooms in houses that are still used as homes. Others are in converted public buildings including, occasionally, former Christian churches. Recently, though, a number of purpose-built mosques have been constructed.

When visiting a mosque, clothing should be modest for both men and women. For women this means an ankle-length skirt or trousers, which should not be tight or transparent, together with a long-sleeved and high-necked top. A headscarf is usually essential for women. Shoes are removed before going into the prayer hall and put on the racks provided. Clean and presentable socks, stockings, or tights are therefore sensible. Before entering the prayer hall to pray, if they have not previously done so, Muslim men and women perform *wudu* (ablutions) which includes washing hands, face, hair, mouth, nose, arms (up to the elbows), and the feet (up to the ankles). This is not necessary for the non-Muslim visitor who will not be joining in the prayer.

Visitors may be greeted by the Arabic greeting *'Assalaam-u-'alaikum'*, which means 'Peace be upon you.' The answer, if the visitor would like to use it, is *'Wa 'alaikum-us-salaam'*, or 'Peace be upon you too'. Visitors should not offer, or expect, to shake hands with people of the opposite sex. There are no seats in a mosque but the floor is carpeted, therefore visitors should enter the prayer hall quietly and sit on the floor. If arriving during one of the five daily prayers known as *salah* (also known, in Persian/Urdu, as *namaz*), non-Muslim visitors are welcome to observe. At such a time, find a place near the rear or side walls and sit quietly. No sacred or blessed food will be offered, nor will visitors be expected to make any particular physical gesture of respect to holy objects, other than adopting a generally respectful demeanour.

No images, paintings or decorations representing living beings are found inside mosques, although in some Arabic calligraphy and perhaps some geometrical patterns may be found on the walls. Music is not played although in some mosques there may be congregational chanting. There is a *minbar* (pulpit or raised steps) to one side of the *mihrab* from which the imam delivers sermons on Fridays and at festival times. There may also be a symbol of the crescent moon and star that has come to be associated with Islam.

Although every mosque is, in principle, open to all Muslims, management committees of particular mosques may, in practice, reflect specific Muslim tendencies or national or regional groupings. Therefore specific languages are often used for instruction and general communication, although the language of the prayers themselves is always Arabic.

Mosques provide a number of services, like the channelling of *zakat* to the poor; providing *imams* to visit Muslims who are sick in hospital or are inmates in prison; and providing educational facilities and instruction in Arabic and in community mother-tongue languages, as appropriate. In addition, many mosques are now registered for the solemnization of marriages, and some mosques have installed morgues ensuring that Muslims can perform Islamic burial rites there.

The main form of *'ibada* (worship) is that of *salah* (Arabic for the five-times-a-day obligatory prayers) or *namaz* (Urdu). The exact times for this vary throughout the year due to the fact that daylight hours vary. Prayer timetables are published and can often be found on display in mosques. Generally speaking, the following prayers take place at around the following times: *Fajr* (dawn), *Zuhr* (midday), *'Asr* (late afternoon), *Maghrib* (after sunset), and *'Isha* (late evening).

Prayers are obligatory from puberty onwards, except for people who are not fully conscious and for women who are menstruating or in the post-natal period. If a Muslim cannot reasonably attend a mosque, they can pray in any clean place using a prayer mat. During prayer, worshippers face Makka, the *qiblah* (direction) of which, in a mosque, is marked by the *mihrab*, which is a small niche in the wall. In the UK, this direction is towards the south-east. Friday is the day for congregational prayers and most male Muslims attend the mosque for this obligatory *Salat al-Jumu'a*.

Attendance at mosque prayers is not obligatory for Muslim women. In practice, many mosques do not cater for their attendance, but this can vary according to both the Muslim culture and tradition and the specific mosque concerned. In some cases women are discouraged from worshipping in mosques and are only expected to attend for special occasions. Where provision is made for women to pray at the same time as men they usually sit separately, for example in a room upstairs that is also considered as part of the mosque, although in some mosques women worship behind the men on the same floor, sometimes separated by a curtain.

Visiting Hindu Mandirs

At present most *mandirs* (temples) in the UK are converted public or religious buildings and private houses, with only a few being purpose-built buildings. One of these is the Shri Swaminarayan Mandir in Neasden, North West London which was opened in 1995 as the first ever traditional *mandir* carved in white marble stone to be built in Europe. Other examples include the Sri Murugan Temple in Newham, London, opened in 2006 and serving mainly Tamil Hindus, as well as the new Balaji Temple in Birmingham, opened in 2006 on a twelve-acre site.

Almost all Hindu *mandirs* welcome those who are not Hindus to visit and, if they wish, to take part in worship. Clothing should be modest for both men and women, with shoes being removed and put on the racks provided before going into the *mandir*. Clean and presentable socks, stockings, or tights are therefore sensible. Women are sometimes requested to cover their heads and some Hindu women do not go to the *mandir* during menstruation. Visitors should walk in quietly and find a place to sit on the floor (usually carpeted). In some mandirs males sit on one side of the room and females on the other.

One should sit with crossed legs or with legs pointing to one side as it can be considered disrespectful to sit with legs forward and feet pointing towards the sacred area at the front of the mandir. There is no expectation that visitors join in formal prayer and worship unless they wish to do so. When visiting a mandir, Hindus generally take some kind of offering for the deity, such as fruit, milk, money or flowers, *haldi* (turmeric) and *kumkum* (red powder). For a visitor who is not a Hindu, this would not be expected, although it would be welcomed. If food is offered, then it should not be cooked food and especially not if it violates the principle of *ahimsa* (not-harming). Fresh fruit or nuts would be appropriate.

There may be a bell for worshippers to ring on entering, to invite the presence of the gods and to ward off evil spirits. Inside the *mandir*, there is usually a main hall with a shrine where the *murtis* of the *mandir* are installed. There may also be other side shrines. For outsiders to the Hindu tradition, it can be difficult to gain a proper accurate understanding of the *murtis*. They are more than purely symbolic representations of deities, being understood as full of divine energy, although at the same time, Hindus do not believe that the reality of a deity is limited to a particular *murti* in a particular place and time.

Murtis are installed following several days of ritual. Once dedicated, they are venerated as deities, being dressed in the finest fabrics and decorated with ornaments, jewellery and garlands of flowers. This is intended to foster a mood of *seva* (sacrifice and selfless service) by centring people's devotion on the deity. *Murtis* are usually made of marble, but can also be made of other kinds of stone, wood or metal. For the believer, the presence of a particular deity is manifested by *murtis* that have specific characteristics. Thus Ganesha is represented by an elephant-headed *murti* with four arms, and Krishna as a cowherd standing with one leg crossing the other at the ankles, playing a flute, and accompanied by his favourite devotee, a *gopi* (cowherd girl) Radha.

Deities are often accompanied by *murtis* of their *vahana* (a vehicle, the animal or bird on which they ride). For example, Shiva rides on the bull, Nandi. Brightly coloured and sweet-smelling flowers are laid before the *murtis* or hung over them as garlands. The *murtis* may be housed in a *garbha-griha* (inner sanctum), which only the priest is permitted to enter. Within individual *mandirs*, there may be different *murtis* and pictures of holy people. Such variety can reflect the range of *sampradayas* (spiritual traditions) use the temple. Partly because of the minority position of Hindus and the financial constraints within which they must therefore operate, *mandirs* in the UK are more likely than in India to cater for a variety of *sampradayas*. But this is also made possible by the generally inclusive approach of the Hindu traditions.

For the Hindu worshipper, coming face to face with the *murti* is called taking *darshan* (sight) of the deity, which is understood to be a blissful experience. The worshipper offers respect to the deity/deities by folding hands or by bowing down, and may offer prayers and a gift, or respectfully sip a few drops of *charnamrita* (holy water used to bathe the deity). The worship of the *murti* with offering of gifts is called *puja*, more formal versions of which are performed by the temple priest.

Inside the main hall one may also see one or more *vyasasanas*, which are decorated thrones on which *swamis* (religious teachers) sit when delivering discourses to religious gatherings. One may also see the *AUM* (or *OM*) symbol to symbolize the primeval sound representing God in the simplest form, and perhaps also the swastika (which is not to be confused with the swastika of Nazism, the original Hindu form of this symbol being a sign of auspiciousness). It is likely that incense will be in use to purify the air and create a spiritual atmosphere for worship.

One might also see a conch shell, the sound of which assists concentration on worship; a *trishul*, which is the trident weapon of Shiva and represents God, the soul and the ignorance through which the soul is held in bondage; and a coconut, which is believed to represent the three-eyed Shiva and is symbolic of life by being hard on the outside but sweet on the inside. There may also be images of the lotus, which is an ancient symbol of the cosmos, of wisdom and of humanity; and a *kalasha*, which is a pot representing the human body. The mouth of a *kalasha* is considered as Vishnu; its base as Brahma; and its middle as Shiva. The water within it stands for purity and love of the divine. It also relates to the *Pancha Mahabhuta* (the five physical elements).

Hindu corporate devotional activities include *bhajan* and *kirtan* (singing songs and mantras); *pravachan* (sermon); *havan* (the sacred fire ceremony); and the *arti* ceremony. Private devotions, in the temple and at home, include *japa* (mantra meditation), prayer, *puja* (worship of the *murti*) and the study of sacred texts. In the *arti* ceremony, performed several times a day in the *mandir*, the priest offers articles of worship, representing the five physical elements of life (earth, air, fire, water and space), to the deity including lighted ghee lamps, incense, water for bathing, coconut, flowers and grains. During this, worshippers play musical instruments, sing *bhajans*, and clap their hands in rhythm, and visitors to some Hindu *mandirs* may be expected to stand.

Prior to *arti*, food is offered to the deity and is blessed for later distribution. Such food, which often takes the form of sweets or fruit offered on a tray, is said to be sanctified and is known as *prasad* or *prasadam*. Visitors are likely to be offered a piece of *prasada* that they can either eat or take home. If receiving this, hold it in cupped hands with the right hand uppermost. A visitor who, for religious reasons, is uncomfortable about being given some of this sacred food to eat, should let the person offering the food know with a quiet 'No thank you', although if possible it would be better to explain to the hosts in advance that such an action would not be out of any disrespect.

In Havan, a fire is lit and Sanskrit *mantras* are recited, while offerings are made to the holy fire. Worshippers offer their obeisance, through the sacred fire, to the formless God, emphasizing the quality of selflessness. No Hindu sacraments, especially weddings, are complete without it.

As well as a worship hall, many *mandirs* have other facilities on their premises, such as social, cultural, educational and administrative rooms. In a country in which Hindus are in a minority, worship at the *mandir* also fulfils an important social function, providing an opportunity to engage in community and cultural activities and consolidate faith together.

Visiting Sikh Gurdwaras

The Sikh place of congregational worship is called the gurdwara, meaning 'doorway of the Guru'. The first gurdwara in the UK was opened in Shepherd's Bush in 1911 at the initiative of Sant Teja Singh, and with funding from Maharaja Bhupinder Singh of Patiala. The majority of gurdwaras in the world, including in the UK, follow guidance from the Shiromani Gurdwara Parbandhak Committee (SGPC), Amritsar, which is based at the Darbar Sahib (Golden Temple) complex at Amritsar in the Punjab.

A gurdwara is usually recognizable from the outside by the *nishan sahib* (*nishan* meaning 'flag' while sahib is an honorific title of respect). This is a triangular saffron-coloured flag with the *khanda* (*Khalsa* emblem) depicted in black, the emblem being a symbolic two-edged sword surrounded by a circle outside of which are two further swords, which symbolize the temporal and spiritual sovereignty of God.

The clothing worn by male and female visitors should be modest. For women it is advisable to wear a long skirt or trousers, while head-covering is essential for both women and men. A large clean handkerchief is adequate for men, and women are expected to use scarves. The gurdwara will usually have some head coverings available for those who have not brought them, but not necessarily enough for a large group of visitors. Because shoes are removed before going into the gurdwara clean and presentable socks, stockings, or tights are sensible.

Tobacco, alcohol or drugs should not be taken into the buildings of a gurdwara (not just the prayer hall). Smokers should therefore remember to leave their tobacco or cigarettes outside. Shoes should be removed before entering the prayer hall and may also need to be left off before entering the *langar* hall (see below). In addition to covering their heads, visitors may also be asked to wash their hands (which Sikhs do before entering to pray).

If arriving during a time of worship, visitors will normally be expected to join the worshippers, but there is no obligation to participate in the worship itself. On entering, the visitor will see the Guru Granth Sahib (the sacred scripture of the Sikhs, which they view as a living presence) placed on a low platform, covered by a canopy. When Sikhs enter they touch the floor before this with their forehead and offer a gift such as food or money. Visitors may also bow in similar fashion as a mark of respect or, if uncomfortable with this for religious reasons, they may if they wish simply stand in silence for a few moments as a mark of respect. No gift would be expected from a visitor although it would be appreciated. If making a gift, leave it with the others either in a wooden box, or on the floor in front of the Guru Granth Sahib.

Seating is on the floor (usually carpeted). Men and women usually sit in separate groups. Seating should be in a position that avoids the feet being pointed towards the Guru Granth Sahib, or with the back being turned towards it since both these positions are considered disrespectful. A cross-legged meditational stance is the usual practice, but simply tucking one's legs in is acceptable.

Sikhs do not consider any specific day of the week to be especially holy. The gurdwara is usually open daily and some Sikhs visit it every morning and evening. In the UK, for convenience, *sadh sangat* mainly takes place on a Saturday or Sunday. *Diwan* usually lasts between two and four hours. The main elements of worship include path (prayer by means of the recitation of scriptures), *simran* (chanting of God's name) and *kirtan* (singing of hymns).

On special occasions the Guru Granth Sahib is read from cover to cover by relays of readers. *Akhand Path* is the uninterrupted recitation of the entire Guru Granth Sahib that takes forty-eight hours to complete. Devotees take it in turns to read, and visitors come, day and night, to listen. *Akhand Paths* are conducted to celebrate festivals and other special occasions. *Saptah Path* is a form of path that is not continuous and which takes seven days. *Sahaj Path* is also not continuous, but is without time limit for the completion of reading.

A typical Sikh religious service consists of *Gurbani kirtan* (hymn-singing), a discourse on the divine Name, followed by *Ardas* (a final corporate prayer). The *Ardas* ends with the invocation of God's blessing on the whole of humanity. Then follows the *Hukamnama*, a random reading of special significance from the Guru Granth Sahib understood as a spiritual message from the Guru to each individual member of the congregation. While reading the Guru Granth Sahib in a gurdwara, the reader or another person close by will wave over it a *chaur sahib* (a whisk made of white yak's hair). Despite the historical origin of this practice, the *chaur* is not intended to serve as a fly-whisk or a fan, but is waved as a sign of respect for the Guru Granth Sahib. At the end of the evening service *Kirtan Sohila* is recited when the Guru Granth Sahib is laid to rest, usually in a separate room.

The service concludes by the offering of *Karah Prashad* (holy food) to all those present at the end of the worship, both members of the congregation and visitors, and is followed by the sharing of *langar*. *Karah Prashad* is a sweet pudding, made of butter, flour, sugar and water, that has been blessed during the service. Because of the way it is made, it is buttery in texture and hands therefore usually need wiping after it has been received. Paper napkins are often distributed to facilitate this. If a visitor is, for religious reasons, uncomfortable about being given some of this sacred food to eat, then the person offering the food should be informed with a quiet 'No thank you', though, if possible, it is preferable in advance to explain to the hosts that this is not out of any disrespect.

The same applies to *langar*, which is a meal that is provided free of charge and served in the communal kitchen at the gurdwara. The *langar* is a meal to which outsiders are also welcomed. Because the food served in the *langar* has been blessed, head-covering is usually maintained in the *langar* hall. The food is vegetarian and will not contain meat, fish or eggs or their by-products. It is generally advisable to ask only for as much food as is actually wanted rather than to accept too much and then have to leave some. Both *langar* and *karah prashad* symbolize universal fraternity and equality since it is intended that all should eat together regardless of their social position and that there are no strangers in the House of God.

The gurdwara is not only a place for formal worship, but it is also a centre for religious education and for other activities such as Punjabi classes, youth clubs, women's groups, welfare provision and elderly day centres. In keeping with the

Sikh tradition of service, gurdwaras often provide temporary accommodation for the needy.

Visiting Jewish Synagogues

The majority of Jews who are affiliated to a synagogue belong to Orthodox synagogues and a minority to the Progressive sector of Reform and Liberal synagogues, with a much smaller number being aligned with synagogues in the Masorti and Sephardi traditions.

Due to the number of attacks that have been made on Jewish buildings many synagogues are fenced and gated and a significant number also have CCTV cameras installed for security purposes. Because of the Orthodox rule of walking to the synagogue on Shabbat and festivals the locations of these have generally moved from inner city areas, where Jewish communities were first established, to the suburbs of towns and cities where the main Jewish communities are now established.

When visiting a synagogue, dress should be modest, with arms and legs covered, but need not be formal. In an Orthodox synagogue, women should wear a skirt or dress of reasonable length and not trousers while married women should cover their heads. Men and boys should cover their heads when visiting any synagogue. Non-kosher food should not be brought into a synagogue. If the community is standing quietly in prayer, then visitors should wait at the back until the prayer has finished since prayer should not be interrupted.

In Orthodox synagogues men and women are separated for reasons of propriety. Women usually sit in a gallery above the section where the men conduct the service. When there is no gallery, the women are seated behind the men with a short curtain or partition separating the two. In some small house synagogues, women and men worship in different rooms.

Sabbath services in Progressive synagogues can last between one and two hours, while those in Orthodox synagogues can be up to two to three hours long. Therefore visitors should take this into account when planning for their arrivals and departures. There is no expectation that visitors join in the worship unless they particularly wish to do so. Orthodox services, and many Masorti services, are conducted entirely in Hebrew except for the rabbi's sermon and the prayer for the Royal Family. However, prayer books with translations are generally available in bookcases at the back of the synagogue. Reform services contain a high proportion of English, and Liberal services are mostly in English.

Inside the synagogue, one can see a range of symbols and objects. The *Magen David* (Shield of David) is a six-pointed star that is a Jewish symbol of no particular religious significance. The *Menorah* is a seven-branched candlestick of a type dating back to the Temple in Jerusalem prior to its destruction by the

Romans. The *Bimah* is a raised platform, usually in the centre of the synagogue, from which the Torah is read. Most synagogues also have a pulpit from which the sermon is preached.

The *Aron Kodesh* (Holy Ark) is an alcove or cupboard with wooden or ornate door panels that contains the Torah scrolls. It has an embroidered curtain across it, which is known as a *Parochet*. A *Ner Tamid* (everlasting light) is a lamp hung in front, reminding the congregation of the eternal presence of God. In western countries the *Aron Kodesh* is usually on the east wall of the synagogue, in the direction of Jerusalem.

The *Sefer Torah* is a handwritten scroll of the Torah. In Orthodox synagogues, it is read four times a week, on Monday and Thursday mornings, Saturday mornings and Saturday afternoons. It is also read on other distinctive days such as the holy days. The Torah scroll is kept inside a velvet cover and is usually decorated with metal breastplates and adornments. It has an honoured place in Jewish worship, especially at the festival of *Simchat Torah*. The sanctity of the *Sefer Torah* is underlined by the use of a *Yad,* that is, a long pointer in the shape of a hand used by the reader so that the place may be kept without touching the parchment.

As another reminder of the Torah a *mezuzah* (literally meaning 'door post') may also be found on the door of synagogue buildings, as well as in private homes. It is a parchment scroll containing two sections of scripture (Deuteronomy 6 vv. 4–9 and Deuteronomy 11 vv. 13–21) that constitute the first paragraphs of the *Shema*, placed in a small, hollow box.

In the larger synagogues services are held every morning and evening. However, *Shabbat* is the key occasion for Jewish communal worship. The most regular and well-attended forms of communal worship on Shabbat are *Kabbalat Shabbat* (the first *Shabbat* service at dusk on Friday evening) and *Maariv* (the evening service said every day including Friday night), as well as *Shaharit* and *Musaf* on Saturday morning.

During the *Shabbat* morning service a portion of the Torah is read. The Torah is divided into the weekly *Sidrah* or *Parashah* (fifty-four weekly portions) to be read each consecutive Saturday in the synagogue. In an Orthodox synagogue a minimum of seven men are called to read the Torah. Following this, the *Haftarah* (an excerpt from the *Nevi'im* which has some connection with the Torah portion) is read. A *Chazzan* leads congregational prayer. In Progressive synagogues, worship may be accompanied by musical instruments, whereas in Orthodox synagogues this does not happen, although there may be unaccompanied singing by a male choir.

Traditionally, during worship (whether at home or in the synagogue) all males and married women cover their heads out of modesty when addressing God although some Progressive Jewish communities do not observe this practice.

Some Jews keep their heads covered at all times in recognition of the continual presence of God. For men, traditionally this is done by means of wearing the small cap known as a *kippah* (in Hebrew) or a *yarmulkah* (in Yiddish), while among married Orthodox women, many maintain head-covering by means of a hat or a *sheitel* (wig).

Male Orthodox Jews over thirteen years old wear *Tephilin* (phylacteries) on the forehead and left arm. These consist of two strap-on leather boxes that enclose parchment sections of the scriptures. *Tephilin* are worn for weekday morning prayers, but not for Shabbat or festival prayers. *Tallitot* (the singular being *tallit* or *tallis*) are traditional prayer shawls, often with black or blue stripes. *Tzitzit* are the fringes that are attached to the four corners and they act as a reminder of the commandments. Traditional style prayer shawls are usually made of wool. Some Orthodox Jewish men may wear the fringes, known as *Arba Kanfot* (meaning 'four corners') at all times on a vest under their clothes. Among Progressive Jews, women are often encouraged to wear a prayer shawl if taking a leading role in corporate worship, but they are not obliged to do so.

Visitors will not be expected to make particular gestures of respect toward any objects and no sacred food is distributed during the service. However, *kiddush* (the Hebrew for sanctification) may take place after the service. In Orthodox synagogues, this food and drink will consist of wine and biscuits or crisps, while in other synagogues bread accompanies the wine (in Orthodox synagogues bread is not shared at *kiddush*, because this would require the ritual washing of hands). Young children are usually given fruit juice instead of wine. Visitors will be invited to join in the blessing that is said or sung over food and drink that is distributed in order to give thanks to God. While visitors are invited to share in this as a sign of hospitality, there is no sense of obligation to participate.

As well as being a place of worship, the synagogue is usually also a central place of administration, cultural and social activities and education programmes. Synagogues are self-financing and may have a *Heder* (room) that is a part-time (usually taking place on Sundays) school for Jewish education where children can gain religious knowledge and learn Hebrew. The synagogue might also offer adult Jewish education.

Visiting Buddhist Places of Worship

Buddhist places of devotion in the UK vary considerably in style and practice, often reflecting the different Buddhist traditions, schools and ethnic groupings of Buddhists. Styles range from small rooms in a converted or private house in which a room has been set apart as the central shrine, through the stark simplicity of meditation halls, to the elaborate ornateness of purpose-built constructions on extensive sites such as the Temple at the Samye Ling Tibetan Centre in

Scotland, the Dhammatalaka Pagoda in Birmingham, and the Theravada Thai Buddhapadipa Temple in Wimbledon. Others are relatively small structures such as the Nipponzan Myohoji Peace Pagodas in Milton Keynes and Battersea Park in London.

A Buddhist temple or *vihara* (or monastery) usually contains at least a *Buddharupa* (statue of the Buddha) and a *stupa/thupa*, which were originally burial mounds built over relics of the Buddha or other saints or other holy objects. If a temple is influenced by Chinese tradition (in other words is Vietnamese, Korean or Japanese) there will be a funerary memorial chapel outside the main place of worship, where memorials of a family's dead are kept.

The temple is commonly a place where teaching, religious observance and meditation take place. Temples may be a part of a vihara (a place where monks or nuns live), or may be found in a general centre. In these ways, the three refuges of Buddhism – the Buddha, the *dharma* and the *sangha* – can be physically focused.

The shrine room is primarily a place for meditation and teaching. However, it may also contain a statue or image of a Buddha or, in some Buddhist traditions, of a Bodhisattva. This will generally be in a central position, commonly with an incense holder, flowers and candles by its side. Candles symbolize the light that the Buddha's teaching brings to the world. There are vases of cut flowers as a reminder of impermanence and sometimes a Buddhist text wrapped in silk represents the teaching. Most Buddhists practise *puja* (a way of expressing one's devotion by means of offerings and chanting) as well as meditation, and the shrine room is a place where *puja* is performed.

Devotional practices are also considered as *bhavana*. These involve the offering of food, flowers, incense and water, together with chanting. The offering of incense is symbolic of the importance of diligent action. Tibetan Buddhists offer bowls of water to represent water for bathing, washing the feet, rinsing the mouth and drinking, as well as food, flowers, incense and light. In the Zen tradition, offerings of fruit, tea and water are made.

There are no particular clothing requirements for visiting a Buddhist temple, except that for reasons of practicality it is best if clothes are loose fitting because of the normal practice of sitting on the floor. Because of the need to remove shoes, clean and presentable socks, stockings or tights are therefore sensible. Before entering the shrine room, as a mark of respect shoes should be removed. Once inside, seating is generally on the floor and it is appropriate to adopt a quiet and meditative demeanour.

On entering a temple or shrine room Buddhists may prostrate themselves three times (representing body, speech and mind, or the Three Refuges) before the shrine, or else bow with hands in the *anjali* (hands together) position. There is no expectation that visitors will do this, although they may do so if they wish. In some traditions it is considered disrespectful to sit with one's legs or feet pointed in the direction of the shrine, or with one's back turned to the Buddha.

Visiting Bahá'í Places of Worship

Globally there are seven purpose-built Bahá'í Houses of Worship, the European one being in Frankfurt, Germany. There are, however, no formal buildings for Bahá'í worship in the UK and therefore worship and most other Bahá'í gatherings, including Local Spiritual Assemblies, generally take place in Bahá'í homes, although in a few cities there are Bahá'í centres.

The Bahá'í religion has no set worship services and no ordained priesthood. Devotional gatherings are simple and consist of prayers, meditations and readings from sections of the Bahá'í scriptures and other world religions. Music is generally encouraged. Most Bahá'í gatherings and meetings – and particularly study circles, devotional meetings, children's classes, and programmes for juniors, youth and women – are open to people of any faith or none.

The exception is that of Nineteen-Day Feasts which may be held in local Bahá'í centres and are generally intended for Bahá'ís themselves. If those who are not Bahá'ís are present, they will not be asked to leave. However, the consultative part of the Feast will be omitted and the Feast will be termed a Unity Feast. A Unity Feast is an informal gathering of Bahá'ís and their friends. It often begins with devotional readings, prayers or songs. Visitors are free to join in or not. During prayers, a reverent silence is requested. There is no sacred food or sacrament. The Feast closes with a period during which people meet each other and share refreshments.

Small regular and informal meetings for discussion, which take place in homes, are known as 'Firesides'. These are organized by individual Bahá'ís or by families and can begin and end with prayers and include information and discussion. Firesides are generally open to anyone who wishes to attend, although some may be by invitation only. Those interested in learning more about the Bahá'í faith may also attend Study Circles, which provide systematic courses of study.

Those wishing to attend a Bahá'í meeting should contact the host or the secretary of the Local Assembly or one of the Cluster Co-Ordinators, to make suitable arrangements. There are no special clothing requirements, although it is appropriate to dress tidily and modestly.

Visiting Jain Places of Worship

Jains have consecrated *mandirs* and also places of worship that are not consecrated. In consecrated *mandirs*, there are images of *Tirthankaras* who are key in Jain sacred cosmology and are depicted as either standing or sitting in the lotus position and meditating. As conducted by a Jain *alaya*, or spiritual leader these images go through a sacred process of conception, birth, renunciation, becoming omniscient, and liberation. Daily rituals are set out in the Jain scriptures, and strict devotees worship only at consecrated *mandirs* and images. At present in the UK, there are only three consecrated *mandirs*. These are the Jain Centre in Leicester – which is also the only purpose-built Jain Temple outside of India; the Oshwal Jain Temple in Northaw, Hertfordshire; and the Shree Digamber Jain Temple in Harrow, Middlesex.

There are also non-consecrated places of worship including the Mahavir Foundation, in Harrow, Middlesex; the Manchester Jain Samaj Community Centre; and the Oshwal Mahajanwadi, in Croydon, Surrey. In areas of the country where there is no temple, Jains meet in homes and halls. While all Digamabaras and the majority of the Shvetambaras worship in *mandirs*, the Shvetambara groups known as Sthanakvasis and the Terapanthis do not participate in these temple rituals. Instead, they emphasize *bhava puja* (mental worship) and perform their rites in *upashraya* (meditation halls).

In India, Shvetambaras and Digambaras worship in separate mandirs, but in Leicester there is a purpose-built Jain mandir that provides places of worship for all Jains. Within this mandir, in addition to the main Shvetambara shrine, there is a also a Digambara shrine and a Sthanakvasi *upashraya* for *pratikramana* (the ritual of confession), as well as a meditation room dedicated to Shrimad Rajachandra (1868–1901), a great spiritual leader and religious counsellor to Mahatma Gandhi. The mandir also contains a museum about the Jain history, philosophy, architecture and way of life.

For visitors to a Jain temple, clothing should be modest for both men and women, but need not be formal. Jain women will be expected not to enter the temple during menstruation. Head coverings are not necessary for either sex. Shoes should be removed before going into the temple and put on the racks provided. Clean and presentable socks, stockings, or tights are therefore sensible. All leather objects should be left outside.

No eating or chewing is allowed in the temple area. When Jains enter the temple they bow to the image in the temple and chant a *mantra*. Devotion to the *Jinas*, as represented by images of the *Tirthankaras*, inspires Jains to engage in meritorious activities. This will not be expected of a visitor, from whom a reverent silence is appropriate. Visitors should therefore enter quietly and find a place to sit on the (usually carpeted) floor, sitting with crossed legs, or with legs pointing to one side. It is considered disrespectful to sit with legs forward with the feet pointing towards the sacred area at the front of the temple or to stand or sit with one's back to the image. There is no expectation that visitors will join in the prayer unless they particularly wish to do so, and there is no custom of offering sacred food to devotees or visitors.

Before coming into a place of worship Jains purify themselves with a bath. At the entrance to the *mandir*, a worshipper puts a sandalwood paste-mark on the or her brow to signify their intention to live a life according to the teachings of *Jina*. Using rice grains, a swastika design (not to be confused with the Nazi swastika) is made on a low table indicating a desire to be liberated from the four destinies of the world cycle. To the chant of mantras, worshippers bathe the images of the *Tirthankaras*, offer flowers and incense, and wave *arati* (lamps) in front of them.

The most important of the Jain mantras is the *Pancanamaskara-mantra* that affirms, 'I pay homage to the *Arhats* (the living omniscient beings), *Siddhas* (the perfected beings), *Acharyas* (the Jain mendicant leaders), *Upadhyayas* (Jain mendicant teachers) and the *Sadhus* (all other Jain ascetics)'. Another important ritual is *pratikramana*, a confession of transgressions against one's religious vows committed knowingly or unknowingly.

Visiting Zoroastrian Places of Worship

The use of temples was introduced into Zoroastrianism during the period of the Achaemenid kings in what is now the territory of Iran, in around the fifth century BCE. Traditionally, Zoroastrian places of worship are known as Fire Temples because a consecrated fire burns perpetually inside them. This has led some people to describe Zoroastrians erroneously as 'fire worshippers', a misunderstanding that is offensive to Zoroastrians. A reverence for fire is found in the broader Aryan tradition that pre-dates Zarathushtra and in which fire was associated with truth and order. However, Zoroastrians do not worship fire, but worship Ahura Mazda.

In the Gathas (key Zoroastrian scriptures) fire (*atar* or *adur/adar*) is linked with *Asha* and is considered a sacred force because it is a source of light and warmth as well as a symbol of truth and righteousness. It is used in virtually all Zoroastrian ceremonies and many individual Zoroastrians keep an oil lamp burning in their homes. The oldest consecrated Zoroastrian fires have been continuously burning in Iran for over 2500 years and in India for over 1000 years, both of which are centres of Zoroastrian pilgrimage.

The consecrated sacred fire in a Zoroastrian Fire Temple is the focal point of worship, praise and propitiation. There is a consecrated chamber in which the fire is housed and into which only priests may enter. Zoroastrian worshippers may bow before the fire and take some cold ash to place on their foreheads in order to receive the divine blessing. Standing before the consecrated sacred fire in a Fire Temple, Zoroastrians believe they are in the presence of the spirit of Ahura Mazda. This philosophy lies behind the *atash Nyaish* (Litany of Fire).

There are no traditional, formally consecrated, Zoroastrian Fire Temples in the UK. There is, however, a room for Zoroastrian worship at the new Zoroastrian

Centre in Harrow. It is assumed that Zoroastrians will have bathed at home prior to visiting a place of worship and, before entering the worship hall, Zoroastrians must remove shoes, wash their hands and faces, cover their heads when praying, and then perform the *kusti* ritual in the entrance to the place of worship.

People from outside the Zoroastrian community may, on occasion, be invited to attend a *jashan* (thanksgiving festival). In these circumstances a general attitude of respectful presence is appropriate, along with appropriately modest clothing. During ceremonies visitors, just like Zoroastrians, should cover their heads with a prayer cap or scarf. During ceremonial occasions, out of respect for Zoroastrians who are praying, non-Zoroastrians are requested not to enter the prayer room, known as the *setayash gah* (place of worship). However, at other times they may enter provided they are accompanied by personnel from the Zoroastrian Centre.

4 Places of Worship, Religious Diversification and Planning Issues

Study Activity 8

In relation to the area in which you live, make contact with the local authority Planning Department and:

(i) *discover* what you can about any buildings locally that may have changed their use (either from a secular use to a religious use, or from one religion to another)

(ii) *discover* if the local authority area in which you live has a specific policy, or a section of a wider policy, on places of worship and planning, and request a copy

(iii) *describe* the principal features of any policy that does exist or, if one does not exist for your local authority area, obtain one for another nearby area and describe that policy

(iv) *discuss* the strengths and weaknesses of that policy with regard to the religious profile of the area and the pattern of religious buildings within it

(v) *evaluate* potential issues in relation to (i), (ii), (iii) and (iv) above and how they might best be dealt with

Places of Worship: Heritage and Change

Pagan sites of worship are to be found in landscape locations throughout Britain, some of which were then later built upon by Christian churches. Church buildings, of course, are a very widespread feature of both the urban and rural landscapes. Apart from pre-Christian Pagan traditions the Christians, followed by Jews, were the first to establish places of worship in Britain. The oldest synagogue in current use is the Bevis Marks Synagogue in London, which was built in 1701. As other communities began to emerge, places of worship within their traditions also began to be established. For example, the first purpose-built mosque was established in Woking in 1889 and the first Sikh gurdwara in Putney, London, in 1911.

After the major post-Second World War migrations the pattern and distribution of places of worship began to change significantly. Gradually, during the 1960s, as migrants decided to settle in the UK and to bring their families here, the question of more permanent provision of worship facilities began to emerge as a community concern. As previously noted, since they were often lacking the economic means to buy or build new facilities, people adapted either existing private dwellings or other buildings for religious purposes. Sometimes, faced with prejudice and misunderstanding from the general population, they turned to a number of more sympathetic local Christian places of worship in order to seek hospitality for their worship gatherings.

This phase coincided with the continuing numerical decline in attendance at churches that resulted in the closure of many Christian buildings, particularly in inner city areas where traditional Christianity was weak. As a result, minority religious organizations often sought to purchase formerly Christian places of worship. This gave rise to considerable debate among Christians because, for some, this seemed tangible evidence of Christianity's lessening significance in British life. In addition, for many minority ethnic groups within the Christian Church, such sales were met with puzzlement. The churches that have predominantly black Christian membership and leadership often could not understand why such redundant buildings were not either given or sold on favourable terms to them as fellow Christians, since they also needed places of worship and often lacked the economic means to build new ones.

In addition to purchasing redundant church buildings, minority religious groups began to convert dwelling-houses and to purchase old warehouses, cinemas and other public buildings and, in a few cases, to construct their own buildings. In this phase it was often the case that, under pressure of numbers and the consequent limitations of economic resources, groups that might normally have remained separate on grounds of ethnicity, caste or sect found that they needed to join together to create premises for shared use within the community.

In areas with the greatest numerical concentrations of the religion concerned, with relatively increased security and prosperity the process of re-diversification into sectarian and ethnically based places of worship has generally taken place, leading to the establishment of purpose-built facilities. Conversely, as has already been noted, among many Christian traditions, pressing economic factors have been influential in bringing about a degree of rationalization and ecumenical sharing of buildings, especially in the inner urban areas. A summary of the findings of a Leverhulme Trust-funded survey (conducted by the School of Geography at Oxford University between 1998 and 2001) of 'Ethnicity and Cultural Landscapes' about registered Hindu, Muslim and Sikh places of worship in England and Wales, explained that,

> ... slightly more than 10 percent of such buildings are conversions of existing religious premises (most commonly the churches and chapels of Nonconformist denominations). However, of the remainder, approximately 14 percent were purpose built premises and approximately 76 percent were conversions from one type of building use to another. As such, approximately 90 percent of these buildings will have had to obtain planning permission. (Quoted in Beckford, Gale, Owen, Peach, and Weller, 2006: 53–4)

Planning Issues: Findings of the Religious Discrimination Research Project

Against this background, there is evidence of considerable tension and sometimes of outright conflict around planning applications. Examples of this can be found in reported interviews with members of minority religious traditions that were conducted as part of the 1999–2001 Religious Discrimination in England and Wales Research Project (Weller, Feldman and Purdam, 2001: 63–78). For example, it was reported that a house-based Buddhist vihara had put up a gate without first obtaining planning permission. As a result of this it received a visit from the local authority following which the vihara was also told to take down a small relief sculpture that was attached to the side of the house, on the grounds that it was a religious symbol.

It was also, however, clear from the project's fieldwork that a wide range of issues other than those relating to the buildings themselves could often become caught up in debates around existing or proposed buildings. For example, it was reported that in one place local opposition to what was to become a Hindu temple centred upon claims about 'cooking smells'. Ironically, this was before anyone had moved into the building and certainly before anything was cooked. It also did not take account of the fact that, in its cooking, the particular religious group concerned uses neither onions nor garlic, and only a few spices.

The procedural aspects of the planning process were also highlighted as a source of considerable frustration to religious groups who seek to establish a place of worship. In one example, an interviewee pulled out a stack of photocopied letters and commented that, 'people come out of nowhere to object', since in that case, none of the objectors was from the immediate area and the individual who initially set up opposition to the application lived half a mile away. One group noted that, 'once petitions go around, councillors and MPs side with the mainstream community and the temple has no chance'. It was also noted that when permissions are actually granted, other planning decisions in the immediate area seem to be made without regard to the presence of the religious building, resulting in what were foreseeable problems. An example was given in which

> The Council gave permission for a mosque, but then gave permission for a night club next door, and later a gay/lesbian club. This was not just a matter of religious beliefs ... it was hard to have little children around for evening activities and lessons as people around the area were often drunk, shouting, and abusive.

Religious groups have also been concerned about inconsistencies within planning policy and practice. Neighbourhood traffic and parking issues are often cited by planning departments as a reason for rejecting planning applications for places of worship. But, an interviewee commented, 'what about the football stadium?', and, in relation to noise problems, then asked 'what about the noise from the pub next door which is open much later·than the temple?'

A number of interviewees found it difficult to understand why it can sometimes seem easier to obtain permission to convert old church buildings into residential flats than to change them into a place of worship for another religion. One Hindu suggested that there seemed to be less difficulty with this thirty years or so ago than he felt there was now. In his opinion, the current difficulties were possibly due to fears of community expansion. 'Newcomers' were seen to be 'making their mark' through the acquisition and use of public space, and buildings that have a religious purpose are charged with symbolic meanings, not only for those who use them, but also for others within the neighbourhood. Thus one interviewee noted that, 'people have fears about religion, about change, especially if you come in and change the neighbourhood' and that, among the majority community, quite a few people are 'mourning the passing of a Christian landscape'.

In fact, on the basis of its fieldwork, the Religious Discrimination project identified more general issues to do with the sense of 'place' and 'territory' as being as much at stake as the more specific planning objections that people raise. A white, female mediation worker noted that it is important to deal with these underlying issues rather than only the presenting ones. This was on the basis that:

> ... the fundamental premise is that underneath the surface of neighbour-hood conflicts or turf battles are unmet needs, fears. Someone saying 'you can't build a mosque here' could also be more about the fact that their

friends have moved away, and they have unmet needs stemming from belonging issues.

In relation to planning policy, however, a planner with a Sikh religious background expressed the conviction that, 'Religious "use" needs to be seen as any other legitimate planning use or need, and must be given the same rigorous analysis rather than assuming that "oh, religion, here comes a problem."' In his view, the way forward must be to 'mainstream' religious needs and use them as part of an overall planning policy rather than continuing to marginalize or make a problem out of religion by 'adding it on' to other issues.

This particular planner's authority had tried to create a package of measures to relate to religious communities and organizations in which there is an explicit policy with regard to places of worship; translators are provided; assistance is given in preparing effective planning proposals; and communities have been assisted to locate appropriate buildings. A local authority worker expressed the view that the council 'must be bold' in pursuing such an approach since, if religion is not incorporated into the mainstream policy, then there would be a likelihood that planning issues connected with religion 'won't be dealt with in a coherent manner'.

The worker concerned noted that what was being proposed was not a 'quick fix' because developing a coherent policy of that kind could take between ten and fifteen years. Interviewees also highlighted the fact that planning policies were inconsistent from one local authority area to the next, with some taking explicit account of religious dimensions and needs, and others not focusing on religious needs as such, but dealing with religious buildings as part of a more general set of criteria for the population and the locality.

Planning Issues: Academic Research and Local Policy Development

A growing body of academic studies (see Edge, 2002; Gale and Naylor, 2002; Gale, 2004a, 2004b, 2005; and Nye, 1996, 2001), together with a number of planning appeal case records, show ways in which new issues have been highlighted as changes have come about in the building requirements of minority religious groups. For example, Hodgins (1981) indicates that the early research literature documents that the conflicts that developed in Birmingham in the 1970s were generally clustered around the use by Muslim groups of houses as places of worship. Use of domestic residences for religious purposes was often perceived, both by local residents as well as by local authority planners, as being likely to call into question the 'amenity' of adjacent properties in what were generally residential areas. As a result of this, in the 1970s and 1980s, planning authorities such as Leicester City Council (1977); Walsall Metropolitan Borough Council (1980); and Wellingborough Council (1979) adopted policies aimed at controlling the conversion of houses into religious facilities.

Recent research in Birmingham (Gale, 2005) shows that the need for places of worship embedded in residential areas continues to be high, and that adaptation of domestic dwellings to meet this need remains a relevant issue. However, as the demand has emerged for the creation of large, purpose-built premises, newer planning issues have begun to emerge – and especially with regard to the appropriateness of aspects of architectural design and location in existing urban landscapes.

As highlighted in the 2006 *Review of the Evidence Base on Faith Communities* (Beckford, Gale, Owen, Peach, Weller, 2006: 54–5) conducted for the Office of the Deputy Prime Minister, an early case of this kind was that of 'Tower Hamlets London Borough Council *and* Esha' Atul Islam' (1993) in which there was a proposal for a mosque that 'drew on Islamic architectural antecedents'. This was rejected by the local planning authority on the grounds that 'it would be "out of character", "unsympathetic" and "not in keeping with the surrounding buildings" that reflected inner London's "traditional architectural heritage"'. The report (Beckford, Gale, Owen, Peach, Weller, 2006: 55) also notes that, as recently as April 2005, plans for a major new mosque in Dudley were put on hold 'due to heavy public opposition to the building's size, style and prominence. Specifically, local residents argued that the minaret was too high, and that the building was architecturally "out of place" in the context of Dudley's "ancient" townscape'.

Partly as a result of issues of this kind, many such buildings have finally been given permission to be built in what are mixed-use zones, including industrial or commercial districts, instead of in residential areas. One of the most famous examples of this is the Swaminarayan Mandir in Neasden, London, which now stands near an Ikea store, a short distance from the North Circular Road, having previously been refused planning permission in suburban Harrow.

In addition to issues around the type and size of buildings, matters to do with conditions placed on the hours during which a religious building can be used have sometimes become contentious. As reported by Beckford, Gale, Owen, Peach and Weller (2006: 55):

> in 1997, a Council in Lincolnshire imposed a condition on a mosque that was housed in a former Baptist church, restricting its hours of use to between nine o'clock in the morning and nine o'clock at night. This was justified on the grounds that to use the site outside of these hours would 'unacceptably harm the general living conditions of neighbouring residents, on account of noise and disturbance'.

This condition effectively prevented the mosque being used for the first and the fifth of the five Muslim daily prayers. In doing so, it showed that local planners had interpreted legislation in such a way that the interests of non-Muslims had been given priority over the religious obligations of Muslims. In this case the Muslims concerned appealed, and the planning inspector overturned the decision of the Council.

Another example of the use conditions relates to broadcasts of the Muslim call to prayer or *azan* from the minarets of mosques that are purpose built. In the Religious Discrimination in England and Wales Research Project report (Weller, Feldman and Purdam, et al., 2001: 67), it was noted that, 'Both Hindu and Muslim interviewees pointed out that ringing of church bells does not seem to be regarded as a problem, and yet great restrictions are placed on the public broadcasting of the Muslim call to prayer.' In Birmingham during the early to mid 1980s, a four-year-long planning controversy ensued after the City Council's decision to prevent the broadcasting of the azan from the Birmingham Central Mosque. Eventually, after a trial period and an exercise in public consultation, the originally imposed condition was partially relaxed, allowing the call to prayer to be broadcast for the midday, afternoon and Friday prayers (Gale, 2005).

John Battle, MP (Personal Communication with the author, 4.09.07), the former Prime Minister's Envoy to the Faith Communities, recounts an example of similar debate in his constituency, in which the potential for conflict without possibility of a resolution by consensus seemed very high. Local Muslims argued that the call to prayer was an important part of their religious practice while other local residents had concerns about this, and it seemed that there might be some extremist groups who could have been poised to take advantage of the resulting difficulties. However, as an example of the kind of creative approach that can be found to such issues when goodwill is deployed, an unexpected solution was found when, instead of pressing for the broadcast of the call to prayer, it was agreed that personal digital alarms would be provided to worshippers at the mosque, thus fulfilling the function of the call to prayer as a reminder to the faithful about their obligations.

The instances highlighted above are examples of the kinds of issues that can easily emerge in the context of planning and places of worship. Underlying these specific issues are debates about the terms of reference of overall planning policies, the way in which they evolved, and the way they are implemented. In connection with this, it is significant that as recently as a 1998 survey (Loftman and Beazley, 1998: 21) of 111 local authorities in England conducted on behalf of the Local Government Association, only eight had policies on places of worship.

More recently, an ODPM (2004: 29) survey on *Planning and Diversity: Research into Policies and Procedures* reported that only slightly more than 25% of all local planning authorities in England stated that they 'always' consulted faith groups when preparing development plans or special planning guidance, whilst 26% stated that they 'never' did so, and (ODPM: 2004: 25) only 10 planning authorities assessed the impact of development plans upon faith groups, once these plans had been adopted. Because of this, the discussion of all these issues in the *Review of the Evidence Base on Faith Communities* (Beckford, Gale, Owen, Peach, Weller, 2006: 57) concluded that:

> local planning authorities appear, on the whole, to have been slow to respond to the planning needs of religious minorities. Nevertheless, there are several local planning authorities that have developed a positive set of policy initiatives in response to the needs of religious minorities, and there is a need for their experience to be extended and circulated to other planning authorities that have only relatively recently been confronted to the need to sensitise their policies and practices to religious group interests. Such an approach to sharing of good practice is a helpful one.

In light of the above, the report by Beckford, Gale, Owen, Peach and Weller (2006: 57–9) went on to outline the history of two local authorities in this regard: Birmingham City Council and Leicester City Council, both of which are in areas with substantial minority ethnic and religious minority populations.

Birmingham City Council is the largest planning authority region in Britain, both in terms of geographical area and the size of the population within its area of administration. Its first policy on places of worship was adopted in 1973. While this signified that the planning authority had begun to recognize the needs of its increasingly diverse population, the basic aim was to limit the establishment of places of worship to the residential areas where South Asian groups had concentrated.

Following an appeal case, the original policy was changed to one that recognized the right of minority groups – and Muslims in particular – to establish religious and community facilities in residential areas. That policy, adopted originally in 1981, has since been reviewed at regular intervals, and continues to inform development control decisions in relation to religious buildings. At the same time, recent analysis (Gale, 2005) has shown that there continues to be a relatively high rate of refusal for planning applications pertaining to mosques and madrasas in Birmingham.

Leicester City Council also has a long experience of planning issues and religious diversity. Over the years it has evolved its policy into what is generally recognized to be quite a sophisticated attempt to systematize planning responses in relation to the needs of its local religious groups. It first adopted a policy on places of worship as early as 1977, although that policy assumed that the issues with which it was concerned would lessen once there was greater awareness of planning system requirements.

Over the years, however, the Council developed (see Gale, 1999: 20–7) a much more proactive approach to the point where, in its revised policy of 1987, it included a clear statement (Leicester City Council, 1987: 3) that it would 'exercise a presumption in favour of proposed new places of worship'. The Council's policy has not since been further reviewed. As summarized by Beckford, Gale, Owen, Peach, and Weller (2006: 58) there were three key elements of Leicester's new policy:

> Firstly, all major new housing developments, and some industrial and recreational sites, were to include land allocated for the development of new places of worship. Secondly, all vacant property owned by the City Council (including both land and buildings) which were to be offered for sale would be assessed pre-emptively according to their suitability for housing religious premises. In addition, in instances when such property was deemed appropriate for use by a religious organisation, the City Council would undertake to sell it to the respective group at a rate below the market value. And thirdly, a register was set up 'of all religious groups approaching the City Council for help'. (Leicester City Council, 1987: 40)

The register was to be used as the basis upon which Council property would be allocated to religious groups. Priority was to be given to groups that had been on the list for the longest time, or whose needs on various other criteria made their case especially compelling.

Consultation, Controversy and Governance

The role of local authorities in making planning decisions in relation to existing and proposed places of worship is a reminder that religious diversity in the UK and how it develops does not exist in a social and political vacuum. Rather, in many different ways religious groups and organizations find that their corporate life takes 'shape' at an intersection between their inherited beliefs, traditions and values and the requirements of the local and national state, the law, custom and practice.

Planning issues are, in fact, only one example where the freedom to manifest religion is not an absolute one. There are legal requirements that must be fulfilled, both by the religious group in terms of plans that meet building regulation requirements, and also by the local authority in terms of its obligations for consultation with the wider community. And it is with this wider arena of the relationships between religion and governance in the context of religion(s), state and society relationships that the next chapter is concerned.

Resources for Further Learning

Beckford, J., Gale, R., Owen, D., Peach, C., Weller, P. (2006), *Review of the Evidence Base on Faith Communities*. London: Office of the Deputy Prime Minister.

Edge, P. (2002), 'The construction of sacred places in English law'. *Journal of Environmental Law*, 14, 2, 161–83.

Finneron, D. and Dinham, A. (n.d.), *Building on Faith: Faith Buildings in Neighbourhood Renewal*. London: The Church Urban Fund.

Gale, R. (1999), *Pride of Place and Places: South Asian Religious Groups and the City Planning Authority in Leicester*. Papers in Planning Research, 172. Cardiff: University of Wales, Department of City and Regional Planning.

Gale, R. (2004a), 'The multicultural city and the politics of religious architecture: urban planning, mosques and meaning-making in Birmingham, UK'. *Built Environment*, 30, 1, 18–32.

Gale, R. (2004b), *The Impact of Urban Planning Law and Procedure upon Religious Groups amongst the South Asian Diaspora in Britain*. Unpublished Ph.D. thesis, submitted to the University of Oxford.

Gale, R. (2005), 'Representing the city: mosques and the planning process in Birmingham, UK'. *Journal of Ethnic and Migration Studies*, 1, 6, 1161–79.

Gale, R. and Naylor, S. (2002), 'Religion, planning and the city: the spatial politics of ethnic minority expression in British cities and towns'. *Ethnicities*, 2, 3, 389–411.

Hodgins, H. (1981), 'Planning permission for mosques – the Birmingham experience'. *Research Papers – Muslims in Europe*, 9, 11–27.

Inter Faith Network for the UK (1995), *Places of Worship: The Practicalities and Politics of Sacred Space in Multi-Faith Britain*. London: Inter Faith Network for the UK.

Leicester City Council (1987). *Places of Worship in Leicester*. Leicester: Leicester City Council.

Loftman, P. and Beazley, M. (1998), *Race, Equality and Planning – Technical Survey Report*. London: Local Government Association.

Magida, A. (1996), *How to be a Perfect Stranger: A Guide to Etiquette in Other People's Religious Ceremonies*. Woodstock, Jewish Lights Publishing.

Nasser, N. (2003), 'South Asian ethnoscapes: the changing cultural landscapes of British cities'. *Global Built Environment Review*, 3, 2, 26–39.

Nye, M. (1996), 'Hare Krishna and Sanatan Dharm in Britain: the campaign for Bhaktivedanta Manor'. *Journal of Contemporary Religion*, 21, 1, 37–56.

Nye, M. (2001), *Multiculturalism and Minority Religions in Britain: Krishna Consciousness, Religious Freedom and the Politics of Location*. Richmond: Curzon Press.

ODPM (Office of the Deputy Prime Minister) (2004), *Planning and Diversity: Research into Policies and Procedures*. London: Office of the Deputy Prime Minister.

Peach, C. and Gale, R. (2003), 'Muslims, Hindus and Sikhs in the new religious landscape of England'. *The Geographical Review*, 93, 4, 469–90.

Weller, P. (1995), 'The changing patterns of worship space provision in Britain', in The Inter Faith Network for the United Kingdom, *Places of Worship: The Practicalities and Politics of Sacred Space in Multi-Faith Britain*. London: Inter Faith Network for the UK, London, pp. 4–16.

Weller, P., Feldman, A. and Purdam, A., et al. (2001), *Religious Discrimination in England and Wales* (Home Office Research Study, No. 220). London: Research, Development and Statistics Directorate, The Home Office.

Religious Diversity, Governance and Civil Society

Learning Outcomes for Chapter 3

After studying this chapter, and referring to a range of its associated Further Learning Resources, you should be able to:

(i) *describe* some key aspects of the existing relationship between religion(s), state and society at UK level

(ii) *discuss* possible changes to the existing relationships between religion(s), state and society at UK level

(iii) *discuss* the relevance of the 'bonding' and 'bridging' forms of 'social capital' to aspects of the role of religious groups in society

(iv) *discuss* new developments in religion and governance at local levels

(v) *evaluate* the appropriateness of a range of theses concerning the relationships between religion(s), state and society

1 Religion(s), State and Society in the UK

Religions and Governance

One of the earliest developments following the appointment of Gordon Brown as Prime Minister was the publication of a Green Paper on *The Governance of Britain* (2007). 'Government' can be understood as the exercise of political authority over the actions and affairs of a political unit and/or as the system by which a community is ruled.

'Governance' is broader than 'government' and relates to the manner of governing, and thus goes beyond the machinery of government to include also those policies, structures and mechanisms through which the legislation that is passed by Parliaments and the policies and practices that are adopted by governments are then translated into the wider social context of civil society. Thus, while 'government' will always include 'governance', it is possible to share in 'governance' without being in 'government'.

There is, in fact, a whole range of ways in which religion(s) interface(s) with civil society, public life and government (Hebert, 2003). Some of these are in critique and tension with the government of the day and are counter-cultural to the broader society, while others partake in the institutional structures of state, government and society (Cohn-Sherbok and McClellan, eds, 1992).

Religion(s), State and Society: The UK and National Inheritance(s)

Study Activity 9

In light of sections 1, 2, 3 and 4 of the chapter:

(i) *describe* the framework for religion, state and society arrangements in two countries of the UK

(ii) *discuss* some of the key arguments that might be used in support of a continuing 'special relationship' between Christianity and governance in the UK

(iii) *discuss* some of the main arguments for (a) continuity and (b) change, with regard to the representation of organized religion in the Second Chamber of Parliament

(iv) *discuss* various ways of understanding the role of religion in 'civil society'

(v) *evaluate* the appropriateness to the current UK landscape of religion and belief of the various ways of understanding a 'secular state' as set out in Panel 1

Christianity, especially in its established forms, still plays a pre-eminent role in the public religious life of the UK (Bradley, 2007). Within this, the established Church of England has a special constitutional position with regard to the UK state as a whole that marks it out from other Churches. However, in contrast with the national Churches of some other European countries, the Church of England is not funded by the state in any direct way and is therefore not technically a 'state Church' in the way that, for example, the Lutheran Church in Norway is. Also, within the constituent nations of the UK there is a range of different arrangements for defining the relationships between religious bodies, the nations of the UK, the state and society (Lamont, 1989; Wolffe, 1994a, 1994b).

Religion(s), State and Society in England

In England, the Church of England is the form of religion 'by law established' (Smart, 1989) and other Christian denominations do not have any formal link with the state. In English history the *Act of Uniformity* (1662), the *Conventicle Act* (1644), possibilities for the *Five Mile Act* (1655) and the *Test Act* (1673) all restricted the religious freedom and civic participation of Roman Catholic and Nonconformist Christians.

Modification of this occurred only gradually (Jordan, 1932, 1936; Edwards, 1992), and initially this was in respect only of Nonconformist Christians. For example, the popularly called *Toleration Act* of 1689 was, in fact, more precisely *An Act for Exempting Their Majesties' Protestant Subjects Dissenting From the Church of England From the Penalties of Certain Laws.* The Act thus produced legal toleration (Barlow, 1962) for Trinitarian Protestant Christians who adhered to the 39 Articles of the Church of England (with the exception of articles 34, 35 and 36) rather than religious liberty for all.

While many things are connected with establishment today, technically what lies at its heart is that the Westminster Parliament has control over legislation relating to the Church of England. In addition, the reigning monarch acts as Supreme Governor (and not, as is sometimes popularly but incorrectly stated, its 'Head') of the Church of England and thus must be in communion with it.

The monarch has the title 'Defender of The Faith'. Although the origins of this title predate the Reformation, since the Reformation it has generally been understood in terms of upholding the particular character and role of the Church of England, although the original Latin title, *Fidei Defensor*, is perhaps better translated as 'Defender of Faith' (Bradley, 2002). This is a style that the present Prince of Wales, Prince Charles, has reportedly expressed interest in adopting in order to reflect and bring about a greater connection between the monarchy and the religious diversity of the contemporary UK (Ipgrave, 2003).

The Church of England continues to have a special role in public ceremonial on both ordinary occasions (such as the daily prayers offered by an Anglican Chaplain in the House of Commons) and special ones (such as the prayers at the Cenotaph on Remembrance Day). Its ecclesiastical law is treated as a part of the public law of England, being passed through parliamentary processes and then receiving the Royal Assent. In addition, its ecclesiastical courts currently have the legal power to call as witnesses individuals of any faith or none.

Religion(s), State and Society in Scotland

In Scotland, following the Reformation, the established Presbyterian Church of Scotland was involved in a series of struggles for supremacy (Brown, 1987). Initially, this was between those of Presbyterian and Episcopalian traditions, with the governance of the Church of Scotland changing five times between 1560 and 1690. But even when the established Church in Scotland became clearly Presbyterian, there was a succession of conflicts between Presbyterians of different traditions contesting control of that tradition.

These conflicts have revolved around the laxity or rigour of the leading party in the Church and/or around the issue of the Church–state relationship. They have led to various secessions from, and reunions with what, even where they were opposed to its established status, most parties to these debates nevertheless continued to see as a National Church in Scotland.

Since the 1603 accession of James VI of Scotland to the English Crown as James I and the union of the Parliaments in 1707, Scotland has had close links with England and Wales through a shared monarch and participation in the political system of the UK. But in many ways Scotland remains distinct, especially in its systems of law and education, as well as in relation to matters of religion (Asponwall, 1982). The re-establishment of the Scottish Parliament in 1999 has reinforced this distinctiveness (Sutcliffe, 2004).

The Presbyterian Church of Scotland (rather than the Anglican tradition's Episcopal Church of Scotland) is the established Church in Scotland (Bisset, 1989) and among Presbyterians in Scotland it is often understood as the national Church. Prior to the recent devolution of powers from Westminster to the Scottish Parliament, the Kirk (as it is known in Scotland), which is governed by a hierarchy of elected clerical and lay Kirk Sessions, Presbyteries and also its General Assembly, was frequently seen as a surrogate Scottish parliament.

The Scottish form of establishment differs from that of the Church of England in that it does not place legal restrictions upon the Church of Scotland's self-government, nor does the British Prime Minister, the Secretary of State for Scotland nor the First Minister of the Scottish Executive, have any role in the appointment of its leadership. Similarly, despite its legal status and role within Scottish history, the Church of Scotland has no right, corresponding to that of the Church of England, for its leaders to have seats in the House of Lords. The Church of Scotland does, however, maintain a formal link with the Crown that is symbolized by the Lord High Commissioner's presence at the Church of Scotland's General Assembly, which meets each May in Edinburgh.

Religion(s), State and Society in Wales

Until the recent creation of the National Assembly for Wales, the country had very little modern constitutional distinctiveness, but its culture and language were vigorously revived during the 1960s through the campaigns of Cymdeithas yr Iaith Gymraeg (the Welsh Language Society).

Following the 1920 disestablishment of the Anglican Church in Wales (Bell, 1969), there is now no established form of religion in Wales. Unlike in Scotland, in Wales there has not been a predominant single denominational tradition that has acted as a focus for national identity (Chambers, 2004; Williams, 1991; Jones, 1992). At the same time, the multiplicity of Free Churches has played a significant role in the social, political and cultural life of Wales, including a role in preserving and promoting the use of the Welsh language.

Religion(s), State and Society in Northern Ireland

Neither Northern Ireland nor the Republic of Ireland has an officially established form of religion. The episcopal Church of Ireland (which is part of the global Anglican Communion) was disestablished in 1871 and the *Government of Ireland Act*, 1920, specifically proscribed the establishment of any particular religion or religious tradition. In Northern Ireland, although the Roman Catholic population is the largest single denomination, it is outnumbered by the combined Protestant groupings of which the Presbyterians (organized in a number of different denominations) are the largest.

Religion has continued to be a significant concern – although the relative weighting of its importance is contested (see Barnes, 2005) – in the context of the wider political and national struggle between Nationalists and Unionists, Republicans and Loyalists. In this context, religion (of the Roman Catholic and Protestant Christian varieties) has melded with other aspects of ethnic and communal identity to maintain a high degree of social and political division (Hickey, 1984; Bruce, 1986; McSweeney, 1989; Badham, 1990; Comerford, Cullen and Hill, 1990; Mitchell, 2006).

Despite the existence of the political border between Northern Ireland and the Republic of Ireland, nearly all the Churches of the island of Ireland are organized on an all-Ireland basis with regional and local bodies existing within a common organizational framework both north and south of the border. In the Republic of Ireland, the Roman Catholic Church originally had a special position within the 1937 constitution which meant that its teachings had a formative effect upon legislation in the Republic, particularly in areas of personal, social and sexual morality. However, in 1972 the 'special position' clause was abolished.

2 Established Religion, Constitutional Change and Reform of the Lords

Established Religion: The Inheritance

Against this background, the changing religious landscape poses questions for the future of the inherited patterns of religion and governance, including the continued Establishment of the Church of England. Debates around the Establishment were very vigorous and played a substantial part in public and political debate especially in the latter part of the nineteenth century. This was especially the case following the 1851 Census of Public Worship, the results of which underlined that, especially in the new urban and industrial areas, the Church of England did not on the ground have the strength and presence that its position in the mechanisms of national governance would seem to imply.

Through the nineteenth century, numerous bodies were formed to campaign against religious privilege and civil disabilities, one of the most well known of these being the Society for the Liberation of Religion from State Patronage and Control (originally known as the British Anti-State Church Association). While fundamental constitutional change of this kind did ultimately happen in Ireland and Wales, in England it did not. Nevertheless, issues concerned with the civil and political rights and disabilities of Nonconformist and Roman Catholic Christians (Larsen, 1999), Jews (Salbstein, 1982), Humanists, Freethinkers and other groups were at the forefront of social, religious and political debate.

Under the terms of the 1829 *Roman Catholic Relief Act*, Roman Catholics were admitted to Parliament. In 1858 the *Jews' Relief Act* allowed Jews basically the same civil rights granted to Catholics in 1829. The 1846 *Religious Disabilities Act* removed the last legal restrictions on Nonconformists, whilst allowing Jews the same rights as Nonconformists in respect of education, charities and property. It also removed the majority of the restrictions on Roman Catholics.

For Atheists and Freethinkers, key debates were focused around the continuing requirement for the swearing of oaths on assumption of public office. In 1833, Joseph Pease, a newly-elected Quaker MP, had been allowed to take his Parliamentary seat on the basis of an affirmation rather than an oath (Quakers having, more generally, from 1749 onwards, been allowed to affirm rather than swear an oath). However, atheists were not allowed to do this and between 1850 and 1855, the atheist Charles Bradlaugh was four times prevented from taking the seat to which he had been elected, with the issue becoming a *cause célèbre* until eventual agreement was reached in 1885.

The contemporary UK is therefore not much more than a century away from a time in which the main (including Christian) religious minorities still had to contend with exclusions that were enshrined in the law and which restricted their civil rights and social participation. In fact, it remains the case that no Roman Catholic is permitted to occupy the Throne. Under the *Accession Declaration Act* of 1910, the oath administered to succeeding monarchs obliges them to uphold the Protestant faith. Conversion to Roman Catholicism disinherits successors to the Throne as does, under the *Royal Marriages Act* of 1772, marriage to a Roman Catholic.

Established Religion: Emergent Debates

During much of the twentieth century these and similar issues were quiescent, with many arguing that the issues involved were no longer important enough to spend time and energy on. But towards the end of the twentieth century and the beginning of the twenty-first, debates around establishment have re-emerged both within the Church of England itself (Buchanan, 1994) and in the wider society (Modood, ed., 1997). At the same time, the growth of religious plurality has meant that the lines of debate are no longer drawn so straightforwardly between the historical alternatives of a continued advocacy of a Christendom model, and of a secularizing disestablishment (Modood, 1992, 1993, 1994; Fergusson, 2005; Weller, 2000, 2005a; and Cranmer, Lucas and Morris, 2006). Rather, alternatives such as that of an 'extended' Establishment, or even the creation of a new National Religious Council, have also been the subject of debate.

At the same time, many of the debates about the relationships between religion(s), state and society that have more recently taken place have not been so focused on the specific question and machinery of establishment, but have been more concerned with the broader questions of governance and civil society within the existing constitutional arrangements of the established role of the Church of England (Beckford and Gilliat-Ray, 1996a, 1996b, 1996c; Hebert, 2003).

While there have been some Private Members Bills brought by Members of Parliament concerning establishment, government itself has largely steered clear from direct action relating to establishment as such. Thus, while the new Green Paper on *The Governance of Britain* proposed changes to the appointment process for Church of England bishops, these were also prefaced with a statement to the effect that 'The Church of England is by law established as the Church in England and the Monarch is its Supreme Governor. The Government remains committed to this position.'

Religious Representation in the Legislature: Reform of the House of Lords

One area in which issues of governance and religious diversity had already come into focus in terms of government policy relates to reform of the Second Chamber of the Westminster Parliament. Reform of the House of Lords had been debated for many years, but until the election of the 1997 New Labour Government, no previous government had grasped the nettle of such reform. Even so, the reform process has proceeded slowly and hesitantly, commencing with the removal of hereditary peers from the Lords. Initiating this process, in December 1998, the government published a White Paper entitled *Modernising Parliament: Reforming the House of Lords*, followed by the establishment of a Royal Commission on the Reform of the House of Lords that reported in January 2000.

One element in the present composition of the Second Chamber is the religious representation in the House of Lords (Edge, 2001). In the present composition of the House of Lords, what is known as 'The Lords Spiritual' is composed of the two

Archbishops (Canterbury and York) of the Church of England; three specified Bishops (London, Winchester and Durham); and the next 21 most senior diocesan Bishops of the Church of England. Their membership of the Lords is often seen as expressing something of the particular and unusual relationship between the Church of England, the Crown and Parliament.

Considered by comparison with arrangements in other countries their presence in the legislature is highly unusual, with the exception of the Tynwald Parliament of the Isle of Man, in which the Lord Bishop of Sodor and Man has a place by virtue of his bishopric (Edge and Pearce, 2003, 2004). Nevertheless, however unusual this representation, it is not, in fact, specifically linked with the Establishment of the Church of England. Rather, historically the Bishops' presence was rooted in their role as major landowners and as counsellors to the monarch and in law they sit in the Lords by virtue of the *Bishoprics Act* of 1878. Thus, the White Paper on *Modernising Parliament: Reforming the House of Lords* (chapter 3, paragraph 6) noted that:

> The Bishops are the only true ex officio members of the House of Lords, as they retire from the House on retirement from their see. Since clergymen of the Churches of England, Scotland and Ireland, and Roman Catholic priests, are not able to be members of the House of Commons, the presence of Bishops in the House of Lords was before the introduction of life peers the only significant non-lay representation of the principal religious denominations in Parliament.

In relation to people of other religions, neither non-Anglican Christian Churches (including the established Church of Scotland) nor other religious groups have such representation, although of course many individual members of the House of Lords are people of religious belief and conviction. In addition, through use of the mechanism of life peerages, a number of individuals were made members of the House of Lords as a result of their profile within their religious group and their contribution to the wider society.

These individual appointees to the House of Lords have included such Christian figures as Lord Donald Soper from the Methodist Christian tradition, and Lord George MacLeod of Fuinary, from the Church of Scotland. The former Chief Rabbi, Lord Jacobovits was also made a life peer, while in more recent times Baron Ahmed of Rotherham was a Labour Peer and the first Muslim in the House of Lords, where he has been joined by Lord Ali of Norbury and Baroness Uddin of Bethnal Green, along with peers of other minority ethnic, cultural and religious backgrounds.

In its *White Paper* (chapter 8, paragraph 7) on reform of the Lords, the government suggested that there were four main possible models for the composition of a reformed House: those of a 'nominated chamber'; a 'directly elected chamber'; an 'indirectly elected chamber'; and a 'mixed chamber'. And, among other things, in its consultation paper, the Royal Commission on Reform of the House of Lords, sought responses in relation to a series of questions on the place, role and possibilities that might exist for what the Commission called a 'formal religious component' in future of a reformed Second Chamber for 'organised religion'.

The government's subsequent White Paper of 2001 envisaged retaining a smaller number of Church of England bishops, together with members from other religions, among the appointed section of a reformed Second Chamber. Its later proposals of February 2007 were for a 'hybrid' House, partly elected and partly appointed, including continued representation of the Church of England. However, both Houses subsequently voted in favour of a wholly elected Second Chamber. At the time of writing it is unclear what the outcome of the current political debate will be and when, although the Prime Minister, Gordon Brown, has given a clear signal that he intends to continue the modernization process of government.

The scenario of a wholly elected Second Chamber would, on the face of it, seem to preclude the continuation in the Second Chamber of Parliament of a 'formal religious component' although it is not, in fact, logically impossible. For example, in some other European countries there are significant political parties that are formed and operate on the basis of an explicitly religious self-understanding. Also within the European Union, Belgium is one country that has experimented with 'sectoral' electorates based on, among other things, religious minority groups.

However, such an approach is not familiar within the UK. Very difficult issues of both principle and implementation would be involved in arriving at definitions of, and mechanisms for, the establishment of such electorates. In addition, the organization of political parties on religious grounds has not been the general pattern of political organization in the UK. Even political groupings such as the Movement for Christian Democracy have found it hard to develop and achieve an impact on UK politics, let alone an explicitly religious political party such as the Islamic Party of Great Britain.

In specific periods of UK history broad swathes of people in various religious traditions have seen one or other political party as best representing their interests. This was, for example, the case with respect to Nonconformist Christians in periods during the nineteenth century when Gladstone's Liberal Party was seen as offering the best hope for the removal of the continuing civil disabilities suffered by Nonconformists (Bebbington, 1975). Today, though, with the exception of Northern Ireland – where many Protestant Christians believe their religious interests to be best served by one of the Unionist or Loyalist parties and many Roman Catholic Christians look to Nationalist or Republican parties to advance their interests – such forms of alignment are not generally found. Rather, the more common and recent pattern has been for religious organizations and formal representatives to distance themselves from any specific party political alignments.

At the same time, committed religious individuals have organized themselves as distinctive sectors within the overall structures of political parties that represent interests on the basis of broader social and economic interests and party political programmes. Thus, within the Labour Party there is the Christian Socialist Movement, while within the Conservative Party there is the Conservative Christian Fellowship.

3 New Developments in Religion(s), Consultation and Governance

Previous Patterns

Despite the debates around reform of the Second Chamber, many of the historical patterns for the involvement of the Christian Churches in 'governance' and public life in the UK and in its constituent nations remain (Moyser, 1985). In light of the 'three dimensional society' questions are increasingly raised about the adequacy, equity and appropriateness of these inherited structures and forms. Religious leaders and other representatives of minority religious communities continue to find it hard to gain access to many public and social institutions on the same basis as most Christian leaders and representatives, bearing in mind that this problem could also affect representatives of the smaller Christian denominations.

Alongside the existing constitutional position on religion and state, government has historically utilized a number of other mechanisms for consulting with religious bodies. In the case of education – which is the main focus of the next chapter – the historical role of the Christian Churches in the provision of school education has required ongoing liaison. At present this is facilitated through the Joint Churches Education Policy Group. In addition, touching on the broader issues of the Religious Education curriculum and the practice of collective worship in schools, the Religious Education Council for England and Wales has, for the past quarter of a century, provided a framework for faith communities more generally to consider together issues on Religious Education and collective worship, and has helped in their engagement with government on these issues.

In relation to other issues, most of the historical mechanisms for consultation extended only to the 'mainstream' Anglican, Roman Catholic and Free Churches although, for some purposes, the Jewish community was also included, as in the case of the so-called Churches' Main Committee, which for many years dealt with questions relating to the employment of ministers of religion and other similar matters. However, in light of the religious landscape having changed in the direction of a much greater religious plurality, over the past decade government has made efforts to consult more widely, although the pattern has been patchy and there has been concern among some minority religious groups that these developments were neither fast enough nor sufficiently developed.

National Developments

An early attempt at broader consultation and engagement was the foundation, in 1992, of the Inner Cities Religious Council (ICRC), that was created as part of the then Conservative Government's response to the issues raised by the *Faith in the City* report from the Archbishops' Committee on Urban Priority Areas (1985). Following its foundation, the Council (Beales, 1994) went on to sponsor regional and local consultancy to secure the engagement of religious groups in urban regeneration (Farnell, Furbey, Al-Haqq-Hills, Macey and Smith, 2003; Furbey and Macey, 2005; Ahmed, Finneron, Miller and Singh, 2006). From this, a number of the current local inter-faith organizations and initiatives developed at regional and local levels. Today this work is located in the Department for Communities and Local Government and continues to play a role via the newly created Faith Communities Consultative Council.

The Inter Faith Network for the UK (Weller, 1988; 1994) has also played a significant role in the broadening of consultation, having opened up dialogue with government across a whole range of issues at the interface between religions and public life. The Network has also provided a forum within which faith community and inter-faith organizations could explore and debate these matters and seek to reach a common mind (Inter Faith Network for the UK, 1996).

In the light of continuing concerns among minority faith groups, in 2003 what had previously been established as the Religious Issues section of the then Home Office Race Equality Unit was reconstituted into the Faith Communities Unit, and the government initiated a review of its interface with Faith Communities. The aim of the review was to highlight good practice and to make recommendations designed to make these processes both more effective and more widespread across government. The outcome of that review was contained in the report, *Working Together: Co-Operation Between Government and Faith Communities* (Home Office Faith Communities Unit, 2004). That review considered the possible need for creating a new national mechanism for consultation with faith communities to act as a single point of reference and consultation across the machinery of government.

At the time of the original report, it was concluded that the case for a single point of reference and consultation had not yet been demonstrated. However, by 2006 a new Faith Communities Consultative Council was established. This brings together the work of the Inner Cities Religious Council and the Working

Together exercise that is now located in the Department for Communities and Local Government and responsibility for the Council passed to that Department. In addition to representatives of the Bahá'í, Buddhist, Christian, Hindu, Jain, Jewish, Muslim, Sikh and Zoroastrian communities, the Inter Faith Network for the UK and the Faith Based Regeneration Network UK have seats on the Council, as do the Northern Ireland Inter Faith Forum, the Scottish Executive Core Liaison Group and the Inter Faith Council for Wales.

At the same time, more focused departmental consultation still takes place. For example, in relation to the agenda of tackling extremism, the government has had particular consultations with the Muslim community. In relation to education, there have been recent consultations on the issue of 'faith schools' that will form the main topic of the next chapter. Finally, recognizing that the new Commission for Equality and Human Rights has an agenda that encompasses 'religion and belief', a Religion and Belief Consultative Group has been set up to facilitate discussion between faith community representative organizations, the British Humanist Association and the National Secular Society on issues arising in this field.

Religion, the 'Secular', Consultation and Governance

This latter development is important with regard to the 'secular' dimension of the 'three-dimensional' nature of the UK religious landscape. The British Humanist Association and National Secular Society in general argue that religions should not be privileged and that the state should assume a position of strict neutrality in relation to the religious commitments and identities of its citizens. Such an approach is based on a sociological model of society that generally seeks to maintain a distinction between the 'public' and the 'private' spheres as a means of managing religious and cultural plurality. It also needs to be understood in the context of the exclusionary discrimination that has, in the past, been exercised by powerful religious bodies, and against the background of a variety of historical struggles between Church and state.

But it is all too easy for protagonists in any debate on religion and governance, and on either side of the substantive debates involved, to refer to the concept of a 'secular state' as if its meaning was always clear and shared among those who use the concept. However, in a Council of Europe (1999) seminar on 'Religion and the Integration of Migrants' held just as the states of Central and Eastern Europe were emerging from their period of Communist rule, it was identified that, just as religion can be understood in varied ways, so also the meaning of the 'secular' is not unproblematic and requires further reflection.

Developed by a writer (Dopamu, 1994) who comes from a different social context than the UK and European one, Panel 1 outlines a number of varied understandings that can impinge on the meaning of the relationship between 'religion' and the 'secular state', suggesting that 'a secular state is one where one or a combination of the following is prevalent':

Panel 1: Possible Meanings of the Secular State

(i)   A state where religion is suppressed

(ii)   A state where religion is not given official recognition

(iii)   A state where the government is neutral in matters of religion

(iv)   A state where there is freedom of worship

(v)   A state where no religion is imposed on the people or where there is no state religion

(vi)   A state where advancing science and technology have limited the sphere of influence of religion

(vii)   A state where there is a waning of institutional religion or where fewer people regularly attend religious services

(viii)   A state where there is a separation of religious from political, legal, economic or other institutions

Source: P. Ade Dopamu (1994: 179)

In a twentieth-century European context that has also suffered greatly from totalizing visions of a secular kind, secular Enlightenment projects do not always appear as obvious and unproblematic solutions to the previous abuse of power by organized religion. Therefore in current debates that have an impact on specific issues of religion and public policy, some have tried to distinguish between an understanding of the 'secular' that is a more 'procedural' one – and can be understood as being a way of trying to facilitate the inclusion and participation of a range of groups within the society and the state – and an approach that attempts to confine religion to the private sphere alone, on the basis of either politically pragmatic and/or ideological considerations.

Religions, 'Social Capital' and Governance

In light of an increasing modesty on the part of governments of all political complexions about what they can achieve on their own there has been a search for social partners to collaborate with in the implementation of social policy (Smith, G., 2002, 2003, 2004). This pragmatic political recognition has also been linked with social theory through application of the work of American political scientist, Robert Putnam, on 'social capital'. Beginning with his article 'Bowling Alone'

(Putnam, 1995), which was later developed into a book (Putnam, 2000) of the same title, Putnam took the idea of 'social capital' that had first been introduced into political theory by Coleman (1988, 1990) and applied it to his country of the USA. In doing so he argued that, in recent years, the country has experienced an overall decline in social capital. While his thesis has been critiqued on a number of grounds connected both with data collection and interpretation, the notion of social capital has now become firmly established in public and general discourse in the UK.

Putnam argues that key aspects of 'social capital' relate to behaviours that can be learned and developed over time in the context of ongoing social relationships that are supported by organizations and groups in the community, including religious ones. Trust and co-operation are seen as central features of this. Within this, both the potential and actual social engagement of religious groups and organizations have increasingly been recognized, leading to the development in government and other public body discourse of reference to the 'faith sector' within what is known, overall, as the 'voluntary and community sector'.

Thus, out of the so-called 'bonding' social capital that is produced within and among each religious tradition (Harris and Harris, 1997; Slesinger, 2003), there is a whole range of resources that can, with benefit, be deployed into the creation also of 'bridging' social capital that can benefit the wider society (Furbey, Dinham, Farnell, Finneron, Wilkinson, Howarth, Hussain and Palmer, 2006). As the Local Government Association's (2002: 7) *Faith and Community* report puts it: 'Among the typical resources which faith groups and local inter faith structures can offer as part of the voluntary and community sector are local networks, leadership and management capacity, buildings with potential community use, and volunteers.'

Local Developments in Religion, Consultation and Governance

While the debate at UK level has not yet resulted in significant changes to the structure of governance in terms of religion, alongside the regional developments highlighted above, at local levels there has been a pattern of substantial change. Here, a range of structures and initiatives have emerged that are concerned with facilitating interaction between religions and the wider society in its Christian, secular and religiously plural dimensions.

For the religions this development has been based partly on the need for representation of their interests in the public sphere. Also, within their self-understanding, most religions also have a commitment to making a contribution to the common good that goes beyond the boundaries of their own membership (Chalke, 2001). On the part of government and other public bodies, there has been a growing interest in the potential of multi-faith mechanisms, as a means of facilitating appropriate consultation with faith communities. But there is also interest in their potential role in unlocking collaborative resources in the delivery of social policies and goals, and in utilizing the human and economic capital that can be found among religious groups.

Religious groups and public authorities are increasingly collaborating at regional (Northwest Development Agency, 2003), county (Bates and Collishaw, 2006) and local city/town level (Ravat, 2004) to document the contributions of religious groups to the wider society. In the case of the North West region (Northwest Development Agency, 2005), this goes so far as to include very specific socio-economic impact analyses, while work by Yorkshire and Humber Assembly (2002) has identified the need for an adequate level of what it calls 'religious literacy' to be developed among public bodies.

Relationships on the ground at local authority level remain complex (Vertovec, 1994) and local inter-faith initiatives have a variety of histories, self-under-standings and methods of working (Inter Faith Network for the UK, 2003; Inter Faith Network for the UK, 2007) that can include focus on inter-faith dialogue and action alone. However, increasingly as government has sought to engage with, and facilitate, the contribution that religions can make to wider public life, a pattern of local inter-faith initiatives has emerged, the main rationale for which lies in the need for religious groups to co-operate in their interface with local authorities, business and other community groups through mechanisms such as City Partnerships, an example of which will be the focus of the remainder of this section.

Developments of this kind have been stimulated by a series of good practice guides in which bodies such as the Inter Faith Network, the Inner Cities Religious Council and also the Faiths Based Regeneration Network have played a part along with government Departments and Units and the Local Government Association. These guides include: the Inter Faith Network for the UK and Inner Cities Religious Council's (1999) *Local Inter-Faith Guide: Faith Community Co-Operation in Action*; the Local Government Association's (2002) *Faith and Community: A Good Practice Guide for Local Authorities*; and the Inter Faith Network's (2003b) *Partnership for the Common Good*. As such initiatives have developed, a range of issues have been identified, a number of which are highlighted in the following quotation from the Local Government Association Guide:

> The value of more formal structures of this kind in multi-faith cities and towns is becoming increasingly apparent. The constitution of a council of faiths is usually designed to ensure that its management committee adequately reflects the faith make-up of the area. The most successful groups regularly check that these representatives are, in the view of their faith communities, the most appropriate people for the committee. But

there are difficult issues to be resolved in deciding which faith groups should be represented on a council and how they should be represented, particularly where effective linking structures with the different faith communities are only beginning to emerge and the nominating mechanisms are, in some cases, in the early stages of development. (Local Government Association, 2002: 24)

4 'Involving Religions': A Local Case Study

Study Activity 10

After reading section 4 of the chapter:

(i) *discover* whether any Forum or Council of Faiths operates where you live or else nearby, and obtain information from it about its history, constitution and work

(ii) *describe* how that Forum or Council of Faiths was originally set up, its aims and objectives, its present composition and work

(iii) *discuss* the issues that underlie the range of questions asked by the Derby 'Involving Religions' project, found in Panels 3–6

(iv) *discuss* what other questions might need to be asked when setting up a Forum of Faiths, either in addition to, or instead of, the kinds of questions asked by the Derby 'Involving Religions' project

(iv) *evaluate* the appropriateness of the Derby project recommendations (see pp. 115–16 and pp. 117–18) in light of what was reported about the project's context, stated aims and findings

Project Context

A recent local development in the author's home city of Derby is illustrative of some of the issues involved. Between March and October 2003, the author and a colleague, Michele Wolfe, conducted a research and development project on 'Religious Group Participation, Inter-Faith Infrastructure, and Capacity-Building in Derby'. Its funding was from the local Community Empowerment Fund and it reported to a project reference group of people drawn from various religious traditions and groups, existing inter-faith initiatives in the locality and the local authority. This section of the chapter therefore draws on text from the project report (Weller and Wolfe, 2004), including a number of direct quotations in Panels 2–6. The aims of the project are set out in Panel 2.

A mailout was issued inviting all identified local religious organizations and groups in Derby to participate in the project. Semi-structured interviews took place with key representative figures among the leadership and membership of

Panel 2: 'Involving Religions' Project Aims

(i)   identify and initiate the most appropriate means of making appointments to the two places on the Board of the Derby City Partnership allocated for participants from local religious groups

(ii) explore the potential for religious group involvement in related developments such as the City of Learning, City of Opportunity, Cultural City, Environment City and Prosperous City initiatives

(iii) identify and develop appropriate means through which the views and experience of the broad range of religious groups in the city might be drawn together and participate in wider public life

(iv) identify how religious groups in Derby might appropriately contribute to the development of community networks more generally

Source: Weller and Wolfe (2004: 3)

organized religious groups in Derby. Focus groups were organized for women and youth who are often less well represented among the formal leaderships of religious groups. Semi-structured interviews also took place with a number of people from key public, private and voluntary sector bodies and groups. In total, 72 participants were involved in project meetings and interviews, of which 62 were from religious groups across the city. Finally, a sample survey of practice drew upon the experience of selected local inter-faith organizations and structures from beyond Derby.

The issues with which the project was concerned needed to be considered in the context of the religious landscape of the city. For this, the 2001 Census question on religious affiliation provided important contextual information. Table 30 shows the actual numbers involved, while Table 31 locates the religious landscape of Derby more broadly within local authority areas in the region of the East Midlands, and then within England and Wales.

Project Questions

Informed by this background information, a range of key questions was used to help to frame and explore the possibilities for future development. The Derby City Partnership (DCP) had made two places available on its Board for representation of religious groups in the city. Given that the Anglican Bishop of Derby already held one of those places, Panel 3 sets out the range of questions that the project asked concerning possible future patterns of representation for the Christian Churches, highlighting the issues involved. But given that the religious diversity of the city had been a key impetus for the initiation of the project, the project

Table 30: Number of People Responding to the Religion Question in the 2001 Census in the city of Derby

Religion	Numbers
Buddhist	448
Christian	149,471
Hindu	1,354
Jewish	141
Muslim	9,958
Sikh	7,151
Other religions	550
Total all religions	169,073
No religion	35,207
Not stated	17,428
Total no religion/not stated	52,635

Source: Weller and Wolfe (2004: 14)

Table 31: Proportionate Ranking of Respondents to the 2001 Census Religion Question in the city of Derby, the East Midlands Region and in England and Wales

Religion	Percentage of Derby Population	Percentage of England Population	Derby Ranking in 376 England and Wales Authorities	Percentage of East Midlands Population	Derby Ranking in 40 East Midlands Local Authorities
Buddhist	0.2%	0.3%	158th	0.2%	9th
Christian	67.4%	71.7%	317th	72.0%	37th
Hindu	0.6%	1.1%	97th	1.6%	9th
Jewish	0.1%	0.5%	255th	0.1%	21st
Muslim	4.8%	3.1%	50th	1.7%	3rd
Sikh	3.2%	0.7%	13th	0.8%	3rd
Other Religions	0.2%	0.3%	192nd	0.2%	10th
No religion	15.9%	14.6%	133rd	15.9%	17th
Not stated	7.9%	7.7%	130th	7.5%	10th

The Derby results are based on a city population of 221,708; for England of 49,138,831; and for the East Midlands of 4,172,174.

The response rates for Derby were 96%; for England and Wales 94%; and for the East Midlands 96%.

Source: Weller and Wolfe (2004: 13)

questions highlighted in Panel 4 focused on how this wider religious diversity might most appropriately be reflected.

The project was also concerned to explore the possible value of developing a formal inter-faith Council or Forum for Derby, and the questions that related to this are set out in Panel 5. Although the city had a longstanding Derby Open Centre and an associated Multi-Faith Group, and is also the location for the Multi-Faith Centre at the University of Derby, unlike many other comparable cities, a formal inter-faith council had never previously existed.

Finally, Panel 6 sets out a range of more general questions and issues concerning the operational realities of local equity, inclusivity and participation in relation both to the DCP Board and any emergent Forum or Council of Faiths.

Panel 3: Derby City Partnership Board: Christian Participation?

In view of the relative size of religious communities in Derby, should one of these places always be taken by a Christian representative?

If so, bearing in mind the position of the Church of England as an established Church, would it be appropriate for this representative to be from that Church?

If not, would it be appropriate for one place to revolve between various broad Christian traditions: Anglican, Roman Catholic, Free Churches?

If so, what about smaller Christian communities in Derby: Churches of predominantly African-Caribbean members; Restorationist/House Churches; the Orthodox and others?

What about smaller traditions that have an historical relationship (Society of Friends and Unitarians) with the Christian tradition, but whose members sometimes understand themselves in more free-standing ways?

Source: Weller and Wolfe (2004: 4)

Panel 4: Derby City Partnership Board: Participation from Other Religions?

How might participation from the largest three (Hindu, Muslim and Sikh) other than Christian traditions be equitably facilitated?

Is there any practical way in which diversities within these traditions can or should be taken account of?

Should there be a possibility for involvement from any of the smaller world religious traditions (at least Bahá'ís, Buddhists and Jews) in Derby?

What about people of other religious traditions, such as Spiritualists, Pagans, and groups often described as New Religious Movements?

Are there completely different ways in which the two places might be distributed with regard to religious equity and the need for some continuity of involvement?

Source: Weller and Wolfe (2004: 4)

Panel 5: A Formal Inter-Faith Council/Inter-Forum for the City?

Might the development of a formal inter-faith Council provide an appropriate vehicle for nomination, support and lines of reporting from the Partnership Board?

Would such a Council enable the nomination of individuals to serve on the Board as representatives of the Council, rather than directly of their individual religions?

If so, how might they be appointed with a view to the issues outlined above (either taking these factors into account for each new nomination, or according to a 'formula' for appointment)?

What *else* might usefully fall within the remit of such a Council if it were developed?

What should *not* be within the remit of any such Council? What might the weaknesses and possible dangers of such a Council be?

In any such Council, should the distribution of membership in some way reflect the relative size of religious communities in Derby?

How far should account of the diversities *within* each religion be taken, and how far is it practicable?

Should any such Council be inclusive of all religions? If not, what criteria might be used to decide membership?

Might there be both 'members' and 'observers', and/or 'full members' and 'associate members'? If so, on what basis?

Given that leaders in religious organizations and groups tend to be predominantly male and older, should there be a specific mechanism to enable the participation of young people and women in the work of any such Council?

Should inter-faith initiatives in the city (such as the Open Centre, and the Multi-Faith Centre at the University of Derby) be part of such a Council?

If so, should they be involved as 'full members', 'associate members' or 'observers'?

What might the appointing mechanisms be for membership of such a Council (especially where at present no city-wide structures exist for particular religions)?

Could a wider religious 'Forum' also be developed, to which all places of worship and religious organizations in Derby could, in principle, apply to join without the constraints of seeking to achieve an inter-religious balance?

Might such a 'Forum', linked with a Council, provide a context for nomination of Council members? Might it also offer a broader network for dissemination of the Council's work and one context for accountability?

Are there completely different issues that should be considered in developing the inter-faith infrastructure in Derby?

Source: Weller and Wolfe (2004: 5)

Panel 6: Issues in Representation and Participation

How might the need for continuity of involvement and stability of communication back to the religious communities, organizations and groups be balanced with equity of representation and opportunities for involvement?

How might members of the Board/possible Council gain and retain the confidence of the religious communities, organizations and groups of the city?

How might representatives on the Board/possible Council maintain communications with the religious communities, organizations and groups of the city?

How might representatives on the Board/possible Council ensure connection with the perspectives of women and young people from among the religious communities, organizations and groups of the city?

Source: Weller and Wolfe (2004: 6)

Project Findings: City Partnership Board Membership

All those interviewed from religious groups welcomed the opportunity for increased involvement in public life represented by the invitation to religious groups to take up two places on the DCP Board. At the same time, there was difficulty in engaging with some religious groups which may have reflected a concern about a potential loss of religious distinctiveness that can, to some, seem to be necessarily implied in inter-faith co-operation. Among other groups there was a concern about the extent to which any initiative might be culturally inclusive enough, particularly bearing in mind the African-Caribbean Christian church presence in the city.

People interviewed from the broader public, private and voluntary sectors of society generally affirmed that religious participation on the Board would be beneficial, articulating this in terms of what they identified as the potential of a 'spiritual' contribution that could be made to the wider society. In particular, it was felt that involvement of people from religious groups, organizations and communities could enhance the overall 'well-being' of the city.

Many interviewees from other than Christian religious traditions felt that, since Christianity was the majority religion, it could be appropriate for one of the two DCP Board places to be taken by a Christian. Some, though, pointed out that while other Board members were not members by reference to their religious background, it was likely that many may, in fact, have a Christian background. Because of this, it was argued that those from other religions should fill the places formally available for religion.

The question was also posed about how far the two religion places available on the DCP Board could adequately reflect the city's religious diversity. But the majority of interviewees from religious groups concluded that the most appropriate function of such individuals would be to contribute to the common good from a broadly religious and spiritual perspective. It was therefore generally felt more important for an individual to carry the confidence of a broad range of religious groups than for them to be expected to represent the interests and perspectives of particular religious groups. Nevertheless some respondents from one religion with a substantial local community argued that it would not be possible for anyone outside of their religion really to represent its concerns.

The DCP Board members interviewed stressed that what would be most valuable was the broader issue of how to secure greater involvement from religious groups across the whole range of local public life. Many interviewees argued that the two places should be filled through some kind of democratic process from among the religions, while an overwhelming majority of interviewees regarded the development of some sort of inter-faith structure as the most appropriate vehicle for this.

Project Recommendations: City Partnership Board Membership

From the project's research, it was agreed that the need to identify individuals to take up the available places on the DCP Board should be seen in the context of the primary aim of facilitating a greater involvement of religions within the work of the DCP. Such an approach emphasized 'participation' in the broadest sense, rather than 'representation' (either based on individual religions and/or size of religious groups) in a narrower sense. In this connection it was noted that much of the work of the DCP takes place in its city or theme groups: City of Learning, City of Opportunity; Cultural City; Environment City; and Prosperous City and that there would therefore be many opportunities for religious groups and individuals to have wider involvement.

It was also agreed that the two available DCP Board places should be filled by individuals with 'best fit' for the general 'job description' required of a DCP Board member. Such an individual should also meet a more specific 'person specification' for this particular role that combines some knowledge of the beliefs, practices and concerns of different religions with being able to command broad confidence among those religions. It was felt that such an approach would enable the individuals concerned to function appropriately in the context of the Board and could command the broad confidence of religious traditions and groups in the City.

It was recommended that the individuals appointed to the DCP Board should serve for up to two years before review, and it was additionally proposed that 'alternates' should be identified who could 'shadow' the two full members and be 'mentored' by them. In this way, participation on the Board of a wider range of religious traditions and groups would be facilitated and a broader pool of people would be developed for future service on the Board. It was recognized that consultation needed to be undertaken among the religious traditions and groups and their 'gatekeepers', 'leaders' and 'elders' in order to identify individuals who might appropriately fulfil these roles.

The project also recommended the establishment of a formal Forum of Faiths to provide an appropriate context within which the two DCP Board members could be appointed. It was felt that a Forum of this kind could provide a means by which these Board members could have some accountability to the broader constituency of Derby's varied religious communities, groups, organizations, and places of worship.

Project Findings: Forum of Faiths

On the question of why such a formal Forum or Council of Faiths had not previously existed in Derby, most interviewees pointed to the existence of informal networks and specific initiatives taken at times of crisis. However, what had been missing was an inter-faith 'champion' along with a lack of resources to translate the evident informal and occasionally specifically focused goodwill into something more permanent.

The vast majority of interviewees felt that a Forum would be desirable and many expressed the view that it should fulfil a wider role than that of merely appointing people to the DCP Board. However, some interviewees were concerned that a Forum might lead to a duplication and dilution of resources already spread thinly between existing local inter-faith initiatives that required diverse religious representation. However, representatives of both the existing inter-faith organizations in Derby – the Derby Open Centre and the Multi-Faith Centre at the University of Derby – felt that they could not 'stretch' their remits to encompass the role that a formal Forum or Council might play.

Interviewees noted a range of other issues. Some raised the question of the location for Forum meetings, arguing that they would best take place in 'neutral' settings. Some felt that a smaller and more 'compact' Forum would be best on the basis that it could facilitate the development of trust among its members. Some expressed the view that, at least initially, a Forum's membership should be restricted to members from the principal 'world religious traditions' with substantial communities in Derby. Others felt that it was in principle important that all religious groups and organizations should have opportunity to participate and that such inclusiveness would be a significant aspect of a Forum's legitimacy and accountability.

In relation to gender composition, in the women's focus group meetings it was pointed out that men often are not in a position to articulate issues from the perspective of women and that women in some communities are not offered opportunities to speak for themselves. Several project participants – both younger and older – noted that adults do not always appreciate and understand the young people's experience. In this context, the possibility of creating a youth 'Forum' or 'Council' was considered as a possible mechanism by which younger people could develop relevant inter-faith skills and experience. However, the majority of interviewees were not in favour of mechanisms such as 'quotas' for ensuring the participation of women and young people. Generally, these were felt to be somewhat artificial and to run the risk of tokenism.

Project Recommendations: Forum of Faiths

It was recommended that a newly established Forum of Faiths should exist not only for the purpose of relating to the DCP or for relationships with the local authority but also to have a remit that should include good relations between the various religious groups. In relation to the Derby Open Centre, the Multi-Faith Centre at the University of Derby, and also the Standing Advisory Conference on Religious Education, it was agreed that they should be invited to 'federate' their existing networks within a 'Forum', the function of which would have points of overlap with each of the existing initiatives, but would not replace any of them.

All groups, organizations and places of worship based in Derby that consider themselves to be religious would be invited to constitute a Forum of Faiths by affirming its aims and objectives and by appointing a representative. It was proposed that the full Forum should meet three times per annum: with one occasion to transact the formal business of an Annual General Meeting; another to hear reports from the two participants on the DCP Board; and a third for a discussion on a topical issue or issues with an invited speaker. It was also agreed that the Forum should seek external funding to support and develop its work.

It was proposed that the Forum should elect a smaller Council to carry forward the work of the Forum throughout the year. The Council would, initially (and also when re-appointments are due), be responsible for nominating individuals to serve on the DCP Board. When existing appointments are reviewed, the Council should bring a nomination or nominations to the Forum, while Forum members may also propose nominees to the Council.

In order to reflect the variety of religions in the city, it was proposed that the Council of the Forum should consist of 12 people elected by the Forum of Faiths including at least: 4 Christians (including not more than one person from any one denomination); 2 Muslims; 2 Hindus; 2 Sikhs; 2 persons (not more than one being from any one tradition) from other 'world religious traditions' (ie. Bahá'í, Buddhist, Jain, Jewish or Zoroastrian) beyond those listed above.

It was also noted that, once constituted, the Council should consider its composition with regard to the relative presence or absence of women and younger people and may co-opt up to a further two people. Finally, it was recommended that the Forum should also include one 'participant observer' from each of the Derby Open Centre; the Multi-Faith Centre at the University of Derby; and the Derby Standing Advisory Conference on Religious Education.

In broad terms, the recommendations of this research and development project were accepted. A Forum of Faiths for Derby was established, and appointments were made from it to the Board of the Derby City Partnership. At the time of writing, the Forum has just secured some public funding from the Neighbourhood Renewal Fund and Connecting Communities Plus to develop and promote inter-faith work with organizations and individuals in the city. This will be carried out by means of the employment of two community development workers (one of whom is to relate specifically to the African-Caribbean churches of Derby) and a number of community researchers with the aim of further identifying issues and opportunities related to the work of the Forum.

5 Theses for Religion(s), State and Society
Origins of the Theses
Having in the earlier parts of the chapter considered aspects of UK, national, regional and local developments in relation to religion and governance, the final section of this chapter introduces seven theses on religion and public life in the

Study Activity 11

Once you have read and considered section 5 of the chapter, in light of your reflection on the chapter as a whole:

(i) *describe* some evidence that might be deployed (a) in support of, and (b) against, each of the theses in Panel 7

(ii) *discuss*, in relation to each of the theses, your agreement or disagreement with, or proposed modification(s) to the thesis concerned

(iii) *evaluate* the adequacy of the theses to the 'three dimensional' religious landscape of the UK

(iv) *propose* some theses of your own to address your view of the relationship between religion(s), state(s) and society in the UK

UK that the author has developed over the past quarter of a century of practical and academic engagement with issues of religious diversity and public life. These are set out in Panel 7.

Since they were first articulated in 1995, these theses have appeared in a range of slightly variant published forms (see Weller, 1990a, 1990b, 2002, 2005a, 2005b – the developmental history of which can be found in Weller, 2005: xiii). The theses are, in a way, the equivalent of newspaper headlines. Like such headlines they are intended to focus attention and to provoke reaction, debate and discussion. As propositions there is much that could be said about them by way of qualification. They do not claim to be either a detailed survey or the last word.

However, especially in a context such as the UK where there is no formal written constitution, but there does exist what the constitutional scholar Peter Hennessy (1995) calls the 'hidden wiring' of the constitution, it is important to have some means of teasing out the fundamental presuppositions that may underlie the particular positions that are taken on a myriad of intersections that exist between religion(s), state and society. Reflection on, and discussion of, the theses provides one way of doing this by stimulating agreement, disagreement or a modification of them.

Panel 7: Theses for Religion(s), State and Society

Thesis 1: The Importance of Not Marginalizing Religions from Public Life

States that assign religions to the private sphere will impoverish themselves by marginalizing important social resources and might unwittingly be encouraging those reactive, backward- and inward-looking expressions of religious life that are popularly characterized as 'fundamentalisms'.

Thesis 2: The Need to Recognize the Specificity of Religions

Religious traditions and communities offer important alternative perspectives to the predominant values and power structures of states and societies. Religions are a reminder of the importance of the things that cannot be seen, touched, smelled, tasted and heard, for a more balanced perspective on those things that can be experienced in these ways.

Thesis 3: The Imperative for Religious Engagement with the Wider Community

Religious communities and traditions should beware of what can be seductive calls from within their traditions to form 'religious unity fronts' against what is characterized as 'the secular state' and what is perceived as the amorality and fragmentation of modern and post-modern society.

Thesis 4: The Need for a Reality Check

National and political self-understandings that exclude people of other than the majority religious traditions, either by design or by default are, historically speaking, fundamentally distorted. Politically and religiously such self-understandings are dangerous and need to be challenged.

Thesis 5: The Need to Recognize the Transnational Dimensions of Religions

Religious communities and traditions need to pre-empt the dangers involved in becoming proxy sites for imported conflicts involving their co-religionists in other parts of the world. But because they are themselves part of wider global communities of faith, religions have the potential for positively contributing to a better understanding of the role of the states and societies of their own countries within a globalizing world.

Thesis 6: The Importance of Religious Inclusivity

Religious establishments as well as other traditions and social arrangements that provide particular forms of religion with privileged access to social and political institutions need to be re-evaluated. There is a growing need to imagine and to construct new structural forms for the relationship between religion(s), state(s) and society(ies) that can more adequately express an inclusive social and political self-understanding than those that currently privilege majority religious traditions.

Thesis 7: The Imperative of Inter-Religious Dialogue

Inter-religious dialogue is an imperative for the religious communities and for the states and societies of which they are a part. There is a need to continue the task of developing appropriate inter-faith structures at all levels within states and societies and in appropriate transnational and international structures.

Religion and Governance: Applications

The theses above are written in a very general way and are intended to apply to broad considerations about the relationship between religion(s), state and society in relation to overall structures of government and governance. However, what is critical is the way in which these issues are worked out in each sector of society and in each institutional setting. One of the areas in which the interaction between religion and 'governance' can still be found to have a permeative and powerful role in modern societies, such as the UK, is in that of the public education system. Education represents an enormous investment of financial and human resources that many argue can play a substantial role in the future development of society in its economic, social and cultural dimensions. It is therefore to the consideration of religious diversity and education that the next chapter turns.

Resources for Further Learning

Ahmed, R. and Salter, J. (1999), *Ethnic and Faith Community Development*. London: Community Relations Section, Royal Borough of Kensington and Chelsea.

Ahmed, R., Finneron, D., Miller, S. and Singh, H. (2006), *Tools for Regeneration: A Holistic Approach for Faith Communities* (revised and expanded edition). London: Faith Based Regeneration Network UK.

Archbishop's Commission on Urban Priority Areas (1985), *Faith in the City: A Call for Action by Church and Nation – The Report of the Archbishop of Canterbury's Commission on Urban Priority Areas*. London: Church House, London.

Asponwall, B. (1982), 'The Scottish Religious Identity in the Atlantic World, 1888–1914', in S. Mews, ed., *Studies in Church History: Religion and National Identity*. Oxford: Blackwell, pp. 505–18.

Avis, P., ed. (2003), *Public Faith? The State of Religious Belief and Practice in Britain*. London: SPCK.

Badham, P., ed. (1989), *Religion, State and Society in Britain*. Lampeter: Edwin Mellen Press.

Badham, P. (1990), 'The contribution of religion to the conflict in Northern Ireland', in D. Cohn-Sherbok, ed., *The Canterbury Papers: Essays on Religion and Society*. London: Bellew, pp. 119–28.

Barlow, R. (1962), *Citizenship and Conscience: A Study of the Theory and Practice of Religious Toleration in England During the Eighteenth Century*. Philadelphia: University of Pennsylvania.

Barnes, P. (2005), 'Was the Northern Ireland conflict religious?' *Journal of Contemporary Religion* 20, 1, 53–67.

Bates, J. and Collishaw, S. (2006), *Faith in Derbyshire: Working Towards a Better Derbyshire: Faith Based Contribution*. Derby: Derby Diocesan Council for Social Responsibility.

Beales, C. (1994), 'Partnerships for a change: the Inner Cities Religious Council'. *World Faiths Encounter*, 8, July, pp. 41–46.

Bebbington, D. (1982), *The Nonconformist Conscience: Chapel and Politics, 1870–1914*. London: George Allen and Unwin.

Beckford, J. and Gilliat, S. (1996a), *The Church of England and Other Faiths in a Multi-Faith Society*. Coventry: Warwick Working Papers in Sociology, University of Warwick.

Beckford, J. and Gilliat, S. (1996b), *The Church of England and Other Faiths in a Multi-Faith Society, Volume I & Volume II*. Coventry, Department of Sociology, University of Warwick.

Beckford, J. and Gilliat, S. (1996c), *The Church of England and Other Faiths in a Multi-Faith Society: Summary Report*. Coventry: Department of Sociology, University of Warwick.

Bell, P. (1969), *Disestablishment in Ireland and Wales*. London: SPCK.

Bisset, P. (1989), 'Kirk and society in modern Scotland', in P. Badham, ed., *Religion, State and Society in Britain*. Lampeter: Edwin Mellen Press, pp. 51–65.

Bradley, I. (2002), *God Save the Queen: The Spiritual Dimensions of Monarchy*. London: Darton, Longman and Todd.

Bradley, I. (2007), *Believing in Britain: The Spiritual Identity of Britishness*. London: I.B. Tauris.

Brown, C. (1987), *A Social History of Religion in Scotland Since 1730*. London: Methuen.

Bruce, S. (1986), *God Save Ulster: The Religion and Politics of Paisleyism*. Oxford: Oxford University Press.

Buchanan, C. (1994), *Cut the Connection: Disestablishment and the Church of England*. London: Darton, Longman and Todd.

Chalke, S. (2001), *Faithworks: Actions Speak Louder than Words*. Eastbourne: Kingsway Publications.

Chambers, P. (2004), 'Religion, identity and change in contemporary Wales', in S. Coleman and P. Collins, eds, *Religion, Identity and Change: Perspectives on Global Transformations*. Aldershot: Ashgate, pp. 69–83.

Cohn-Sherbok, D., ed. (1990), *The Canterbury Papers: Essays on Religion and Society*. London: Bellew.

Cohn-Sherbok, D. and McClellan, D., eds (1992), *Religion in Public Life*. London: Macmillan.

Coleman, J. (1988), 'Social capital in the creation of human capital'. *American Journal of Sociology*, 94, 95–120.

Coleman, J. (1990), *Foundations of Social Theory*. Cambridge: Cambridge University Press.

Coleman, S. and Collins, P., eds, *Religion, Identity and Change: Perspectives on Global Transformations*. Aldershot: Ashgate.

Comerford, R., Cullen, M. and Hill, J. (1990), *Religion, Conflict and Coexistence in Ireland*. London: Gill and Macmillan.

Council of Europe (1999), *Religion and the Integration of Migrants*. Strasbourg: Council of Europe.

Cranmer, F., Lucas, J. and Morris, B. (2006), *Church and State: A Mapping Exercise*. London: The Constitution Unit, University College.

Dopamu, P. (1994), 'Religion in a secular state: problems and possibilities within the Nigerian context'. *The Indo-British Review*, 20, 1, 177–89.

Edge, P. (2001), 'Religious remnants in the composition of the United Kingdom Parliament', in R. O'Dair and A. Lewis, *Law and Religion: Current Legal Issues, 4*. Oxford: Oxford University Press, pp. 443–57.

Edge, P. and Harvey, G., eds (2000), *Law and Religion in Contemporary Societies: Communities, Individualism and the State*. Aldershot: Ashgate.

Edge, P. and Pearce, C. (2003), *Religious Representation in a Democratic Legislature: A Case Study of the Lord Bishop of Sodor and Man in the Manx Tynwald*. Oxford: Oxford Centre for Legal Studies.

Edge, P. and Pearce, C. (2004), 'Official religious representation in a democratic legislature: lessons from the Manx Tynwald'. *Journal of Church and State*, 46, 3, 1–42.

Edwards, D. (1992), 'A brief history of the concept of toleration in Britain', in J. Horton and H. Crabtree, eds (1992), *Toleration and Integrity in a Multi-Faith Society*. York: Department of Politics, University of York.

Farnell, R., Furbey, R., Al-Haqq Hill, S., Macey, M. and Smith, G. (2003), *'Faith' in Urban Regeneration? Engaging Faith Communities In Urban Regeneration*. Bristol: Policy Press.

Fergusson, D. (2005), *Church, State and Civil Society*. Cambridge: Cambridge University Press.

Francis, L. (2003), 'Religion and social capital: the flaw in the 2001 Census in England and Wales', in P. Avis, ed., *Public Faith? The State of Religious Belief and Practice in Britain*. London: SPCK, pp. 45–64.

Furbey, R., Dinham, A., Farnell, R., Finneron, D., Wilkinson, G., with Howarth, C., Hussain, D., and Palmer, S. (2006), *Faith as Social Capital: Connecting or Dividing?* Bristol: Policy Press.

Furbey, R. and Macey, M. (2005), 'Religion and urban regeneration: a place for faith?'. *Policy and Politics*, 33, 1, 95–116.

Ghanea, N., ed. (2003), *The Challenge of Religious Discrimination at the Dawn of the New Millennium*. Leiden: Martinus Nijhoff.

Harris, M. and Harris, R. (1997), *The Jewish Voluntary Sector in the United Kingdom: Its Role and Its Future*. London: Institute of Jewish Policy Research.

Hastings, A. (1991), *Church and State: The English Experience. The Prideux Lectures for 1990*. Exeter: University of Exeter.

Hebert, D. (2003), *Religion and Civil Society: Rethinking Religion in the Contemporary World*. Aldershot: Ashgate.

Hennessy, P. (1995), *The Hidden Wiring: Unearthing the British Constitution*. London: Victor Gollancz.

Hickey, J. (1984), *Religion and the Northern Ireland Problem*. Dublin: Gill and Macmillan.

Home Office Faith Communities Unit (2004), *Working Together: Co-Operation Between Government and Faith Communities. Recommendations of the Steering Group Reviewing Patterns of Engagement Between Government and Faith Communities in England*. London: Faith Communities Unit, The Home Office.

Horton, J. and Crabtree, H., eds (1992), *Toleration and Integrity in a Multi-Faith Society*. York: Department of Politics, University of York.

Inter Faith Network for the UK (1996), *Britain's Faith Communities: Equal Citizens?* London: Inter Faith Network for the UK.

Inter Faith Network for the UK (2003a), *Local Inter Faith Activity in the UK: A Survey*. London: Inter Faith Network for the UK.

Inter Faith Network for the UK (2003b), *Partnership for the Common Good: Inter Faith Structures and Local Government*. London: Inter Faith Network for the UK.

Inter Faith Network for the UK (2007), *Inter Faith Organisations in the UK: A Directory* (fourth edition). London: Inter Faith Network for the United Kingdom.

Inter Faith Network for the UK/Inner Cities Religious Council (1999), *The Local Inter Faith Guide: Faith Community Co-Operation in Action*. London: Inter Faith Network for the United Kingdom in association with the Inner Cities Religious Council of the Department for the Environment, Transport and the Regions.

Ipgrave, M. (2003), '"Fidei Defensor" revisited: Church and state in a religiously plural society', in N. Ghanea, ed., *The Challenge of Religious Discrimination at the Dawn of the New Millennium*. Leiden: Martinus Nijhoff, pp. 207–22.

Jones, R. (1992), 'Religion, nationality and state in Wales, 1840–1890', in D. Kerr, ed., *Religion, State and Ethnic Groups*. Aldershot: Dartmouth Publishing, pp. 261–76.

Jordan, W. (1932, 1936), *The Development of Religious Toleration in England* (2 volumes). London: George Allen and Unwin.

Kerr, D., ed. (1992), *Religion, State and Ethnic Groups*. Aldershot: Dartmouth Publishing.

Lamont, S. (1989), *Church and State: Uneasy Alliances*. London: Bodley Head.

Larsen, T. (1999), *Friends of Religious Equality: Nonconformist Politics in Mid-Victorian England*. Woodbridge: The Boydell Press.

Lewis, J. and Randolph-Horn, E. (2001), *Faiths, Hope and Participation: Celebrating Faith Groups' Role in Neighbourhood Renewal*. London: New Economics Foundation and Church Urban Fund.

Local Government Association (2002), *Faith and Community: A Good Practice Guide*. London: Local Government Association Publications.

McSweeney, B. (1989), 'The religious dimension of the "Troubles" in Northern Ireland', in P. Badham, ed., *Religion, State and Society in Modern Britain*. Lampeter: Edwin Mellen Press, pp. 68–83.

Mews, S., ed. (1982), *Studies in Church History: Religion and National Identity*. Oxford: Blackwell.

Mitchell, C. (2006), *Religion, Identity and Politics in Northern Ireland: Boundaries of Belief and Belonging*. Aldershot: Ashgate.

Modood, T. (1992), 'Minorities, faith and citizenship'. *Discernment: A Christian Journal for Inter-Religious Encounter, 6*, 2, 58–60.

Modood, T. (1994), 'Establishment, multiculturalism and British citizenship'. *Political Quarterly, 65*, 1, 53–73.

Modood, T., ed. (1997), *Church, State and Religious Minorities*. London: Policy Studies Institute.

Moyser, G., ed. (1985), *Church and Politics Today: The Role of the Church of England in Contemporary Politics*. Edinburgh: T. & T. Clark.

Northwest Regional Development Agency (2003), *Faith in England's Northwest: The Contribution Made by Faith Communities to Civil Society in the Region*. Warrington: Northwest Regional Development Agency.

Northwest Regional Development Agency (2005), *Faith in England's Northwest: Economic Impact Assessment*. Warrington: Northwest Regional Development Agency.

Parsons, G., ed. (1994), *The Growth of Religious Diversity: Britain From 1945. Volume II: Issues*. London: Routledge.

Putnam, R. (1995), 'Bowling alone: America's declining social capital'. *Journal of Democracy*, 2, 65–78.

Putnam, R. (2000), *Bowling Alone: The Collapse and Revival of American Community*. New York: Simon and Schuster.

Race, A. and Shafer, I., eds (2002), *Religions in Dialogue: From Theocracy to Democracy*. Aldershot: Ashgate.

Ravat, R. (2004), *Enabling the Present: Planning for the Future: Social Action by the Faith Communities of Leicester*. Leicester: Leicester Faiths Regeneration Project.

Salbstein, M. (1982), *The Emancipation of the Jews in Britain: The Question of the Admission of the Jews to Parliament, 1828–1860*. London: Associated University Press.

Slesinger, E. (2003), *Creating Community and Accumulating Social Capital: Jews Associating With Other Jews in Manchester*. London: Institute for Jewish Policy Research.

Smith, G. (2002), 'Religion and the rise of social capitalism: the faith communities in community development and urban regeneration in England'. *Community Development Journal*, 37, 2, 166–77.

Smith, G. (2003), *Faith in the Voluntary Sector: A Common or Distinctive Experience of Religious Organisations*. (Working Papers in Applied Social Research, No. 25, Department of Sociology). Manchester: University of Manchester.

Smith, G. (2004), 'Faith in community and communities of faith? Government rhetoric and religious identity in urban Britain'. *Journal of Contemporary Religion*, 19, 2, 185–204.

Sutcliffe, S. (2004), 'Unfinished business – devolving Scotland/devolving religion', in S. Coleman and P. Collins, eds, *Religion, Identity and Change: Perspectives on Global Transformations*. Aldershot: Ashgate, pp. 84–106.

Vertovec, S. (1994), 'Multi-cultural, Multi-Asian, Multi-Muslim Leicester: dimensions of social complexity, ethnic organisation and local Government interface'. *Innovation: European Journal of Social Sciences*, 7, 3, 259–76.

Weller, P. (1988), '"Inheritors together": the Inter Faith Network for the United Kingdom'. *Discernment: A Christian Journal of Inter-Religious Encounter*, 3, 2, 30–4.

Weller, P. (1990a), 'Freedom and witness in a multi-religious society: a Baptist perspective. Part I'. *Baptist Quarterly*, 33, 6, 252–64.

Weller, P. (1990b), 'Freedom and witness in a multi-religious society: a Baptist perspective. Part II'. *Baptist Quarterly*, 33, 7, 302–15.

Weller, P. (1994), 'The Inter Faith Network for the United Kingdom'. *Indo-British Review: A Journal of History*, 20, 1, 20–26.

Weller, P. (2000), 'Equity, inclusivity and participation in a plural society: challenging the Establishment of the Church of England', in P. Edge and G. Harvey, eds, *Law and Religion in Contemporary Societies: Communities, Individualism and the State*. Aldershot: Ashgate, pp. 53–67.

Weller, P. (2002), 'Insiders or outsiders?: propositions for European religions, states and societies', in A. Race and I. Shafer, eds, *Religions in Dialogue: From Theocracy to Democracy*. Aldershot: Ashgate, pp. 193–208.

Weller, P. (2005a), 'Religions and social capital: theses on religion(s), state(s) and society(ies): with particular reference to the United Kingdom and the European Union'. *The Journal of International Migration and Integration*, 9, 2, 271–89.

Weller, P. (2005b), *Time for a Change: Reconfiguring Religion, State and Society*. London: T. & T. Clark.

Weller, P. and Wolfe, M. (2004), *Involving Religions: A Project Report on Religious Group Participation, Inter-Faith Infrastructure, and Capacity-Building in Derby*. Derby: School of Education, Health and Sciences, University of Derby.

Williams, G. (1991), *The Welsh and Their Religion*. Cardiff: University of Wales Press.

Wolffe, J. (1994a), *God and Greater Britain: Religion and National Life in Britain and Ireland, 1843–1945*. London: Routledge.

Wolffe, J. (1994b), '"And there's another country …"': religion, the state and British identities', in G. Parsons, ed., *The Growth of Religious Diversity: Britain From 1945. Volume II: Issues*. London: Routledge, pp. 85–159.

Yorkshire and Humber Assembly (2002), *Religious Literacy: A Practical Guide to the Region's Faith Communities*. Wakefield: Yorkshire and Humber Assembly.

Religious Diversity and Education

4

Learning Outcomes for Chapter 4

After studying this chapter, and referring to a range of its associated Further Learning Resources, you should be able to:

(i) *describe* key aspects of the framework within which publicly funded faith-based schools in England and at least one other country in the UK operate

(ii) *discuss* some of the key arguments for and against publicly funded faith-based schools from (a) a selected faith community perspective (b) a 'secular' perspective

(iii) *discuss* some of the issues that have recently emerged at the interface between religion and higher education

(iv) *discuss* some ways in which it might be possible for higher education institutions positively to benefit from the diversity of religion and belief among their staff and students

(v) *evaluate* the challenges involved for higher education institutions in supporting values of freedom of enquiry, religion and speech while at the same time protecting students and staff against incitement of hatred and other potentially threatening actions of extremist individuals and groups

1 Religion and Education: Complementarity and Conflict

Education in a Society of Diverse Religion and Belief

The formal education system is of great importance. At school level, it directly impacts upon the lives of almost the whole of the population, while higher education is becoming part of the adult experience of an ever-greater proportion of the population. Education is, at least potentially, a lifelong means to individual achievement, personal growth and the expansion of economic opportunity.

The education system is also an arena within which family traditions and identities, including religious identities and convictions, come into interaction with the beliefs and values of the wider and more diverse society. Such interaction can result in significant tensions for parents, children and teachers alike. These tensions can either take the form of conflict and/or negotiation. The education system is also important because at school level it can be the means by which attitudes and values are initially formed and, later, for those who enter higher education, critically evaluated. It can thus play a significant role in shaping perceptions and approaches to issues of religious diversity.

Religion and Education: Some Roots

There is a long and shared history in the relationship between religion and education, sometimes mutually reinforcing and sometimes in tension. Sometimes religious authority has been pitched against independent learning, as in the kinds of tensions that emerged during the rise of Humanism in the European Renaissance and during the industrial and scientific revolutions of the nineteenth and twentieth centuries.

At the same time, there is a long historical connection between Islam, literacy and learning, and within Christianity, monasteries were often places of literacy and learning while in the UK, the earliest schools were founded in connection with the Church. The ancient Universities were places for clerical training, as at Oxford and Cambridge, and the Church of England became a provider of education before either national or local government did (Murphy, ed., 1971).

2 Publicly Funded Faith-Based Schools: The Inheritance

Study Activity 12

After reading section 2 of the chapter:

(i) *discover* where is the nearest (a) Christian, and (b) other than Christian publicly funded faith-based school to where you live, and obtain a prospectus/newsletter and material about them

(ii) *describe* the main features of the arrangements governing publicly funded faith-based schools in one of the countries of the UK

(iii) *discuss* some of the key arguments for and against publicly funded faith-based schools from (a) a specific faith group perspective and (b) a 'secular' perspective

(iv) *evaluate* what is likely to be the place of publicly funded faith-based schools in the future of educational provision in one of the countries of the UK

Publicly Funded Faith-Based Schools: The Legislative Framework

Schools in both England and Wales share much of the same legislative framework, despite education administration in Wales now being the responsibility of the devolved National Assembly. Education in Scotland is devolved to the Scottish Parliament. The presence of religiously-based schools is one of the key ways in which religion is firmly embodied in the fabric of the UK society but, as in so many other aspects of life in the UK to do with religion, there are both commonalities and also important differences with respect to the relationship between religion and education in the different national contexts of the multi-national UK state.

England and Wales

When, early in the twentieth century, educational provision generally came under government administration, the Church of England's denominational schools became part of a national education framework as a result of an agreement between it and the state embodied in the 1902 *Education Act* which was generally known as the 'dual system'. Following the 1944 *Education Act*, the continuing Anglican denominational schools preserved a degree of autonomy as 'voluntary aided' or 'voluntary controlled' schools.

Both categories of school received public funding, but a proportion of the financial responsibility for 'voluntary aided' schools has remained with the sponsoring religious body. The Church of England, the Roman Catholic Church and (to a much lesser extent) the Methodist Church have schools that are 'voluntary aided', while there have also been a number of 'voluntary aided' Jewish schools too. These schools also have more autonomy with respect both to admissions policies as well as arrangements for Religious Education and Collective Worship. Also, 'voluntary aided' schools can, in their appointment of teachers (but not other staff), include criteria designed to ensure that there is a sufficient proportion of teachers who are related to the religious tradition upon which the school is founded, in order to maintain its fundamental character and ethos.

'Voluntary controlled' schools – the vast majority of which are Church of England schools – are much more fully integrated into the local authority system. For example (except where parents make a request for denominational teaching), they follow the Agreed Syllabus of the Local Education Authority. However, 'collective worship' in 'voluntary controlled' schools should be in accordance with the foundation trust deed of the school, as in 'voluntary aided' schools.

Scotland

From the years of the Reformation in Scotland until 1872, two approaches to school education evolved. In rural areas, the established Church of Scotland shared responsibility for education with the civic authorities. This partnership underpinned the 1696 *Education Act's* requirement that there should be a school established, and a schoolmaster appointed, in every parish 'by advice of the Heritor and Minister of the Parish'.

These schools were, in practice, Presbyterian in outlook. But eventually, during the first half of the nineteenth century, the Scottish Episcopal Church and the Roman Catholic Church established their own denominational schools. In the burghs, a variety of schools developed. By the nineteenth century these included denominational schools established by the Scottish Episcopal Church, the Roman Catholic Church and the Free Churches.

The 1872 *Education (Scotland) Act* aimed to transfer responsibility for education in Scotland wholly to the state. However, in a Preamble to this Act, the right to continue religious instruction was secured, subject to the operation of a conscience clause that gave 'liberty to parents, without forfeiting any other of the advantages of the schools, to elect that their children should not receive such instruction'. Under the 1918 *Education (Scotland) Act*, Roman Catholic schools, which had not been transferred in 1872, became part of the state system, thus establishing in Scotland a system of denominational schools that continues to be fully publicly funded.

Historically, therefore, in Scottish schools it has been the custom for religion to be practised and instruction in religion to be provided together with some form of religious observance or practice. Indeed, it is unlawful for an education authority to discontinue religious observance or instruction unless the proposal to do so has been the subject of a poll of the local government electors in the area concerned and has been approved by the majority of those voters.

Every school run by the education authority must be open to pupils of all denominations and faiths, and the law continues to provide a 'conscience clause' whereby parents may withdraw their children from any instruction in religious subjects and from any religious observance in the school. It also continues to be laid down that no pupils must be placed at a disadvantage as regards their secular education at the school, either because they have been withdrawn from such classes or because of the denomination to which they or their parents belong.

Northern Ireland

In Northern Ireland, more than 90% of students attend schools in which the pupil body is predominantly of Catholic or Protestant background. Against the background of the Northern Ireland conflict many have argued that this pattern of schooling reinforced sectarian divisions and have wanted to promote so-called 'integrated' schools, which serve approximately 5% of school-age children. At present, all pupils who apply to 'integrated schools' gain admittance although, in surveys, parents generally express the view that more integrated provision should be made available.

It is important to understand that, in the sense that 'Catholic schools' are 'Catholic' there are only a few 'Protestant schools' in Northern Ireland. 'Catholic' schools have an overtly confessional orientation and ethos and the Catholic Church has a significant measure of control over them. Since 1993, and in contrast with the funding for equivalent Church schools in other parts of the UK, in Northern Ireland both the capital and maintenance costs of Roman Catholic schools have been met entirely by the state.

By contrast, what are colloquially referred to as being 'Protestant schools' are state schools, the Presbyterian, Church of Ireland and Methodist Churches having transferred their schools to the state system in 1930. Of course, this was in the context of a Northern Ireland state that was established on the basis of a Protestant identity and majority. Therefore, although such schools are, in principle, open to pupils of any religious persuasion or none, in practice their pupils are generally of Protestant background. However, in their general school activities and pastoral support programmes these schools do not normally reflect or commend particular religious values or beliefs, although most of them do provide broadly Christian assemblies and collectively celebrate the festivals of Harvest, Christmas and Easter.

The *Education Reform (Northern Ireland) Order* of 1989 made provision for a common Core Syllabus of Religious Education in Northern Ireland to be taught in all schools and those Protestant Churches that had transferred their schools to the state system were invited, along with the Roman Catholic Church, to draw up the new statutory Syllabus. This historic achievement provided a commonly agreed programme of Religious Education from across both sides of the traditional Catholic–Protestant divide. At the same time, it was characterized by an exclusively Christian content. While schools were free to include teaching relating to religions other than Christianity within their Religious Education programme this has not, in practice, been very widespread.

3 Faith-Based Schools and Religious Diversity: Emerging Debates

Developments

As was noted in chapter 1, the religious composition of the UK is uneven with regard to the spread and extent of religious plurality. Because of their role in the development and education of young people in society, schools are the institutions that very often have first to deal with, and adapt to, the consequences of major social and cultural change, such as the development of the 'three-dimensional' society.

Thus it has been in England – which, as we have seen in chapter 1, has the greatest religious plurality in the UK – that the most significant debate has developed around the desirability or otherwise of extending the traditional pattern of predominantly Anglican, Roman Catholic and Jewish schools to include also schools with a character rooted in other minority religious traditions. In Scotland there is one publicly funded Jewish primary school, but denominational schools are mainly Roman Catholic and the devolved Scottish Executive has so far not made any change to guidance on denominational schools. Some Muslim groups in Glasgow have lobbied to establish a state-funded Muslim school in the city, but so far they have been unsuccessful.

In England the debates emerged initially and particularly in relation to the possible creation of Muslim voluntary aided schools. Within the independent, fee-paying sector, there have for some years been a significant number of institutions based on a religious foundation or ethos, including around sixty Muslim schools. During the 1980s and 1990s, a significant body of opinion among Muslims pressed the government to grant public funding to a number of Muslim schools that applied under government criteria for recognition as voluntary aided schools. At this time it was frequently pointed out that, although the government affirmed that, in principle there could be Muslim schools alongside Jewish and Christian ones, no applications had been successful, leading to a significant concern that discrimination may well have been at work.

However, the government's decision to fund two Muslim primary schools represented a new development that is now being followed by some groups in other religious communities. Under the provisions for 'Foundation Schools' made in the 1998 *School Standards and Framework Act*, such schools receive funding directly from national government rather than through the Local Education Authority. There remains a body of opinion, however, that the designation of Voluntary School status for Muslim and other faith-based schools is necessary as a signal of parity of esteem with the Christian and Jewish Voluntary Schools.

By 2006 there were in England 6,874 state-funded schools with a religious character, representing around 35% of all the schools in the state sector. These included 4,659 Anglican schools, 2,053 Roman Catholic schools, 1 Greek Orthodox school, and 1 Seventh-day Adventist school, with other Christian denominations accounting for 115 schools. There were also 36 Jewish schools, 7 Muslim schools, and 2 Sikh schools.

Arguments

In the Religious Discrimination in England and Wales Research Project (Weller, Feldman and Purdam, 2001: 31–2), a number of interviewees raised the issue of faith-based schools for Muslim children. Their responses are summarized below, including some direct quotations from the report. One group felt that, in general, 'Islamic schools' could offer a conducive and appropriate environment and that, specifically, they could avoid conflicts around issues such as sex education. In connection with this, one informant expressed the conviction that: 'religious organizations can run schools better because they are independent and are supported by the community they serve'. A white, female, educational specialist noted that it is also important to consider the point that such schools allow the students to attend school without the constant fear of the effects of racism, bullying and harassment.

In contrast to this, others, both from within religious traditions and communities and outside them, expressed a concern that separate schools 'don't create a harmonious society', and that they may even create further divisions. One Christian educationalist acknowledged that, compared with the many Church of England, Catholic and Jewish schools, the difficulty of getting state funding for Islamic schools 'is an historical unfairness'. However, he also stated that: 'Just because there is one not particularly helpful way of schooling that we have to live with, we shouldn't extenuate division by using an unhelpful model.'

Just as in debates about the nature of 'secular' society (see chapter 3), in considering the debates around religiously based schools it is also important to clarify what, precisely, is at stake and what specific presuppositions may be operating in the arguments put forward by the protagonists for and against such schools. This is because while schools may share a common legal status they may, in practice, have quite different self-understandings with consequent important differences for the way in which they are organized.

For example, there are generally important differences between Roman Catholic and Anglican Church schools. Many Anglican (especially primary) schools function as general neighbourhood schools. It would appear that a number of these have (perhaps because of a basic religious sympathy) been more sensitive to questions related to the faith and practice of Muslim, Hindu and Sikh parents and children than have some county schools. Because of this some parents of children of other than Christian religions have chosen to send their children to such Church schools in preference to 'secular' schools on the basis that they believe these schools will provide some form of religious environment which, even though it is not that of their own religion, is viewed as being preferable to schooling understood as 'secular'.

While some Church of England schools do have an explicitly religious and Christian ethos, it is generally of a broadly Christian kind. Roman Catholic schools, by contrast, are usually specifically Catholic in ethos, while the majority of them are secondary rather than primary schools. This difference needs to be understood in the context of the history of the Catholic community in England that (as outlined in chapters 3 and 6) suffered a history of civil disabilities until well into the nineteenth century, and has been closely aligned with immigrant groups. To that extent, the history of the development of Catholic schools finds echoes with some who wish to establish schools for other religious minorities, and particularly among Muslims.

However, it is also important to examine the social implications of these religiously based schools within the context of a multi-religious society. In the 1980s, it had already been noted (Christians Against Racism and Fascism, 1982) that if Christians and Jews have access to public funds for religiously based schools, and such access is to continue, then others would, as a matter of equity, justly demand this for themselves.

But it can also be argued that removing religious believers from the county schools can damage the potential for social mixing and mutual understanding that is provided by the county system. Religiously based schools might, in practice, contribute to a structurally reinforced religious ghettoization in which it becomes possible for children of one religious background to grow up without ever meeting or knowing children of another religion and in a society where differences of religion are often overlaid by differences in race or ethnicity this can entail particular dangers. Similarly, the effects of admissions policies based on religious affiliation criteria can, in such a society, and in certain localities, contribute to ethnic differentiation and possibly effective segregation in schooling.

It is, though, important to realize that not all religious groups have, in principle, always been supportive of religiously based schools. The advocacy of an educational system without religious privilege, segregation or what was identified by Christian opponents as 'denominational teaching on the rates' is a part of the heritage of the Baptist tradition of Christianity, a number of whose leaders conducted a civil disobedience campaign around these issues in the early years of the twentieth century.

However, in the intervening years the 'dual system' has been so entrenched that from within the Christian community even to raise the question of whether Anglicans and Roman Catholics should reconsider their position in relation to these schools has been to invite a storm of controversy of the kind that occurred some years ago in relation to the Christians Against Racism and Fascism discussion leaflet on *Church Schools in a Multi-Faith Society*.

The Labour Government of Tony Blair discovered just how sensitive these issues could be when, in February 2005, Stephen Twigg, the then Schools Minister for England, published a list of best practices about how 'faith schools' could contribute to inclusiveness and collaboration. Following this, a substantial controversy developed when, against the background of growing concerns about the potentially negative implications of faith schools for social cohesion (see chapter 6), the government made proposals to implement a quota of children to be taken from outside of the faith community concerned. While a number of faith schools were content with this, and the Church of England was not opposed, the Roman Catholic Church strongly opposed the move, which was eventually dropped.

Whatever side of the debate one comes down on, it is important to remember that by far the majority of children in the UK attend what used to be known as 'county' schools and are now known as 'community' schools rather than religiously based or 'denominational' schools, whether these are Foundation Schools, Voluntary Schools or fee-paying schools. Because of this, the debate on faith schools in the context of religious diversity is only one specific aspect of the issues that arise in the relationship between religious diversity and education.

However, rather than exploring these other dimensions in relation to school-based education, and since, in general, rather less attention has been paid to issues of religious diversity in higher education than in schools, the remainder of this chapter focuses on these issues in higher education.

4 Religious Diversity and Higher Education: Context and Inheritance

The Context for Religious Diversity in Higher Education

Writing in the year 2000, in her seminal study on *Religion in Higher Education: The Politics of the Multi-Faith Campus*, Sophie Gilliat-Ray noted that: 'Issues of religion and higher education hit the headlines … very rarely: more usually the religious and spiritual lives of academic staff and students go unnoticed, even within the universities themselves.' However, Gilliat-Ray (2000: 1) also went on to note that, 'The outbreak of disturbances between different religious groups on campuses does occasionally, however, subvert the normal lack of interest.'

What perhaps now seems a somewhat understated observation was entirely understandable at the time. At that point, campus unrest around religion was largely restricted to the activities of radical student groups such as the radical Muslim group Hizbut-Tahrir whose rhetoric had been of particular concern to Jews and Hindus, as well as to gay people and others who had experienced some of its members as behaving in a threatening and intimidatory manner.

On 1 November 1996, the newspaper for higher education, *The Times Higher Education Supplement* (THES), carried a report entitled 'Free Speech Limits Probed' which reported that the then Committee of Vice Chancellors and Principals had set up a group, to be chaired by Professor Graham Zellick (at the time Vice Chancellor of the University of London) to 'consider the issues raised for universities by groups which incite racial, religious or political hatred. Its report … will provide institutions with guidelines on coping with such problems'.

In relation to the work of his Committee, Professor Zellick was reported as saying: 'We have to ensure freedom of speech on campus – that is fundamental to academic institutions. But it is equally fundamental that it should not deny other people their freedom of speech or subject anyone to harassment, fear, intimidation or anxiety.' Of course, issues to do with student radicalism in general and concern about what to do about this were not new. During the 1960s, 1970s and 1980s, the politics of campus life had often given rise to investigations and concerns related to perceived political extremism. But what was new with the inception of the Zellick Committee was the inclusion of religion making an appearance in the public sphere of university life – and doing so in the context of conflict and controversy concerning the specific behaviour and activities of some religious groups.

To this extent, the Zellick Committee marked a watershed in UK higher education, following a long period in which religion, if recognized as being present at all had, in many institutions (other than those with Church foundations) been generally perceived as being in decline, of marginal institutional importance, and of relevance only to the recreational sphere of student clubs and societies.

Religion and Higher Education: The Christian Inheritance

The origins of the ancient universities of the UK were deeply rooted in the institutional life of the Christian Church and the role of monastics and clergy in relation to the literary and artistic heritages of these islands. Before that, there was also the pre-eminent role of great Islamic libraries and institutions of learning which were at the forefront of the spirit of scientific enquiry and the preservation and transmission of cultural inheritances that did so much to make possible what eventually became the Renaissance in Europe.

Because of the very close links that have historically existed between religion, universities and the social and political structures of states and societies in which they are set, universities have very often been wrapped up with the reproduction of certain kinds of 'sameness' and religion has been one of these. Therefore in England, it is only just over a century and a half ago that the universities first allowed other than Anglican Christians to have access to study in them, and then (only later) the possibility to graduate with a degree. In the nineteenth century, for Free Church and Roman Catholic Christians, the universities were one of the bastions of religious and social privilege (Sanderson, 1975).

It was, in fact, only in 1854 that the *Oxford University Act* abolished religious tests for matriculation for the award of the Bachelor of Arts degree (although not for higher degrees). In 1856, the *Cambridge University Act* followed suit. It was not until 1871 that the *University Tests Act* removed religious tests for all degrees except Divinity, and for all official university posts with the exception of Professorships of Divinity. It was against this background, which was, of course, especially acute and lasted longest in relation to the study of religion, that Free Church Christians who were excluded from qualifying for degrees in universities set up their own Dissenting Academies. It was also the context for the foundation of some of the civic universities that were brought into being in the late nineteenth and early twentieth centuries on the basis of an explicitly secular institutional ethos, an inheritance also reflected in the ethos of many of the Robbins' era 'new universities' of the 1960s, as also among the 'new universities' of the 1990s that were the former polytechnics.

Even though it is *still* a requirement that some occupants of some Chairs of Theology be clerks in holy orders of the Established Churches of the UK, one might feel that all this was really a long time ago, and in one sense that is manifestly true. But it was also not much more than thirty years ago or so in one of the precursor bodies of the author's own institution (the University of Derby) – the Bishop Lonsdale College of Higher Education – that, as a Church of England voluntary teacher-training college it was expected that staff (and certainly senior staff) should have an active connection with the Christian faith and that students and staff should attend college chapel on designated occasions.

But in other institutions not operating on the basis of a specifically religious foundation, if religion has a profile at all it continued predominantly to be Christian religion. In part this was because, aside from the presence at a number of institutions of significant numbers of Jewish students, the impact of the cultural and religious diversity of UK society took longer to filter into the universities than it did to the schools. Initially, religious diversity in higher education was associated with overseas students. Therefore, in 1958, the scholar of comparative religion A.C. Bouquet (1958: 251) could be found writing with a faintly surprised air that, 'Indian students in the University of London publicly present their votive offerings to the goddess of learning, Sarasvati, and get photographed in the act of doing so.'

Religion and Higher Education: Secularity and Religious Plurality

However, by the 1960s, with the acceleration of secularization, the previous public significance of religion on campus in many places declined. Furthermore, among the many institutions in the Polytechnic and Colleges Funding Council sector that eventually became the 'new universities' of the early 1990s, religion never had much of a public profile. Indeed, because of their strong connection with urban local authorities some of these institutions were not only 'secular' in the sense of not privileging one or any religious tradition. They were also sometimes quite 'secularist', at least in their institutional ethos or what, by analogy with schools, might be called their 'hidden curriculum'. Thus, in 1985, the National Standing Committee of Polytechnic Chaplains (1985: 6) published a report called *Going*

Public in which it was stated that: 'by comparison with the religious foundation of the traditional ancient universities, it is PLURALISTIC. The Church has no right of access, formal or informal, indeed in most cases they are perceived at best as irrelevant to and at worst as pernicious in the institutional ethos of the public sector.'

Nevertheless, as a part of the currents in youth culture described in Kenneth Leech's (1973) *Youthquake*, during the 1970s and in some places persisting into the early 1980s, there was also something of a flowering of interest in matters of religion amongst students. This interest was in what were often 'pop' versions of Eastern mysticism – and literally so, as the musical world of the 1970s included bands such as the Mahavishnu Orchestra, and former Beatle, George Harrison's foray into Krishna Consciousness. Trevor Ling's article on 'Counterculture: towards a new perspective' gives a typical flavour of those times with Ling (1975: 168) observing that 'Even in the most prestigious universities, displays of books on the occult can now take over whole floors of major bookshops' and then explaining:

> Bewildered (but not yet bewitched), the middle-aged find that their children are taking an interest in (of all things) religion, and often oriental religion at that. Not stopping at yoga, tantra and meditation, however, the student generation espouses witchcraft, magic, kabbalism, astrology, and any other available form of ecstasy and the occult ...

Nevertheless, whilst that upsurge of religious interest was real (and, within certain limits, plural), it was often confined to late-night conversations in the haze of marijuana smoke-filled rooms – the *Drugs, Mysticism and Make-Believe* of Robert Zaehner's (1972) book of the same title. It had relatively little impact on the public life of universities, their curriculum, or matters of their institutional policy and practice. With the death of sixties' idealism and the channelling of seventies' alternatives into the new cultural establishment, religion on campus was often seen by the wider student and staff body as a faintly quaint backwater of the private sphere, detached from the monetarist and managerialist imperatives that were increasingly impinging upon the institutional and student consciousness of higher education under the ideological and economic influence of Thatcherism.

These developments impacted not only upon older universities and polytechnics, but its effects were also visible among those institutions based on an explicitly religious foundation, such as Church Colleges of Higher Education. Here the secular zeitgeist had the effect of eroding the public profile of religion as evidenced by the growing self-questioning of the role and mission of the Church Colleges (Brighton, ed., 1999). This can again be illustrated from the history of one of the precursor institutions to the author's own university.

Before becoming a university in 1993, the University of Derby was the Derbyshire College of Higher Education. This was, in turn, the product of a previous institutional merger (1977) combining the former local authority Derby College of Art and Technology and the Church of England's Bishop Lonsdale College of Higher Education to form the Derby Lonsdale College of Higher Education. It then joined in 1982 with Derbyshire County Council's Teaching Training College at Matlock to create the Derbyshire College of Higher Education finally, in 1990, joining with a number of health-related training institutions from the Southern Derbyshire Health Authority to create the Derbyshire Institute of Health and Community Studies within the College.

In an article that appeared in a volume celebrating *150 Years: The Church Colleges in Higher Education* John Hey (1989: 80), the former Head of Theology and Religious Studies at the institution, summarized the late 1980s position at Derby following the abolition of the clauses of governance that had previously privileged the position of the Anglican Church:

> Gone is the protection of Church interests and power, to be replaced by a Church commitment to the world. The new clauses express the Christian conviction that the Church's vision of the world has something to contribute: conversations about the meaning we can attach to our life in the world, and the value we discover there. Moreover, the Church will no longer be seen as providing a normative reference in such conversations but as offering a rich resource to encourage and enable.

This brief historical excursus brings us back from the Christian inheritance in higher education, through the secular challenge and to the threshold of a new phase of development in which religious plurality began to make its impact on higher education.

At what was to become the University of Derby, this took shape in the establishment, jointly by the College and the Church of England Diocese of Derby, of a new Religious Resource and Research Centre (Weller, 1992b). The aim of the Centre was to facilitate engagement with Christianity, secularity and religious plurality in terms of both teaching and research and in the development of a more inclusive approach to religious and pastoral care. This, in turn, eventually issued in the development of what was to become the Multi-Faith Centre at the University of Derby, which was formally opened in 2005.

5 Religious Diversity in Higher Education: Emerging Debates and Policies

---

Study Activity 13

After reading sections 3, 4 and 5 of the chapter:

(i) *discover* whether your university/the university closest to where you live has specific policies and/or codes of practice on religion, belief and equal opportunities

(ii) *describe* some of the key themes that are emerging at the interface of religion and higher education institutions

(iii) *evaluate* the principle and practicality of acting on the kinds of questions raised for institutional practice, as set out in Panel 9

Identity Shifts

The end of this brief historical excursus brings us back to the Zellick Committee, the establishment of which signalled that religion was again impinging on the public life of higher education institutions, and that this impact was coming particularly in the form of the challenges arising from aspects of religious diversity and plurality. As previously noted, the immediate source of this was to do with conflicts around the activities of groups such as Hizbut-Tahrir. However, to be properly understood, these developments need to be set in the context of the more general shifts that have, during this period, occurred.

Such underlying shifts were prefigured in Vincent Cable's (1994) prescient Demos booklet, *The World's New Fissures: Identities in Crisis.* Cable, now a leading Liberal Democrat politician, argued that in the contemporary conditions of globalization, the old polarities of the world were giving way to what he called an 'identity politics' that he argued would emerge as the dominant theme at the end of the previous Millennium and the beginning of the new one. Of relevance to radical religious groups among students Cable (1994: 21) observed that many of those who felt threatened by globalization felt the need 'to identify with a recognised, settled value system which gives their lives meaning and dignity'.

Religion is one of the forms by which this identity politics finds expression. In British society and politics of the 1970s, young people from minority communities often defined themselves in terms of the common political colour of 'Black'. But by the late 1980s the agenda had moved to ethnic self-identification and, gradually, through the impact on South Asian youth of events such as the storming of the Golden Temple and *The Satanic Verses* controversy, religion emerged as an increasingly significant dimension.

Religious Diversity and Discrimination in Higher Education

Against this background, institutions of higher education began, hesitantly, to address the public significance of religion and religious diversity in their emergent equality and diversity policies. In the early days of such policies, references to religion were relatively infrequent, although some developments are identifiable from a review of the literature. Thus a *New Community* article on 'Universities and ethnic minorities: the public face' (Jewson, Mason, Bowen, Mulvaney and Parmar, 1991) reported on research conducted by the authors into the texts and images used by the 'old universities' in their prospectuses.

While the predominant frame for this research concerned 'ethnicity', the article noted that, at least at the level of image, universities were beginning to take account of religious change. Thus the researchers (Jewson, Mason, Bowen, Mulvaney and Parmar, 1991: 187) noted that: 'The most common type of information concerned the availability of prayer or meeting rooms. Often names and addresses of people who might be contacted within local communities were supplied where no provision was made on the University campus.' In relation to this, out of Jewson et al.'s sample of 53 prospectuses, whilst 86% contained references to provision for Christian students, 54.7% referred to facilities available to students who practised faiths other than Christianity, with Judaism mentioned in 23 prospectuses; Islam in 22; Buddhism in 4; Hinduism in 3; and Sikhism in 1.

Aspects of the experiences of religious minorities in higher education were reflected in the findings of the Religious Discrimination in England and Wales Research Project (Weller, Feldman and Purdam, 2001: 26). In higher education the highest reported incidence of unfair treatment was from the attitudes and behaviour of students, although substantial levels of unfair treatment were also reported in relation to the attitudes and behaviour of staff. Comparatively less unfair treatment was reported from the practices of universities and colleges, and even less from university and college policies. In relation to Muslims in particular, 'Around two thirds or more of Muslim organisations reported unfair treatment from the behaviour of staff and students in higher education, and from the policies and practices of universities/colleges.'

Quotations from the project's postal survey highlighted comments from Muslims to the effect that 'core texts had anti-Islamic strains' and 'hard to obtain prayer rooms'. Concerns were also raised by Jews about 'events scheduled on religious days' and 'exams set on religious days' and by Pagans and members of New Religious Movements reporting 'Pagan society blocked' and the 'patronising attitude that British equals Christian'.

Developing Policies and Codes of Practice

The evidence highlighted above underlines the importance of policy development in relation to religion and equal opportunities in the universities. A systematic review of such developments was mapped by Sophie Gilliat-Ray, working in association with the Inter Faith Network for the UK. This examined how institutions are developing structures for: relating to the various religious groups on campus; the provision of worship facilities; how chaplaincy arrangements are being developed in multi-faith contexts to respond to the pastoral needs of students of the various faiths; the emergence of inter-faith organizations on campus; and how faith communities are developing national structures to respond to the religious needs of their students.

The results of the research were published in Gilliat-Ray's 1999 report, *Higher Education and Student Religious Identity*. This was circulated to all institutions of higher education in order to enable sharing of good practice and to stimulate opportunities for developing strategies appropriate to multi-faith campuses. Finally, the specific findings of the report were built upon further by Gilliat-Ray's (2000) book on *Religion in Higher Education: The Politics of the Multi-Faith Campus*.

An example of some early developmental work was undertaken in the University of Derby which, during the early 1990s, developed a *Code of Practice on Religion and Equal Opportunities*. In two articles on 'Religion and equal opportunities in higher education' (Weller, 1991, 1992a) the present author set out a series of principles (see Panel 8) and questions addressed to specific areas of institutional practice (see Panel 9).

Panel 8: Principles for Religion and Equal Opportunities in Higher Education

In order to act fairly and to attract staff and students from a wide range of religious traditions, the following matters need to be addressed as key issues in the religious dimensions of equal opportunities:

Institutions need to examine their images, policies and practices in relation to the religious needs and obligations of students and staff of various religious traditions.

Institutions need to examine how far a variety of religious belief and practices among their students and staff is viewed primarily as a positive enrichment of the institutional life rather than as a source of problems or a matter of indifference.

Source: Weller (1992: 55)

Panel 9: Specific Questions for Religions and Equal Opportunities

On those occasions when days which are religious holy days for some are regarded by the institution as ordinary working days, is there a consistent institutional policy with regard to meeting requests for time off from employment and study in order for staff and students to meet their religious obligations?

Where examination dates clash with days of obligatory religious observance for some students (e.g. the Muslim month of Ramadan with its fasting during the daylight hours) how far is it possible to make alternative arrangements for examination where such decisions are under the local control of the institution?

How far does the planning, preparation and presentation of the food which is sold or provided by the organization take into account the religious beliefs and practices of staff and students?

How far are staff sensitive to the religious dimensions of modesty in dress and to the religious significance of particular items of dress in some religious traditions?

To what extent do administrative and academic staff have an understanding of cultural and religious naming systems which differ from the Western European and Christian ones?

To what extent do members of staff have an appreciation of the community mores, family structures and gender traditions of students from minority religious/cultural groups?

How far does the institution facilitate the prayer/worship/meditation needs of employees and students and how far do institutional occasions which incorporate a religious dimension reflect the diversity of religious traditions within the institution?

Source: Weller (1992: 56–60)

Religious Diversity, Higher Education and Legal Developments

For the first time in England, Wales and Scotland, the *Employment Equality (Religion and Belief) Regulations* (2003) made it illegal to discriminate in employment and training on grounds of religion. Since in European law universities are seen as providing vocational training, higher education institutions, their staff and students were also covered by these regulations. They deal with matters of direct discrimination, indirect discrimination, victimization and harassment. To help employers and trainers to prepare for the new Regulations in the specific context of higher education, NATFHE, The National Association for Teachers in

Further and Higher Education (2002), produced *Discrimination on the Grounds of Religion or Belief: A NATFHE Discussion Document*, while the Universities' Equality Challenge Unit (2005) produced *Employing People in Higher Education: Religion and Belief*.

As with the introduction of policies affecting other equality and diversity 'strands', in order for benchmarking of targets and monitoring of achievement to take place, it is necessary to consider statistical monitoring. At the author's own institution, this has been carried out on a voluntary basis since the mid-1990s, most recently using the 2001 Census categories of response. As can be seen from Table 32, in comparison with the religion data for the general population of Derby, the religion profile of the University of Derby student population appears to differ significantly.

For example, taking the University data for the same year as the Census, it can be seen that less than half of the University of Derby students declared themselves as 'Christians' as compared with around two-thirds of the population of Derby. There was also a smaller proportion of Muslims than is the case in the city. At the same time, though, the University student population appeared to contain relatively higher percentages of Buddhists, Hindus, Jews, and members of 'other religions'. There were also much larger percentages either with no religion or declining to answer.

6 Religious Diversity and Higher Education: Continuing Tensions

Study Activity 14

After reading sections 6 and 7 of the chapter:

(i) *discover* what student religious groups are active in your University/your local University through making contact with the University Student Union, obtaining information about their constitution, aims, objectives and activities

(ii) *describe* the activities of these student religious groups and how, if at all, they relate to other student religious groups in the same institution

(iii) *discuss* the relationship between critical thinking, religion and belief

(iv) *evaluate* how universities might be able to continue to promote freedom of thought and speech, while also fulfilling a duty of care to staff and students not to be exposed to incitement to hatred and intimidation

Two Examples of Tensions

Tensions can sometimes emerge because of, rather than in spite of, attempts to plan and act in a more inclusive way. For example, when the Multi-Faith

Table 32: Comparative Data on Religion for Derby and for University of Derby students, in the Context of the East Midlands and England

Religion	England %	East Midlands %	Derby %	Derby numbers	University %	University numbers
Buddhist	0.3%	0.2%	0.2%	448	0.6%	72
Christian	71.7%	72.0%	67.4%	149,471	46.7%	5,626
Hindu	1.1%	1.6%	0.6%	1,354	2.5%	304
Jewish	0.5%	0.1%	0.1%	141	0.3%	33
Muslim	3.1%	1.7%	4.5%	9,958	3.7%	449
Sikh	0.7%	0.8%	3.2%	7,151	3.3%	396
Other Religion	0.3%	0.2%	0.2%	550	2.3%	273
Total Religions	77.7%	76.6%	76.2%	169,073	59.4%	7,153
No religion	14.6%	15.9%	15.9%	35,207	28.4%	3,429
Not stated	7.7%	7.5%	7.9%	17,428	12.2%	1,473
No religion/ not stated total	22.3%	23.4%	23.8%	52,635	40.6%	4,902
Grand Total	100.0%	100.0%	100.0%	221,708	100.0%	12,055

University data from University of Derby enrolment statistics 2001–2, excluding data on the University's Further Education sector mainly operating from Buxton, as well as students based in overseas collaborations. The questions as asked upon enrolment are on a voluntary basis, as also in the 2001 Census questions on religion.

Centre (http://www.multifaithcentre.org) at the University of Derby was planned, although the project was developed over a period of years and now plays a significant role in the life of the University as well as of the local community, not everything has always gone smoothly.

The Centre was developed in a context in which there was previously no dedicated religious space in the University and it would not, from the institution's perspective, have been possible to create a series of separate spaces for different religions. One intended aspect of the Centre (the other being to engage with issues to do with religion in an adult education context) was that it should be a facility that offers space for religious practice, spirituality and the exploration of issues in the context of a publicly funded and accessible environment (Hart, 2001).

In connection with this, it was never intended for the Centre to be an ersatz church, mandir, mosque or gurdwara. In this regard the Multi-Faith Centre is part of an increasing trend that can be observed in terms of the development of similar facilities in a whole variety of public institutions and environments, of which designated multi-faith spaces in airports and hospitals can also provide other pertinent examples. However, it was matters relating to its worship function that, in the development of the Centre, proved to be the most contentious. This is because it is in connection with worship and devotion that people within all individual religious traditions tend to be most anxious and concerned about the possibility of loss of distinctiveness.

Thus, in the late 1990s a leaflet produced from within the University's Christian Union attacked the Centre in relation to the fact that a number of different forms of worship would take place there. The Christian Union leaflet acknowledged that 'Some people that would not want to come to CU, might become interested through the multi-faith centre because some people are merely searching for God, and might begin their search at the multi-faith centre.' However, because of a particular view of demonology, as the Christian Union leaflet put it, 'Concerns have been raised of the spiritual implications of the multi-faith centre. The worry is that prayer to false gods and spirits will attract demons to the multi-faith centre and to Kedleston Road.'

The leaflet went on to say that 'Most members of CU are not strong enough (e.g. new Christians) or have not had experience (with the physical manifestations of) spiritual warfare, and so would be unprepared for the effects of demonic activity (which can be devastating). Also although Christians would have some defence from this, demons would not be hindered in their attacks upon non-Christians in the multi-faith Centre or at Keddleston [sic].'

The issue being raised was one of whether, if Christian worship takes place in a space that is 'time-shared' with people who have a different focus for their devotions, it is possible for some kind of 'spiritual contamination' to occur. Perhaps paradoxically this was raised from within the perspective of an Evangelical Christian tradition in which the physicality and particularity of sacred space is not usually emphasized. On the basis of an aphorism that had been developed in the thinking of the Centre that 'another time is a different space', David Hart (2001: 20) explained that, 'the building will not be consecrated by any one tradition or set of principles. In common with the presuppositions of a post-Einsteinian universe, the designers believe that the sacredness of space is a dynamic rather than a static reality.'

However, rather than simply offering its own position, the Centre set about engaging in serious discussions with representatives of the Christian Union in order to try to explain its approach and to see if it was possible to secure, if not active support, then at least a position that would not encourage active opposition to the Centre. In the end, following the opening of the Centre, Christian groups of a wide variety have readily used the Centre to meet for worship and prayer as well as for discussion and debate.

Aspects of the Centre connected with religious worship were also problematic for some people of other religions. Thus, for the student Islamic Society of the period leading up to and following the opening of the Centre, the Millennium

Commission's financial support to the Centre proved to be a stumbling-block in using the Centre for daily Muslim prayers, because of the origin of Millennium Commission funds in the gambling of the National Lottery. This was despite the fact that the Centre had specifically consulted with Muslim scholars in relation to this matter and that the student Islamic Society at the time of that consultation had accepted the understanding reached then which was, among others, based on the advice of Muslim scholars.

As with the debate with the Christian Union referred to above, so also with the student Islamic Society, the relatively rapid turnover of student society membership on a two- to three-year cycle can bring about significant changes in the present when compared with the position taken by the former leaders of student organizations. In this case while, from its opening onwards, individual Muslim students did pray in the Centre and a local Muslim group used it as a venue in which to celebrate religious festivals, with regard to the Islamic Society as such, once again patient engagement with the issues and concerns was needed on the part of the Centre and the University until a position could be reached that enabled movement in this matter so that today, Muslim students in membership with the society do routinely use the Centre for their regular daily prayers.

Christian Unions and Student Unions

During 2007, in a number of higher education institutions around the country tensions emerged in relation to the affiliation of Christian Unions to university and college Student Unions. Christian Unions are student Christian organizations that are generally of a strongly Evangelical Christian orientation. They are often one of the largest student membership bodies on campuses.

Student Unions have generally been in the vanguard of the adoption of equal opportunities policies and have a strong commitment to reflecting the diverse student body. Tensions have arisen in relation to conflicting stances on gay and lesbian rights and opportunities. While Student Unions have worked to prepare for implementation of the new equality and diversity 'strand' being introduced through the government's Sexual Orientation Regulations, significant sectors of Christian opinion have had concerns about the implications of what is perceived to be an affirming approach to gay lifestyles on the basis that gay and lesbian sexual activity is believed to contradict Biblical teaching.

As a consequence, some Student Unions have sought to prevent Christian Unions from meeting on campus on the basis that their religious teaching is said to undermine the sexual orientation strand of equal opportunities and is seen as homophobic. The Christian Unions concerned have, however, argued that there is a distinction between homophobia and a conscientious position on a matter of morals in relation to which they should have the right to free speech in accordance with the protection offered to the expression of religious convictions under human rights legislation.

The Archbishop of Canterbury, Rowan Williams (2006) intervened in these debates in a short essay written in the THES entitled 'It is not a crime to hold traditional values'. In this he argued the position that, even if some find Christian Union views objectionable, 'The mere expression of a controversial belief, independently of any evidence of violent and disruptive results, should not be grounds for suppression.'

In making this point, Williams endeavoured to draw a distinction between 'an offence that is and should be legally actionable' because it 'so undermines basic human respect that it in effect denies a person's or a group's dignity and puts them materially at risk' and what he described as 'a moral challenge to somebody on the grounds of their choices', which Williams argued should be seen as 'a tribute to human dignity' on the basis that, 'If I challenge what you do, I take you seriously as a moral agent, a free person whose choices matter.'

There have been significant conflicts involving issues of this kind at the Universities of Birmingham, Edinburgh, Exeter, Glasgow and London. At Exeter University (Newman, 2007) there has been a different kind of conflict. There, the Students' Guild suspended the privileges of the University's Evangelical Christian Union (ECU) and froze its bank account on the basis of a position that the ECU's insistence that its members and leaders must be Christian was contrary to the Guild's equal opportunities policy.

The Guild had already also required the group to change its name from Christian Union to 'Evangelical Christian Union' on the grounds that it did not include non-Evangelical Christians. In the dispute that developed, an Independent Adjudicator issued a 100-page report upholding the correctness of the Guild's action on requiring the change of name, while observing that it would have been better not to do so and that this should be changed back. Commenting on this, the General Secretary of the Baptist Union of Great Britain, Revd. Jonathan Edwards (2007) expressed a perspective that would be shared by many Christians when he said, 'Whereas we all accept the principle of equal opportunities, to insist that a Christian group does not have the right to restrict its membership and its leadership to Christians is palpably absurd.'

7 Religious Diversity, Extremism, Terrorism and Free Speech on Campus

Security Issues and Incitement to Hatred: A Week of Headlines on Campus

Post 9/11 and 7/7, issues concerning the relationship between religion, understanding, tolerance, intolerance and higher education have become much more visible than only half a decade ago when Gilliat-Ray's seminal study was published. This is not only because of conflicts on campus, but also, and perhaps especially, because of events in the wider social context and shifts in the political climate.

As illustrative of this, the headlines and other reports in the general and specialist higher education press for the week 16–23 September 2005 underline the change that has taken place. Thus *THES* of 23 September contained a piece by Anthony Glees, the Director of Brunel University's Centre for Intelligence and Security Studies, entitled, 'Beacons of Truth or Crucibles of Terror?', with a subtitle 'Fears Grow, Post 9/11 and 7/7 that universities may be an explosive cocktail of the clever and the gullible, the shadowy recruiters and the would-be warriors'. This was based on a report by Glees and Chris Pope that had been published and was itself widely reported elsewhere, for example, in the *Guardian* of 16 September under a headline 'Extremist Groups Active Inside UK Universities, Report Claims'.

In a piece by Paul Hill on 'Extremism on campus overstated' in the 23 September edition of *THES* it was reported that since February of that year the Special Branch had been compiling evidence about extremism on campus and that this had resulted in a Special Branch report. In the same week, The National Union of Students published the findings of its internal review of anti-Semitism, set up after the April 2005 resignation of three Jewish NUS committee members. While clearing the union of being 'apathetic' in relation to anti-Semitism, its findings included a proposal to review procedures at the annual conference to ensure faster response to 'incidents' and the provision of kosher food for conference delegates.

In the same issue of *THES* there was a report on a survey by the Federation of Student Islamic Societies (FOSIS) which highlighted that one in four Muslim students said they had experienced physical or verbal Islamophobia on campus, while identifying day-to-day issues such as the provision of halal food and prayer rooms as matters to address. At the same time, it included a finding that the higher education minister, Bill Rammell, described as 'extremely worrying': namely that one in ten Muslim students would not inform the police if they found out that a fellow Muslim was planning an attack.

This, in turn, led to Rammell's commissioning of a report on Islam in Universities in England (Siddiqui, 2007) that was concerned both with the teaching of Islam, but also with the provision of religious and pastoral care for Muslim students. The government saw both foci of the report as related to its post-9/11 and 7/7 'Preventing Extremism' (see also chapter 6) agenda. This brings us back to the report by Glees and Pope that argued that universities were becoming a hotbed for the breeding of dangerous religious radicalism and therefore advocated measures being taken which would, in effect, restrict the religious freedom of individuals and groups.

Others argued that it is important there are no knee-jerk reactions taken in this regard. Thus the 23 September 2005 issue of *THES* which reported on Glees and Pope's work also contained a piece by Gordon Johnson, President of Wolfson College, Cambridge and Deputy Vice-Chancellor of the University of Cambridge, entitled 'Cause to pause before starting witch trials'. In this he argued that concerns about subversion on campus are best tackled in a wider social context. He also critiqued the Glees and Pope report of having a narrative that is 'decidedly thin' and 'the analysis weak' and that it is a 'hasty appraisal of recent events' for which the 'sources are not wholly convincing'.

There are, of course, very real security issues posed by the willingness of some people claiming a religious identity and motivation to commit the atrocity of the London bombings. But again, during the armed campaign of the Provisional IRA one could also find individuals and groups on campus who were sympathetic to the Troops Out position, as well as other left-wing political groups who went further to support the right of Republicans to take armed action.

In the post-7/7 climate it should also be noted that there are issues of importance for universities as places of freedom of enquiry arising from some of the government measures for combating terrorism that relate to what could be construed as either the 'glorification' and/or the 'justification' of 'terrorism'.

Building on the human rights provisions with regard to religion and belief, the challenge for universities and for the religious groups and individuals active within them is that of how to balance the *absolute* rights to freedom of religion and belief under the *European Convention on Human Rights and Fundamental Freedoms* (see further, chapter 6) with what are, under the Convention, only the *relative* rights to their manifestation, especially in contexts where such manifestation may be seen or experienced as impinging negatively upon the freedom of religion or belief of another individual or group.

This is an area in which the organization Universities UK (2005) has done work, issuing in guidelines published under the title of *Promoting Good Campus Relations: Dealing with Hate Crimes and Intolerance*. These guidelines, in fact, updated previous guidance from the Committee of Vice-Chancellors and Principals that was, in turn, based on work of the Zellick Committee and others, but which also takes account of the legal developments that were emerging and which eventually issued into legislation on the incitement to religious hatred (see chapter 5).

Truth-Seeking, Robust Debate, Freedom of Enquiry and Expression

The education system, and especially higher education, has traditionally been associated with the nurturing and development of critical thinking and freedom of expression from censorship. One of the important roles of universities in modern liberal societies has been as zones in which student experience could embrace personal exploration alongside vocational training, while scholarship and research, as well as being applied, could also be concerned with a truth-seeking that builds on repositories of inherited knowledge and wisdom, while pushing at the boundaries of conventional and received wisdom.

For some in the religions, this has been a reason why universities have sometimes been profoundly challenging and disturbing environments. While fostering critical thinking is widely acknowledged as necessary for the creation and development of a healthy society, this can come into tension with perspectives that are rooted in tradition and authority, including religious authority – and especially in relation to particular understandings of, and claims to, revealed truth. At the same time, for others in the religions, universities have extended their social experience and opened up their intellectual horizons to explore wider horizons of life and belief than previously thought possible.

The kinds of tensions related to religion and belief that can emerge in a higher education context are unlikely to be completely resolvable. But a commitment to living with them and engaging with their consequences is important both for higher education institutions and for the religions. When dealing with competing truth and value claims, Durwood Foster, Professor of Theology of the University of Berkeley, California, advocates a position and practice of what he calls a 'committed pluralism'. Living according to such a 'committed pluralism' is, Foster (1994: 161) underlines, about 'having been really encountered in mind and heart by the truth of the other, without being able either to dismiss it or to subsume it under one's own truth'. Such a committed pluralism is 'committed to the truth of the other even though that truth cannot (yet at least) be understood as part of its own truth'.

Because of their history and their place within society, universities arguably have an opportunity to facilitate the kind of vision set out by Foster. Since people of Christian, other religious, and secular convictions are all needing to wrestle with the kinds of issues with which this book is concerned, a vision of this kind is as vocationally relevant as it is epistemologically important. And it is in light of this that we turn in the next chapter to the wider field of tension that exists in the contemporary 'three-dimensional society' between respect and religious hatred, freedom of expression and social responsibility.

Resources for Further Learning

Barnes, P. (2005), 'Religion, education and conflict in Northern Ireland'. *Journal of Beliefs and Values*, 26, 2, 123–38.

Bouquet, A. (1958), *The Christian Faith and Non-Christian Religions*. London: James Nisbett.

Bradney, A. (1987), 'Separate schools, ethnic minorities and the law'. *New Community*, 13, 3, 412–20.

Brighton, T., ed. (1989), *150 Years: The Church Colleges in Higher Education*. Chichester: West Sussex Institute of Higher Education, Chichester.

Bristol City Council (2004), *Demand for a Muslim School in Bristol. Final Report*. Bristol. Bristol City Council.

Cable, V. (1994), *The World's New Fissures: Identities in Crisis*. London: Demos.

Cairns, J. and Gardner, A., eds (2004), *Faith Schools: Conflict or Consensus?* London: Kogan Page.

Christians Against Racism and Fascism (1982), *Church Schools in a Multi-Faith Society*. Leicester: Christians Against Racism and Fascism.

Commission for Racial Equality (1990), *Schools of Faith: Religious Schools in a Multi-Cultural Society*. London: Commission for Racial Equality.

Edwards, J. (2007), 'Judge backs Exeter Guild in CU row'. *The Baptist Times*, 19 July 2007.

Equality Challenge Unit (2005), *Employing People in Higher Education: Religion and Belief*. London: Equality Challenge Unit.

Foster, D. (1994), 'The quest for a universal ultimology', in C. Storey and D. Storey, eds, *Visions of an Inter-Faith Future: Proceedings of Sarva-Dharma-Sammelana, Religious People Meeting Together, Bangalore, India, 19th–22nd August 1993*. Oxford: International Interfaith Centre, pp. 155–63.

Gilliat-Ray, S. (1999), *Higher Education and Student Religious Identity*. Exeter: Department of Sociology, University of Exeter, Exeter, in association with the Inter Faith Network for the United Kingdom.

Gilliat-Ray, S. (2000), *Religion in Higher Education: The Politics of the Multi-Faith Campus*. Aldershot: Ashgate.

Glees, A. and Pope, C. (2005), 'Beacons of truth or crucibles of terror? Fears grow post 9/11 and 7/7 that universities may be an explosive cocktail of the clever and the gullible, the shadowy recruiters and the would be warriors'. THES, 23 September 2005.

Guardian, The. (2005), 'Extremist groups active inside UK Universities, report claims'. 16 September 2005.

Halstead, M. (1986), *The Case for Muslim Voluntary-Aided Schools: Some Philosophical Reflections*. Cambridge: Islamic Academy.

Hart, D. (2001), 'A theology of multi-faith design', in *Multi-Ethnic Britain: What Future? The Report of a Conference held in Leicester. Leicester. 5–7 August 2001*, Leicester, 19–20.

Hewer, C. (2001), 'Schools for Muslims'. *Oxford Review of Education*, 27, 4, 515–27.

Hey, J. (1989), 'The Church in the world and the role of the Anglican College. Part II. The Anglican connection', in T. Brighton, ed., *150 Years: The Church Colleges in Higher Education*. Chichester: West Sussex Institute of Higher Education, pp. 69–83.

Hill, P. (2005), 'Extremism on campus overstated'. *THES*, 23 September 2005.

Jackson, R. (2003), 'Should the state fund faith based schools? A review of the arguments'. *British Journal of Religious Education*, 25, 2, 89–102.

Jewson, N., Mason, D., Bowen, R., Mulvaney, K., Parmar, S. (1991), 'Universities and ethnic minorities: the public face'. *New Community*, 61, 2, 183–99.

Johnson, Gordon (2005), 'Cause to pause before starting witch trials'. *THES*, 23 September 2005.

Judge, H. (2001), 'Faith-based schools and state funding: a partial argument'. *Oxford Review of Education*, 27, 4, 463–74.

Leech, K. (1973), *Youthquake: Spirituality and the Growth of a Counterculture*. London: Sheldon Press.

Ling, T. (1975). 'Counterculture: towards a new perspective in religion'. *Religion*, Autumn, 5, 168–74.

McKinney, S.J. (2007), 'Symbol or stigma? the place of Catholic schools in Scotland'. *The Catalyst* (an online publication of the Commission for Racial Equality), 7 January 2007.

Murphy, J., ed. (1971), *Church, State and Schools in Britain, 1800–1970*. London: Routledge and Kegan Paul.

National Association for Teachers in Further and Higher Education (2002), *Discrimination on Grounds of Religion or Belief: A Discussion Document*. London: National Association for Teachers in Further and Higher Education.

National Standing Advisory Committee of Polytechnic Chaplains (1985), *Going Public*. London: National Standing Advisory Committee of Polytechnic Chaplains.

Newman, M. (2007), 'O come all ye faithless – join the Christians'. *THES*, 27 July 2007.

Parker-Jenkins, M. (2002), 'Equal access to state funding: the case of Muslim schools in Britain'. *Race, Ethnicity and Education*, 5, 3, 273–89.

Parker-Jenkins, M., Hartas, D. and Irving, B. (2005), *In Good Faith: Schools, Religion and Public Funding*. Aldershot: Ashgate.

Siddiqui, A. (2007), *Islam at Universities in England: Meeting the Needs and Investing in the Future* (Report Submitted to Bill Rammell MP, Minister of State for Lifelong Learning, Further and Higher Education), 10 April 2007.

Social Policy Group of the British Council of Churches Committee on Relations with People of Other Faiths and the Race Relations Unit (1992), 'Religiously-based voluntary schools'. *Discernment: A Christian Journal of Inter-Religious Encounter*, 6, 2, 32–40.

THES (1996), 'Free speech limits probed'. *THES*, 1 November 1996.

Universities UK, Equality Challenge Unit, and the Standing Conference of Principals (2005), *Promoting Good Campus Relations: Dealing with Hate Crimes and Intolerance*. London: Universities UK.

Weller, P. (1991). 'Religion and equal opportunities in Higher Education'. *Cutting Edge*, 2, 26–36.

Weller, P., Feldman, A. and Purdam, K. (2001), *Religious Discrimination in England and Wales* (Home Office Research Report 220). London: Research, Development and Statistics Directorate. The Home Office.

Weller, P., Feldman, A. and Purdam, K. (1992a), 'Religion and equal opportunities in Higher Education'. *The Journal of International Education*, 3, November, 53–64.

Weller, P., Feldman, A. and Purdam, K. (1992b), 'A new way forward in Church and Higher Education?'. *Collegium*, 1, 2, 44–73.

Zaehner, R. (1972), *Drugs, Mysticism and Make-Believe*. London: Collins.

Religious Diversity, Hatred, Respect and Freedom of Expression

5

Learning Outcomes for Chapter 5

After studying this chapter, and referring to a range of its associated Resources for Further Learning, you should be able to:

(i) *identify* the laws that may have a bearing on creative works that some believers may find unacceptable

(ii) *describe* the nature of (a) faith-based concerns and (b) secular concerns about at least one controversy involving religion and creative work

(iiii) *discuss* if the blasphemy laws should be abolished, extended or simply left as they are

(iv) *discuss* the difference between robust criticism of a religion and incitement to religious hatred

(v) *evaluate* the extent to which in a society of varied religion and belief it is possible or acceptable to have legal constraints on artistic freedom and/or safely to do without them

1 *The Satanic Verses*, Blasphemy and Respect

The Controversy and the Author

What became variously known as 'the Rushdie affair', '*The Satanic Verses* Controversy' or 'the Salman Rushdie controversy' broke out soon following the publication, on 26 September 1988, of the book, *The Satanic Verses*. The book was written by Salman Rushdie, a writer who had already made his literary mark in a number of other novels, including the Booker Prize-winning *Midnight's Children* (Rushdie, 1980) that dealt with controversial themes of religion and politics interwoven into the partition of India and Pakistan, and his *Shame* (Rushdie, 1983) which picked up on the disappointments of post-partition Pakistan's attempt to form a state informed by Islam and a Muslim identity.

Especially during the period 1989 to 1997, and particularly in the year 1989, issues related to *The Satanic Verses* controversy were a regular feature of life in British society at every level – from household discussions of media reports, to the everyday life of localities such as Bradford, on through to the agendas of national and international politics (Appignanesi and Maitland, eds, 1989; Modood, 1990; Ahsan and Kidwai, 1991). The vehemence and drama of the Muslim outrage about the book was difficult for many of a secular outlook to understand (Modood, 1989). As Hugh Hebert (1989) observed, 'the central puzzle the Rushdie affair sets for the liberal mind is how reasonable men and women can be so incensed by a work of the imagination, a fiction, that his book is burned and its author is put in genuine fear of his life'.

The Syrian writer and UK resident Rana Kabbani (1989: 1) wrote at the time that 'The Salman Rushdie affair has brought home to me the immense, perhaps unbridgeable, gulf between the world I belong to and the West.' And, in a letter to *The Church Times* Roderick Palmer (23 March 1989) argued that, '*The Satanic Verses* will now go down in history as a book which has had as much impact, in its own way, as did Darwin's *Origin of the Species* in 1859' since it has 'brought to a head the fact that there is a sizeable and increasingly vocal Muslim community in this country which is no longer willing to be quiescent'.

The Controversy as Microcosm

Almost two decades on from the outbreak of *The Satanic Verses* controversy, it is perhaps now more possible to identify some of the key broader issues for which the elements of the historical controversy served as a lightning rod, a magnifying glass and a catalyst. Through the literary material itself, and the range of actions and reactions to it, questions and issues of diversity of religion and belief emerge in a multi-faceted way and from multiple perspectives. In relation to the controversy and the issues that it raised, the political scientist and former Chair of the Commission for Racial Equality, Bhikhu Parekh (1989) pointed out that:

> A political crisis is like a magnifying mirror reflecting some of the deepest trends and tendencies developing in society. A wise nation meditates on it, and uses it as a means for self-knowledge. The Rushdie affair has raised issues likely to preoccupy us for a long time.

These include the question of physical security for the author as a novelist and understanding for Muslims whose sensibilities were wounded by the text. They touch upon the relationships between rights and responsibilities, and between individuals and groups. The questions reveal the existence of differing value-systems that can inform contrasting and sometimes conflicting world-views. They focus on the relationship between the provisions of national and international law with regard to freedom of expression and constraints upon it, the rule of law, the claims of religion in relation to secularity and secularity in relation to religion, and issues to do with religiously sanctioned violence. However, at the height of the controversy itself, as Ziauddin Sardar and Merryl Wyn Davies (1990: 1) put it:

> The 'Rushdie affair' became a matter of taking sides, defending positions and erecting barricades. So frantic has been the activity of defending high ideals from presumed onslaughts that it is questionable whether the opponents can any longer hear, much less understand, each other.

Thus, in the fraught atmosphere of the times, it was difficult to engage in the measured reflection that Bhikhu Parekh called for. In many ways it has now become more possible to view the controversy with a little more distance as a kind of 'paradigmatic case study' for some of the key issues that were at stake. There are many complex issues involved here and in the space of a short chapter it will be possible to select and highlight only a few. However, the issues raised in *The Satanic Verses* controversy have not gone away. As will be touched on later in this chapter, many of the issues involved have been reprised again through more recent and in some ways similar, though less high-profile, controversies.

The Satanic Verses: The Book Itself

The Satanic Verses itself is a novel dealing with a story of migration and exile, dealing with themes through fantasies that utilize historical elements in the format known as 'magical realism'. It is therefore very difficult to summarize in any straightforward way. However, its title comes from a story related by two early Muslim commentators, al-Tabari and Ibn Sa' d. In al-Tabari's version (see Guillaume, 1987: 165f. for English translation) the Prophet Muhammad wanted to help the pre-Islamic people of the city of Mecca to more easily accept his teaching of monotheism. According to the story of these 'satanic verses', following the Qur'anic Surah known in English by the name of 'The Star' (*Surat al-Najm*, Qur'an 53: 19–30) – which deals with the topic of what were the female tribal deities of the Meccans – Satan put upon Muhammad's lips the words: 'These are the exalted swans [in other words, beautiful ladies] whose intercession is to be hoped for.'

According to the story, because of this the Meccans then joined Muhammad in prostration. But then it is said that the Angel Gibreel showed Muhammad his error and the so-called 'satanic verses' were replaced with what is now in the text that, instead, in the light of the indigenous Meccan practice of killing female offspring, critiques their worship of a female deity as being illogical in the light of such infanticide.

This story was dismissed by a number of early Muslim authorities on the grounds that its chain of transmission in the tradition was weak. Hence it was not included in any of the six authoritative collections of the *Hadith* that were put together in the centuries following Muhammad's death. However, there is a widespread Muslim perception that, in the history of Christian attacks on Islam – and especially those attacks that majored on attacking the integrity of Muhammad with the charge that he was a liar and imposer – the story has been used against Islam. Thus Razi (quoted in Ruthven, 1990: 39) wholly rejected it, describing it as 'a fiction invented by apostates' that is 'unfounded'.

Like many of the references in the novel, those to this story of the 'satanic verses' are likely to be lost on the average western reader who is not Muslim and/or does not have the cultural capital necessary to locate and understand them. But these same references are full of resonances and meanings for readers brought up within the Muslim and South Asian cultural and linguistic universe. To mention only a few in order to give a flavour of the way in which the sanctities of Islam are dealt with by the author: Rushdie uses the name of Mahound, itself a corruption of the name Muhammad, and used in Christian attacks on Islam. Mecca, the holy city of Islam, becomes Jahiliya, traditionally the name given to the time of 'ignorance' before the revelation of Islam, but among many modern Muslims seen now as being linked with a contemporary world system of arrogance, immorality and enmity towards Islam.

The main characters of the book are Gibreel Farishta and Saladin Chamcha. The character of Gibreel Farishta is a flamboyant movie-star of Bombay religious films. In Urdu, his name translates as Gabriel Angel. Saladin Chamcha is an Anglophile making his living from adverts, named after the medieval defeater of Crusaders who restored Islamic rule to Egypt. Many of the crossed-over web of narratives in the book take place in the dreams of Gibreel, beginning with Gibreel and Saladin falling from a jumbo jet that exploded over the English channel after being hijacked by terrorists. Both survive, with Gibreel acquiring a halo, while Saladin disintegrates into a satanic half-man, half-goat, with a monstrous penis.

Gibreel dreams about the brothel called 'The Curtain' in which prostitutes act out the parts of Mahound's wives. The clients of this brothel are said by the author to go round the so-called 'Fountain of Love' in its inner courtyard 'much as the pilgrims rotated for other reasons around the ancient Black Stone' – a reference to the Kabbah in Mecca, which lies at the heart of the Muslim ritual universe.

As indicated previously, it is not really possible completely to summarize the book. But these examples will give a sense of its flavour, and of the way in which it interweaves traditional references and pieties with speculative elements combined with a ribald undertone. All of this raises the question of what Salman Rushdie was intending in writing the book. Of course, subjective motivation is notoriously difficult to uncover. Before the publication of the book, Rushdie told Madhu Jain of *India Today* (15 August 1988) that:

I have talked about the Islamic religion because that is what I know the most about. But the ideas about religious faith and the nature of religious experience and also the political implications of religious extremism are applicable with a few variations to just about any religion.

In the *Independent Magazine* (10 September 1988) Rushdie told Gerald Mazzorati that, 'I am no longer an observant Muslim and I wanted to explore this hole. And of course, that's what novels do, isn't it? Explore.' Or as he later told Shrabani Basu of the Indian magazine *Sunday* (24 September 1989), *The Satanic Verses* was 'a serious attempt to write about religion and revelation from the point of view of a secular person.' Later in the controversy, though, Rushdie was to claim it wasn't about Islam, but was about 'migration, metamorphosis, divided selves, love, death ...'

2 *The Satanic Verses* Controversy: Key Issues

Study Activity 15

Having read sections 1 and 2 of the chapter:

(i) *describe* some of (a) the key Muslim concerns about the novel, and (b) the main wider concerns about the Muslim reaction to the novel

(ii) *discuss* whether you think the controversy could have been handled differently by (a) the author, (b) the publisher, (c) Muslims, (d) the government and, if so, how

(iii) *evaluate* the extent to which it is possible or desirable to have complete artistic freedom of publication and dissemination in a society of diverse religions and beliefs

The Satanic Verses: Debates

In broad terms, Muslim concerns around the book can be examined under two headings: there were philosophical issues and there was emotional outrage. In relation to philosophical issues, the title of the novel goes to the heart of these concerns. Islam rests on the claim that the Prophet Muhammad received a truthful and final revelation, and the notion of there being some 'satanic verses' is one that suggests it was, at least in principle, possible for the Prophet to have been deluded.

As Malise Ruthven (1990: 17) explains it in his book on the controversy '*The Satanic Verses* ... is a kind of "anti-Qur'an", which challenges the original by substituting for the latter's certainties a theology of doubt.' Thus Shabbir Akhtar, author of *Be Careful With Muhammad: The Salman Rushdie Affair!* (1990), commented in a piece on 'Whose light, whose darkness?' published in the *Guardian* (27 February 1989) that, 'Rushdie's attack on the authoritative integrity of a fallible Koran is part of a larger indictment of Islam as a faith which routinely confuses good with evil, divine with diabolical imperative.'

Of course, traditional Islamic epistemologies have been critiqued before, including from within the Muslim cultural tradition itself. So, although these concerns did form part of the response articulated to the controversy by Muslim intellectuals and community leaders, it was the other – emotional outrage – aspects of the response to the book that were the more visible and were extensive among ordinary Muslims. Writing much earlier in the twentieth century, the historian of religion Wilfred Cantwell Smith (1946: 235) pointed out that 'Muslims will allow attacks upon Allah: there are atheists and atheistic publications, and rationalistic societies; but to disparage Muhammad will provoke from the most 'liberal' sections of the community' what Smith, from his liberal religious perspective, described as 'a fanaticism of blazing vehemence'. This emotional attachment – and hence the potential strength of reaction – is particularly strong among those movements and tendencies in Islam that, in terms of piety in the South Asian context, hold the person of the Prophet in particularly high esteem.

In contrast to the perceptions of a number of western commentators on the controversy, it is important to understand that this outrage and hurt, and the sense of powerlessness to which these gave rise, were not something manufactured by Islamist extremists or by the later *fatwa* of the Ayatollah Khomeini. While Islamist groups and the interventions of Khomeini undoubtedly did seek to capture and channel the energies so released, the outrage and hurt themselves formed part of the genuine emotional orientation of ordinary Muslims. When linked with other cultural factors such as a burning sense of the importance of 'honour', the potential for combustion was always going to be substantial. Thus in November 1989, in a *Guardian* newspaper interview with Hugo Young, Kalim Siddiqui (now deceased but then Director of the Muslim Institute) said that 'This is going to run and run. It is a matter, if you like, of honour.'

The concept of *izzat* is one that is not sufficiently understood outside of the communities in which it operates with significant contemporary power. In her work on Asian women in Britain Amrit Wilson (1978: 31) sought to explain *izzat* as: 'the sensitive and many-faceted male identity which can change as the situation demands it – from family pride to honour to self-respect, and sometimes to pure male ego.' In connection with this it is striking how frequently, in seeking to explain the impact of *The Satanic Verses* upon ordinary Muslims, its impact was articulated in language strongly related to *izzat* and its relationship with sexuality.

It is therefore no accident that Dr Zaki Badawi, the head of the Muslim College in Ealing, in an interview with Paul Martin (1989) in the *Guardian*, and reported under the title 'Spurn the book, spare the man', tried to explain the nature of the offence as perceived by Muslims by making the startling analogy that:

> What he has written is far worse to Muslims than if he's raped one's own daughter. It's an assault on every Muslim's inner being. Muslims see Muhammad as an ideal on whom to fashion our lives and conduct, and the Prophet is internalised into every Muslim heart. It's like a knife being dug into you – or being raped yourself.

In trying to convey the sense of shock and outrage that Muslims experienced as a result of the publication of the novel it is not without significance that, as with Badawi's explanation above they often utilized sexual imagery. Thus the Tanzanian Muslim scholar Ali Mazrui (1989: 3) recalled that when he was in Pakistan he had heard the book compared to child abuse in reverse:

> It's as if Rushdie had composed a brilliant poem about the private parts of his parents, and then gone to the market place to recite that poem to the applause of strangers, who invariably laughed at the jokes he cracks about his parents' genitalia – and he's taking money for doing it.

The Controversy as Media Event

Ironically, although hurt and outrage, and the asymmetry of cultural and economic power, were key constitutive features of many Muslim responses to *The Satanic Verses*, it was not these factors themselves but their packaging as a media event that led to one of the two key aspects of the controversy that most outraged western secular liberal opinion. When Sayyid Abdul Quddus burned a copy of the book in Bradford during a demonstration on 14 January 1989, and thus gained a media spotlight, it was not, in fact, the first occasion on which a copy of the book had been burned.

Already in December 1988, outside Blackburn Town Hall, some religious leaders had called for the book to be burned as a distortion of Muslim history and, six weeks prior to the Bradford burning, on 2 December 1988, in a seven thousand strong demonstration in Bolton, a copy had actually been set alight. In Bolton, the burning of the book had been ignored. In Bradford, though, the media had been alerted about the incident in advance.

Thus the first major event that led to a vehement reaction against the Muslim concerns was itself an explicitly arranged media event in which Muslims – like Rushdie in a different way – found themselves at the centre of a cultural storm for having transgressed cultural and symbolic codes, and reaped the consequences of this. The title of one of the chapters of Richard Webster's 1990 book on the controversy and its roots – *A Brief History of Blasphemy* – underlined the ambiguous and contextual nature of the symbolism involved: the chapter was called, evocatively: 'On Not Burning Your Enemy's Flag'.

Flag-burning has a long history when associated with radical critique under-taken from *within* societies – as in American opposition to the war in Vietnam. However, burning the symbols of 'the other' – either literally or figuratively – can often inflame. In this context it could be said that by dealing with the figures and sanctities of Muslim history in a phantasmagoric novel Rushdie, so to speak, had been engaged in burning 'Muslim flags', while in burning a copy of his book, Muslims were also engaged in 'flag-burning' in relation to European cultural concerns. At one level this action succeeded – in the sense of bringing into public view concerns that the wider public had hitherto largely been oblivious to and/or had ignored. But it did so at the price that, in the minds of many secular artists and the general public, Muslims became linked with cultural and historical resonances that, in the living memory of European history, were associated with Nazism.

In this context, writers and other artists took up strongly expressed positions on the barricades of public debate, characterizing the Muslim campaign and concerns as a threat to freedom of expression. Thus, writing in the *Daily Mail*, Anthony Burgess (1989) quoted Heinrich Heine's comment on the Nazi burning of books that 'If you burn books you will soon be burning men and women.' Then he launched an attack on the Muslim protest, declaring that:

> The Bradford Moslems are not within their moral rights in demonstrat-ing such intolerance of the printed word. Britain, nominally a Christian country, has always accepted the presence of other faiths. But when these faiths indulge in barbarous rituals which contradict its humanitarian principles then secular opinion has to step in.

Of course, in reality things cannot be so simply contrasted. Book-burning is not entirely alien to British history. Burgess, for example, had to acknowledge the fact that the law had ordered the burning of D.H. Lawrence's *The Rainbow* in 1916 and that the British customs authorities had burnt James Joyce's *Ulysses* in 1922. At the same time it is precisely because these episodes are, for Europeans, framed in the ongoing tension between forms of collective authority and individual freedom that any such event does become perceived as a kind of 'flag-burning' that is – just like the original Muslim response to the contents of the novel – likely to produce a reaction of a kind that is not always characterized by a measured response.

The Controversy as Global Politics

Thus while the initial emotional reaction among Muslims was strong, it is important in explaining this not to fall into what might be called an 'Orientalism of explanation' in which the emotional Muslims are pitted against the rational secularists. The reaction of artists and writers to the burning of a copy of the novel shows that this was not the case. Any such Manichean division between obscurantist Muslims and enlightened secularists, besides being a travesty of cultural history, fails to take account of the degree to which, in protesting against *The Satanic Verses*, Muslims were actually keying into the asymmetry of cultural and economic power from which they and their societies have suffered since the victory of colonialism and post-colonialism.

It is a failure to understand this political and economic aspect of the context that means that Carlos Fuentes' view that, 'In the novel, realities that are normally separated can meet, establishing a dialogic encounter, a meeting with the other' and that the novel is therefore a 'privileged arena' which can be instrumental in 'bringing together, in tension and dialogue, not only opposing characters, but also different historical ages, social levels, civilisation and other, dawning realities of human life' can – although important – only be a one-dimensional view of how writing and other works of art function in an asymmetrical world. In both a domestic and a global context where it is felt that Islam and the inheritance of Muslim culture and tradition is routinely, and indeed often wilfully misrepresented and denigrated, the somewhat ahistorical approach to the novel in terms of the personal space that the leisured classes can enjoy is not fully adequate.

However, it was the 14 February 1989 *fatwa* or legal judgement issued by Iran's Ayatollah Khomeini that really sent shock-waves through the literary community and galvanized it into organizing protests on Rushdie's behalf. Khomeini, of course, was a leader within the minority, Shi'a branch of Islam, who had come to power in the Iranian revolution against the Shah of Iran's western-backed regime, transforming it into an Islamic revolution that, in its attempt to establish a theocratic form of government, offered a role model for Muslims struggling against corrupt leaderships in predominantly Muslim societies.

The significance of Khomeini's *fatwa* was that Salman Rushdie was to be viewed as an apostate to Islam – and as such became subject to the traditional punishment of death in a perspective in which apostasy to Islam should be understood as treason to the polity of Muslims. Thus Khomeini (quoted in Ruthven, 1991: 112) pronounced that:

> I would like to inform all the intrepid Muslims in the world that the author of the book entitled *The Satanic Verses*, which has been compiled, printed and published in opposition to Islam, the Prophet and the Qur'an, as well as those publishers who were aware of its contents, have been declared *madhur el dam*. I call on all zealous Muslims to execute them quickly, wherever they find them, so that no one will dare to insult Islam again. Whoever is killed in this path will be regarded as a martyr ...

Although sometimes popularly linked with something like an *ex cathedra* statement of papal infallibility, a *fatwa* should not be understood in this way. In Islam, as in Judaism, the giving of legal judgements is part of an organic tradition of interpretation, application and debate. Thus in his interview with Paul Martin (1989) Zaki Badawi pointed out that no individual Muslim has the power to sentence Rushdie to death and that, 'I must state with all the authority under my command that anyone who seeks or incites anyone to kill Rushdie is committing a crime against God and the Islamic Sharia', and furthermore that:

> The Prophet himself tolerated many people who left Islamic beliefs but were not considered dangerous to the fabric of the state. Those who were put to death were killed because of rebellion, not because of their beliefs ... Putting an apostate to death stems from tradition and not from the Koran itself.

It is, though, important to try to contextualize what lies behind this *fatwa*. Thus, in a 22 February 1989 address to the students and instructors of religious seminaries, broadcast on *Tehran Radio*, and appearing in an edited and abbreviated version in the *Guardian* newspaper of 6 March 1989 under the title of 'A challenge to the world-devourers', Khomeini said of the western powers' defence of Rushdie that

> The issue for them is not that of defending an individual, the issue for them is to support an anti-Islamic current, masterminded by those institutions – belonging to Zionism, Britain and the USA – which, through their ignorance and haste, have placed themselves against the Islamic world.

Furthermore, Khomeini went on to explain that, 'God wanted this blasphemous book, *The Satanic Verses*, to be published now', in order that 'the world of conceit, of arrogance and of barbarism, would bare its true face in its long-held enmity to Islam'. It is this global sense of struggle and of conflict that forms a significant part of the context of the debate. Post 9/11 this can perhaps now be seen more clearly than many could understand at the time, when the ideological fault-lines of the world were still concerned with capitalism and communism. But while Samuel Huntingdon had not yet penned his thesis on the coming clash of civilizations, Muslim activists and many thinkers, too, were increasingly coming to see the world in polarized terms based on the history of western imperialism and colonialism, and their experience of corruption at the hands of the secular parties and rulers of many of their post-colonial societies. Coupled with this were strong currents of a conspiracy theory that has a strong plausibility structure through its material basis in the history of colonialism and what was to be clearly revealed in the contours of the coming 'War on Terror'.

Lessons and Reflections

In the early days of the controversy Bhikhu Parekh was one of the few writers to attempt a nuanced exploration of the issues involved. In his important essay, 'Between holy text and moral void', Parekh (1989) identified that one of the difficulties in this whole debate is that the category of the 'sacred' that religious people are concerned should not be besmirched is not adequately understood by secular people who, because of this, have difficulty in connecting with why it might be that religious people do not want certain limits to be transgressed. In the light of this, Parekh thus attempted a description of what religious people mean by the sacred that he believed might also be accessible to secular people:

> By sacred, I mean that which is beyond utilitarian consideration and has an intrinsic or non-instrumental significance, which transcends and links up individuals with something greater than themselves and gives their lives depth and meaning. The holy represents sacredness anchored in, and defined in terms of divine principle. Religion is the realm of the holy par excellence, but it does not exhaust sacredness. Even the atheist regards certain relationships, activities, experiences, life and fellow-human beings as sacred. Broadly speaking, holiness is a religious category, sacredness a spiritual category; and respect a moral category.

In summary Parekh suggested that just as 'We have taken centuries to learn how to explore sexuality in literature without becoming either puritanical or porno-graphic' so also 'religion calls for extremely delicate and sensitive handling'. In fact, he argues that compared with the handling of sexuality it 'requires a greater degree of sensitivity'.

3 Blasphemy Laws, Religious Sensibilities and Freedom of Expression

The Nature of the Laws

The laws of blasphemy and blasphemous libel have been in existence for many centuries, but many in twentieth-century Britain thought that they had long since vanished into the mists of history in terms of any possible active use of them. Thus, already in the middle of the twentieth century Lord Denning (1949: 46) had said of the blasphemy law that:

> The reason for this law was because it was thought that a denial of Christianity was liable to shake the fabric of society, which was itself founded on the Christian religion. There is no such danger to society now and the offence of blasphemy is a dead letter.

The *Blasphemy Act* of 1697 had disqualified from 'Ecclesiastical, Civil or Military' office anyone who had been brought up in or professed faith in Christianity and who then denied its truth, the inspiration of the Bible or Trinitarian doctrine, or who advocated polytheism. The provision relating to Trinitarian belief had been abolished in the eighteenth century, but the rest of the Act remained on the statute book until, on the advice of the Law Commission, the 1967 *Criminal Law Act* removed it.

But laws of blasphemy and blasphemous libel do remain in force in England and Wales. They are no longer part of statute law enacted by Parliament, but they are still part of the common law inheritance. As part of this common law inheritance, interpreted and applied in the courts with reference to custom and case-law, blasphemy in books, broadly speaking, became defined as something concerned with the publication of scurrilous, offensive or abusive matter concerning God, Christ, the Christian religion, the Bible or a sacred subject. The offence of blasphemous libel, however, appears to have related specifically to attack upon the tenets of the Church of England.

Blasphemy and Modern Precursors to *The Satanic Verses*

The offences evolved over the years with respect to both their meaning and the burden of proof required for conviction. Originally, objective statements and actions were considered sufficient for conviction, but as time went on, the presence of subjective elements was increasingly thought to be necessary in order to secure a conviction. Although Denning's conclusion was that, by the late 1940s, they had in effect become a dead letter, an attempt was made to revive the laws in 1972 with Mary Whitehouse's complaint to the Director of Public Prosecutions about an episode of the TV programme *Till Death Us Do Part* in which irreverent remarks were made about the Virgin Birth.

The Director of Public Prosecutions thought a blasphemy prosecution unlikely to succeed, but the National Viewers and Listeners Association had received legal advice that it would be possible to bring a common law prosecution for blasphemy. Following this, in 1976, Jens Jorgen Thorsen proposed making a film in Britain which would have shown Jesus in explicit sexual activity with John the Baptist, Mary Magdalene and a Palestinian girl of today. The then Archbishop of Canterbury said he would consider invoking the blasphemy law, but in the end the film was never made.

It was, however, the cases of *R v. Lemon* and *R v. Gay News*, brought as successful test case private prosecutions by Mary Whitehouse that finally revived the use of these laws. The cases concerned the publication of a poem by Professor James Kirkup entitled, 'The love that dares to speak its name' which portrayed the centurion in attendance at the crucifixion of Jesus as having homosexual fantasies about him. The jury convicted the editor and the paper of blasphemy. A fine was imposed upon the paper and a suspended sentence on the editor. There was an appeal to the Court of Appeal but this was rejected. A further appeal to the House of Lords was rejected by three votes to two.

Historically, the laws provided for the prosecution of blasphemy and of blasphemous libel in relation to Christian religion in general and, in particular, to the rites and formularies of the Church of England. The 1838 Gathercole case clarified that attacks on Judaism, Islam, or other Christian denominations outside of established Christianity were not covered by the law although, later in the nineteenth century, the Lords Macauley and Campbell argued that blasphemy could apply to other religious traditions as well as to Christianity (St. John Robilliard, 1984: 36).

Blasphemy Laws: Abolition, Extension or Status Quo

When it became clear that the current terms of reference for the blasphemy laws did not include Islam, the extension of these laws to include Islam and other religions became one of the central demands of the Muslim campaigns and Muslim leaders called for a change to the current position. During the controversy, The Home Office made it clear that the government was not intending to extend the scope of the blasphemy laws.

A *Church Times* editorial (24 February 1989) argued that the Home Office's decision was, in this respect, 'well judged' on the basis that, 'Defining blasphemy for legal purposes would be as difficult as defining religion itself; and if a Bill were ever drawn up and passed, the writs would be endless'. In a letter to *The Times*, the Archbishop of York, John Habgood, agreed while adding the observation that 'if there has to be an alternative' then the development of the aspect of the law that deals with 'the shaking of the fabric of society when widespread sensibilities are offended' might prove to be the best way forward since the simple abolition of existing legislation without replacement would, in the words of Habgood's letter to *The Times*, 'signal, however inadvertently, that in the last resort our society holds nothing sacred, apart from the freedom of writers to write whatever they like'.

In contrast, critics of blasphemy legislation, such as Nicholas Walter of the Rationalist Press Association, pointed out (in a letter to the editor of the *Independent*) that, in fact, 'the blasphemy law doesn't work. It has been used in this country for three centuries, but in every single case the main practical effect has been not the suppression but the increased circulation of the offending material.' Paul O'Higgins (1989) Professor of Law at King's College, London argued that, 'Today, the crime of blasphemy is an historical accident consisting of the residue of a crime which in its original form should have no place in the 20th century.'

In the tradition of such opposition to the blasphemy laws there have long been attempts to abolish them. Bills to abolish the law of blasphemy had been introduced to Parliament in 1886 by Professor Courtney Kenny; in 1889 by Charles Bradlaugh; and also in 1890, 1894, 1914, 1922, 1930, and 1936. However, all such attempts were unsuccessful including when, just prior to the *Gay News* case, there was a further attempt on 23 February 1978 to abolish the law without replacement on the grounds that it was outdated; that particular groups should not be privileged in law; and that if material was offensive it could be dealt with under obscenity laws. Significantly, this latter attempt at abolition was rejected on the basis that England, its institutions and monarchy were still basically Christian and that the law needed to give expression to this because repeal could give a signal that would unlock the floodgates of attacks upon religion.

During the Rushdie controversy, on 12 April 1989, the centenary of Charles Bradlaugh's bill for the repeal of statutory blasphemy laws, Tony Benn, MP presented to the House of Commons the first formal reading of a Private Member's Bill entitled *The Religious Prosecutions (Abolition) Bill* which was again unsuccessful although supported by MPs of all parties including Sir David Steel and Sir Ian Gilmour.

As part of their response to the Rushdie controversy, the Inter Faith Network for the UK and the Commission for Racial Equality jointly organized two seminars. Among the papers at the first conference was a presentation by Keith Ward (1990: 30–9), at that time Regius Professor of Divinity in the University of Oxford. As well as being at that time chair of the inter-faith organization, the World Congress of Faiths, Ward had previously been a member of a working party that had been appointed by the Archbishop of Canterbury to report on the Law Commission proposals with regard to the blasphemy law (General Synod of the Church of England, 1988).

As a member of that working party Professor Ward had supported the extension of the blasphemy laws to include other than Christian religions. In the seminar, however, Ward explained that he had since changed his mind on this issue. Part of the argument for his new position was theological – that yesterday's heresy often becomes today's orthodoxy and that yesterday's heretics are often later proclaimed as prophets. From a specifically Christian perspective he also noted that Jesus was crucified, at least in part, on a charge of blasphemy and so it would be peculiar for a religion based on one who was accused of being a blasphemer to invoke legal sanctions against blasphemy. However, in the end, in discussion within the seminar, Professor Ward commented with respect to the Archbishop's Working Party that, 'while its members did not want legal protection for themselves on a personal basis, they did not think it would be right simply to surrender it'.

At the time of writing, however, the common law provisions remain, neither abolished nor reformed. As such, they are a continuing expression of the enshrined privilege in the structures of the state and of society for one section of one religious community as well as being a reminder of the exclusion of others. At the same time, over the years the issues involved have been subject to considerable scrutiny, in particular by the Law Commission. In 1981, as part of its programme of review of the provisions of common law, the Law Commission had published its *Working Paper No. 79* on *Offences Against Religion and Public Worship*. In this, the history of the common law offences was outlined and issues surrounding the desirability and practicability of creating new statutory offences were examined.

The Commission saw four possible justifications for such law. First, as a response to a crime against God – for which penal sanctions were not thought to be appropriate today. Second, for the protection of society from damaging views, but this was judged to run counter to the interests of free speech. Third, for the protection of religious sensibilities, as in the 1981 *Indecent Displays (Control) Act's* protection for offended sensibilities with regard to the portrayal of sex. The fourth argument was one for the protection of public order that it was felt could generally be dealt with under Public Order legislation.

The Law Commission (1981: para 7.15) also argued that, in the context of 'overwhelming social pressures ... the general presumption in favour of freedom of speech both as to matter and manner may require modification either for the benefit of particular members of society or for the benefit of society as a whole'. It identified incitement to racial hatred as such an issue but, at that time, judged that the likely social dangers to result from attacks upon religion were not so great.

As alternatives to the blasphemy laws, the Commission considered the possibility of introducing offences of 'publishing insulting matter likely to provoke a breach of the peace by outraging the religious convictions of others' (Law Commission, 1981: para 8.3–4); 'incitement to religious hatred' (Law Commission, 1981: para 8.6); and 'publicly insulting the feelings of religious believers'. On balance, if it were thought expedient to have a law at all, then the Commissioners favoured the first of these options, qualified by the necessity to prove intent and allowing a valid defence in the instance of attacks upon 'particular religious sects'.

In this context, since the Christian religion could no longer be assumed to be the given religion, the issue of defining religion would need to be addressed. The Commissioners (1981: para 8.17–22) therefore argued that, if offences of this kind were to be introduced then, by a small margin, they favoured the adoption for this purpose, too, of the list of those religions recognized as such by the Registrar-General for the purpose of registration as places of worship.

In 1985, after receiving submissions on this *Working Paper* from many different organizations, the Commission published its *Report No. 145* entitled *Criminal Law Offences Against Religion and Public Worship*. By a majority of three Commissioners to two the Report recommended abolition of the common law offences of blasphemy and blasphemous libel without replacement by statute law, on the grounds that, 'where members of society have a multiplicity of faiths or none at all it is invidious to single out that religion [the Church of England], albeit in England the established religion, for protection'. However, the two outvoted Commissioners felt so strongly that a new statutory offence should be enacted and extended to other religions that they produced a minority Note of Dissent that also appears in the Report. In this, they advocated the enactment of a new offence that 'would penalise anyone who published grossly abusive or insulting material relating to religion with the purpose of outraging religious feelings'. These dissenters included Lord Scarman, who had played such a significant role in race and community relations with his Committee of Enquiry into the disturbances of the summer of 1981.

During the Rushdie controversy John Vincent (1989), Professor of History at Bristol University, argued that protection should be given to Islam under blasphemy legislation commenting in respect of the Law Commission's arguments for and against that, 'The balance is still a fine one. The arguments have not changed, but the sociology has' citing the significantly changed composition of English society. Reflecting on such debates, as the historian John Wolffe (1994: 101) put it, 'The problem, in a nutshell, was whether the law should treat England as a secular society in which religion had no special protection; or as a multi-religious one in which all faiths were accorded some legal recognition.'

Just as *The Satanic Verses* controversy in many ways reprised aspects of the previous *Gay News* controversy but, in doing so, opened out issues that had previously been concerned with the law, Christianity and blasphemy to a wider sphere in terms of tensions between the 'secularity' and 'religious plurality' of the UK three-dimensional religious landscape, so, in the early years of the new Millennium, a number of the issues previously highlighted in both the *Gay News* and *The Satanic Verses* controversies were reprised in relation to the play *Jerry Springer: The Opera* and its proposed televised transmission, and the play, *Behzti*.

4 The Issues Reprised: *Jerry Springer: The Opera* and *Behzti*

Jerry Springer: The Opera, TV and Christian Protest

Jerry Springer: The Opera is a musical, written by the British writers Stewart Lee and Richard Thomas, and based on reference to *The Jerry Springer Show*, a US television talk show that established a reputation for loud and controversial interactions with its interviewees and audiences. As a live musical the play had run for two years (2003–5) in London before starting to tour the UK more widely in 2006.

The musical was catapulted into national and international controversy at the start of 2005 when the BBC2 television channel planned to broadcast it on

8 January despite receiving many thousands of complaints prior to broadcast. Public protests were organized at a number of BBC offices and were co-ordinated by the campaigning organization, Christian Voice, which also announced its intention to initiate blasphemy charges against the musical as a result, particularly, of its depiction of characters in the Jewish and Christian tradition.

As with *The Satanic Verses* controversy so with *Jerry Springer: The Opera*, the way in which the play constructed an intersection between revered and loved figures of religion and lewd sexuality proved particularly controversial, with a character of Jesus being introduced who bears similarity with a previously introduced character who had a nappy fetish. Furthermore, in other echoes of *The Satanic Verses* controversy and the confusion or reversal of good and evil, in *Jerry Springer: The Opera*, the figures of Jesus and of Satan are made to indulge in a battle of wits in which Eve is called as a witness and ends up attacking Jesus. Finally, a character of Mary the mother of Jesus is introduced but who in this story, leads a general condemnation of him.

The Christian Institute tried to initiate charges against the BBC but these were rejected by the High Court. Many Christians, however, were left feeling that the play's depiction of what they held sacred had been attacked in a gratuitous way. At the same time, the tactics of some of the Christian campaigning groups caused concern to other Christians who felt that through their actions, the show received far more publicity than it would otherwise have had.

Behzti: The Play and Sikh Protest

Behzti was a play written by a British-born woman of Sikh background, Gurpreet Kaur Bhatti. The play originally opened at the Birmingham Repertory Theatre on 9 December 2004 and it was originally planned that it should run until 30 December. The title of the play means, in English, 'dishonour' and it was the writer's intention to use the play to uncover the kinds of hypocrisy that can be found among Sikhs and, by extension, all people, including religious people. The play was billed as a 'black comedy'. It featured three lead characters, one of whom was male and two were female.

The mix of issues that the play sought to explore was wide ranging, including issues to do with social status, mixed-race relationships, corruption, drug-taking, domestic violence, rape, paedophilia and murder, with the play set in the context of the precincts of a Sikh gurdwara. Because the management of the theatre realized that this might represent a controversial and potentially explosive cocktail of topics, in contrast to the publication of *The Satanic Verses* (where there was no dialogue ahead of publication and precious little in the early days of the controversy until the *fatwa* issued by the Ayatollah Khomeini), the theatre had decided to undertake proactive consultations with the local Sikh community.

Significantly, these consultations broke down before the play opened. The issue around which this happened was not in relation to the content of the play itself but related to the request of the community representatives that the play should be staged as being set in a community centre rather than in a gurdwara. This was because, in their view, such a staging would violate their sense of Sikh sacred space. The theatre management did not feel themselves able to accede to this view, which they felt would be an acceptance of censorship.

As an echo of what some Muslim groups had asked for, but had not received from Viking Penguin as the publishers of *The Satanic Verses* – though Bradford City Council had done in relation to copies of the book in their libraries – the theatre management offered the possibility for the Sikh community representatives to compose a written statement concerning their views. Not only would this be handed out in printed form to all those attending the play, but the theatre also offered that it could be read out publicly before the beginning of each performance of the play.

Because the talks had broken down, the play faced daily protests by Sikhs which were at first peaceful. However, on 19 December around 400 Sikhs attempted to storm the theatre. A foyer door was destroyed, windows were broken in the restaurant, and theatre security guards were attacked. Police were called and arrived in force, including a proportion in riot gear. Five police officers were injured and two protestors were arrested. In due course, it became clear that many of those taking violent action on 19 December had come from Sikh communities well outside the local area. Following these events, the play was cancelled for an indefinite period. The theatre stressed that this cancellation was not in deference to the views of Sikhs, but was based on its 'duty of care' to its audiences, staff and performers.

As with *The Satanic Verses* controversy, the issue reached the global media and many Sikhs in other parts of the world expressed concern and outrage, while the local Sikhs who had been involved in negotiations with the theatre expressed their concern that there was no legal protection for their religious sensibilities. Again, in echo of what happened in support of Salman Rushdie, leading artists, both white and South Asian pulled together an *Open Letter* in support of Gurpreet Kaur Bhatti's artistic freedom of expression, which was published in the *Guardian* newspaper. Like Rushdie, Bhatti found herself forced to go into hiding following receipt of hate mail, including death threats and, like the situation with Rushdie for many years, she has since not appeared in public.

5 Incitement to Religious Hatred

Study Activity 16

Having read the remainder of this chapter and reflected on the chapter as a whole:

(i) *describe* some of the reasons why legislation on 'incitement to religious hatred' has been pursued by the Government rather than reform of the blasphemy laws

(ii) *discuss* how far it may or may not be possible to distinguish between robust criticism of a religion; irreverent mockery of religious leaders; and activity that is likely to 'incite hatred'

(iii) *evaluate* any likely benefits and problems for implementation now that legislation on 'incitement to religious hatred' is on the statute book across the UK

Proposals and Concerns

In the context of the atmosphere of heightened tension following the 9/11 attacks in the USA, the UK government brought forward new legislative proposals relating to aspects of discrimination and unfair treatment on the grounds of religion. In particular, the *Anti-Terrorism, Crime and Security Bill*, introduced in the weeks following September 11, included provisions to make 'incitement to religious hatred' an offence in England and Wales alongside the existing offence of 'incitement to racial hatred'.

These proposals, however, gave rise to fairly widespread concern (including among a range of religious groups) that such a law might have the effect of constraining robust debate and criticism of religion (Cumper, 2007). In response, the government emphasized that there is an important distinction to be made between robust verbal debate and the kind of incitement activity that the Bill was intended to address.

Nevertheless, in the end, the 'incitement to religious hatred' clauses of the Bill did not pass into law, although public and political debate has continued on the possible future introduction of similar legislation. However, the Bill, when passed as the *Anti-Terrorism, Crime and Security Act* (2001), did create a new category of religiously 'aggravated' offences. This now provides some additional means of redress for Muslims and others who may be subjected to religiously aggravated forms of existing assault, criminal damage, harassment and public order offences.

Incitement Law in Northern Ireland: the Public Order Act

In the Northern Irish context, the *Prevention of Incitement to Hatred Act (Northern Ireland)* 1970 had already made it an offence intentionally to stir up hatred against, or rouse the fear of, any section of the public on the grounds of religious belief, colour, race or ethnic or national origins. This covered the publication or distribution of written or any other matter that is threatening, abusive or insulting as well as the use of words of a similar nature in a public place or in a public meeting. These provisions were further developed in part III of the *Public Order (Northern Ireland) Order*, 1987.

Although these provisions have only rarely been used, their scope is not only concerned with incitement directed to or against religious groups, but is also concerned with incitement against any group when such incitement is carried out on religious grounds. In England and Wales, the *Public Order Act,* 1986, did not address incitement to religious hatred, but in part III contained provisions relating to incitement to racial hatred. As in Northern Ireland, this law has only rarely been used over the two decades that it has been in force, with 76 prosecutions taking place, resulting in 44 convictions.

However, it had been partly because the original measures were rushed that they did not find a consensus of support, even among religious groups (Iganski, ed., 2002). Further attempts to legislate followed with the Private Members' *Religious Offences Bill*, 2002, and in the government's *Serious Organised Crime and Police Bill*, 2004. Each of these attempts was based on modifications to the existing provisions for incitement to racial hatred found in the *Public Order Act*, 1986. The proposals have remained controversial throughout, because of the inevitable difficulties involved in trying to balance the freedom of people within religions to live without fear of intimidation and hatred being stirred up against them, and the freedom of people to satirize religious topics and also advance either strong religious convictions or convictions critical of religion.

At the same time, according to the *Racist Incident Monitoring Annual Report* of the Crown Prosecution Service (which covered the period April 2004 to May 2005) for offences under the *Anti-Terrorism, Crime, and Security Act* in England and Wales, 27 of 34 defendants were prosecuted for religiously aggravated offences, and in 23 of these, the actual or perceived religion of the victim was Islam.

Manifesto Commitment and Passage of the Law

The 2005 Labour Party Manifesto for England and Wales (though not for Scotland) contained a commitment to legislate balancing protection, tolerance and free speech, on the basis of which the government introduced further measures into Parliament. Despite this being a Manifesto commitment, in October 2005, the

Racial and Religious Hatred Bill, 2005, was defeated in the House of Lords, with amendments from the Lords separating out racial and religious hatred; making the offence refer only to 'threatening' words and behaviour and not 'threatening, abusive or insulting'; and requiring the prosecution to prove an intention to stir up hatred.

In January 2006, the government attempted to reinstate reference to 'abusive and insulting behaviour' and the notion of being 'reckless' about stirring up hatred, but suffered its second defeat in the Commons, losing by one vote. The measure was finally passed in an amended form, referring only to England and Wales, and being concerned with 'acts intended to stir up hatred' where religious hatred is understood as being hatred against a group of persons defined by reference to religious belief or lack of religious belief.

At the time of writing, these provisions have not yet been brought into force, although an announcement about the timetable for this is expected. Specific explanation was included that the provision of this law should not be read in a way that prohibits or restricts debate, antipathy, dislike or even ridicule or insult of religions, their beliefs and practices, nor to exclude proselytism. It was also made clear that prosecution of an offence under these provisions can only proceed with the permission of the Attorney General.

6 The Management of Diversity

This chapter has highlighted one cluster of areas in which very considerable tension has emerged between religious diversities, secularity, toleration and respect in the public sphere (Horton, 1992; Horton and Crabtree, eds, 1992; Murphy, 1992; Horton, ed., 1993) raising wider questions, in terms of how far it might be possible for diverse societies to find ways of holding together (Inter Faith Network for the UK: 1997). The importance, explosiveness and sensitivity of the issues involved flag up the need for these and other issues arising from the new 'three-dimensional' religious landscape to be approached within an overall framework of law informed by social policy. It is therefore to a consideration of Religious Diversity, Discrimination and Equal Opportunities that the final chapter of the book turns.

Resources for Further Learning

Ahsan, M. and Kidwai, A., eds (1991), *Sacrilege Versus Civility: Muslim Perspectives on The Satanic Verses Affair*. Leicester: The Islamic Foundation.

Akhtar, S. (1989), *Be Careful with Muhammad! The Salman Rushdie Affair*. London: Bellew.

Akhtar, S. (1989), 'Whose light, whose darkness?'. *Guardian*, 27 February 1989.

Appignanesi, L and Maitland, S., eds (1989), *The Rushdie File*. London: Fourth Estate.

Burgess, A. (1989), 'The burning truth'. *Daily Mail*, 31 January 1989.

Cohn-Sherbok, D., ed. (1990), *The Salman Rushdie Affair in Interreligious Perspective*. Lampeter: Edwin Mellen Press.

Commission for Racial Equality (1990), *Britain a Plural Society: Report of a Seminar*. London: Commission for Racial Equality.

Commission for Racial Equality (1990), *Law, Blasphemy and the Multi-Faith Society: Report of a Seminar*. London: Commission for Racial Equality.

Cumper, P. (2007), 'Inciting religious hatred: balancing free speech and religious sensibilities in a multi-faith society', in N. Ghanea, A. Stephens and R. Walden, eds, *Does God Believe in Human Rights?: Essays on Religion and Human Rights*. Leiden: Martinus Nijhoff Publishers, pp. 233–58.

Denning, A. (1949), *Freedom Under the Law*. London: Stevens and Sons.

General Synod of the Church of England (1981), *Offences Against Religion and Public Worship, G.S. Misc. 149*. London: General Synod of the Church of England.

General Synod of the Church of England (1988), *Offences Against Religion and Public Worship, G.S. Misc. 286*. London: General Synod of the Church of England.

Ghanea, N., Stephens, A. and Walden, R., eds (2007), *Does God Believe in Human Rights?: Essays on Religion and Human Rights*. Leiden: Martinus Nijhoff Publishers.

Guillaume, A. (1987), *The Life of Muhammad: A Translation of Ishaq's Sirat Rasul Allah*. Oxford: Oxford University Press.

Habgood, J. (1989), Letter to the Editor. *The Times*, 1 March 1989.

Hebert, H. (1989), 'The liberal taboos'. *Guardian*, 9 May 1989.

Horton, J. (1992), 'Religion and toleration: some problems and possibilities', in J. Horton and H. Crabtree, eds, *Toleration and Integrity in a Multi-Faith Society*. York: University of York Department of Politics, pp. 62–70.

Horton, J. ed. (1993), *Liberalism, Multiculturalism and Toleration*. London: Macmillan.

Horton, J. and Crabtree, H., eds (1992), *Toleration and Integrity in a Multi-Faith Society*. York: University of York Department of Politics.

Iganski, P., ed. (2002), *The Hate Debate: Should Hate Be Punished as a Crime?* London: Profile Books.

Inter Faith Network for the UK (1997), *The Quest for Common Values: Conference Report*. London: Inter Faith Network for the United Kingdom.

Inter Faith Network for the UK and Commission for Racial Equality (1990), *Law, Blasphemy and the Multi-Faith Society*. London: Commission for Racial Equality.

Kabbani, R. (1989), *Letter to Christendom*. London: Virago.

Law Commission, The (1981), *Offences Against Religion and Public Worship: Working Paper No. 79*. London: Her Majesty's Stationery Office.

Law Commission, The (1985), *Criminal Law Offences Against Religion and Public Worship: Working Paper No. 145*. London: Her Majesty's Stationery Office.

Martin, P. (1989), 'Spurn the book, spare the man'. *Guardian*, 27 February 1989.

Mazrui, A. (1989), *The Satanic Verses or a Satanic Novel? The Moral Dilemmas of the Rushdie Affair*. New York: The Committee of Muslim Scholars and Leaders of North America.

Modood, T. (1989), 'Religious anger and minority rights'. *Political Quarterly*, 60, 3, 280–5.

Modood, T. (1990), 'British Asian Muslims and the Rushdie affair'. *Political Quarterly*, 61, 2, 143–60.

Murphy, T. (1992), 'Toleration and the law', in J. Horton and H. Crabtree, eds, *Toleration and Integrity in a Multi-Faith Society*. York: University of York Department of Politics, pp. 50–61.

O'Higgins, P. (1989). 'Relic that has no role'. *Guardian,* 3 March 1989.

Palmer, R. (1989), Letter to the *Church Times*, 23 August 1989.

Parekh, B. (1989), 'Between holy text and moral void'. *New Life*, 12 May 1989.

Parsons, G., ed. (1994), *The Growth of Religious Diversity: Britain From 1945: Volume II: Issues*. London: Routledge.

Robilliard, St. John (1984), *Religion and the Law: Religious Liberty in Modern English Law*. Manchester: Manchester University Press.

Rushdie, S. (1980), *Midnight's Children*. London: Picador.

Rushdie, S. (1983), *Shame*. London: Jonathan Cape.

Rushdie, S. (1988), *The Satanic Verses*. London: Viking Penguin.

Ruthven, M. (1990), *A Satanic Affair: Salman Rushdie and the Rage of Islam*. London: Chatto and Windus.

Sardar, Z. and Wyn Davies, M. (1990), *Distorted Imagination: Lessons From the Rushdie Affair*. London: Grey Seal.

Smith, W. (1946), *Islam in Modern India*. Lahore.

Vincent, J. (1989), 'Outrage we cannot ignore'. *The Times*, 2 March 1989.

Walter, N. (1989), Letter to the Editor. *Independent*, 1 March 1989.

Ward, K. (1990), 'Third introductory paper', in Commission for Racial Equality, *Law, Blasphemy and the Multi-Faith Society, Report of a Seminar*. London: Commission for Racial Equality, pp. 30–9.

Webster, R. (1990), *A Brief History of Blasphemy: Liberalism, Censorship and 'The Satanic Verses'*. Southwold: The Orwell Press.

Weller, P. (1990a), 'The Rushdie Affair, plurality of values and the ideal of a multi-cultural society'. *National Association for Values in Education and Training Working Papers*, 2, October, 1–9.

Weller, P. (1990b), 'Literature update on the Salman Rushdie affair'. *Discernment: A Christian Journal of Inter-Religious Encounter*. 4, 2, 35–41.

Weller, P. (1990c), 'The Rushdie Controversy and Inter-Faith Relations', in D. Cohn-Sherbok, ed., *The Salman Rushdie Affair in Interreligious Perspective*. Lampeter: Edwin Mellen Press, pp. 37–57.

Weller, P. (1996), *The Salman Rushdie Controversy, Religious Plurality, and Established Religion in England*. Unpublished Ph.D. thesis, Department of Theology and Religious Studies, University of Leeds.

Wilson, A. (1978), *Finding a Voice: Asian Women in Britain*. London: Virago.

Wolffe, J. (1994), '"And there's another country ..."': religion, the state and British Identities', in G. Parsons, ed. (1994), *The Growth of Religious Diversity: Britain From 1945: Volume II: Issues*. London: Routledge, pp. 85–121.

Young, H. (1989), 'Life, death and Mr. Rushdie'. *Guardian*, 24 November 1989.

6

Religious Diversity, Discrimination and Equal Opportunities

Learning Outcomes for Chapter 6

After studying this chapter, and referring to a range of its associated Resources for Further Learning, you should be able to:

(i)   *describe* some key aspects of the historical development in the interface between religious diversity, social policy and law

(ii) *discuss* how far it is possible for the law to protect religious identity without privileging it in relation to secular perspectives

(iii) *discuss* examples of tension between the various 'strands' of contemporary law and machinery to support human rights and anti-discrimination

(iv) *evaluate* the strengths and weaknesses of the law in promoting a more inclusive society

1 Diversity, Social Policy and the Law: Possibilities and Limitations

Equality, Diversity and The Law

Liberal democratic governments no longer believe, as some of them once did, that defining appropriate policy and planning for its successful implementation necessarily leads to the solution of issues, especially in the economic field. At the same time, in recent years, especially in the field of social policy, the law has been given a more enhanced role as an instrument of social policy.

Some see such extension of the law into equality and diversity matters as a flawed and unhelpful attempt at 'social engineering'. Others understand this as necessary for redressing the balance and opening up opportunities (Parekh, 1990) in relation to groups and categories of people who have otherwise been disadvantaged by reference to their age, disability, race, religion or belief, sex or sexual orientation. The past forty years in the UK have seen the development of such legislation, beginning with law on sexual and racial discrimination, moving through disabilities, and now encompassing also age, religion and belief and sexual orientation.

At the same time, the making of law itself is now increasingly subject to the scrutiny of international norms and conventions. With the introduction into the UK law of the *Human Rights Act*, 1988, both the public policy pursued by the executive and legislation developed by Parliament should conform with the norms and principles of the *European Convention on Human Rights and Fundamental Freedoms* to which the UK is a state party.

Multiculturalism and Religion

Since the mid-1960s, the social policy and political consensus in the UK, under-lying the equality and diversity policies of central and local government and other significant social institutions, has shaped the development of law in this field and has been predicated on support for, and promotion of, an approach generally known as 'multiculturalism' (Rex, 1995; Modood and Werbner, eds, 1997a, 1997b; Parekh, 2000; Dusche, 2005).

The content of such 'multiculturalism' was classically and perhaps mostly clearly articulated by the former Labour Government Home Secretary, Roy (now Lord) Jenkins who was the architect of the UK's 1968 *Race Relations Act*. Jenkins' (1967: 269) argument was that: 'I do not think that we need in this country a melting-pot, which will turn everybody out in a common mould, as one of a series of someone's misplaced vision of the stereotyped Englishman.' Rather, he clarified that the aim of the government's policy was for 'integration' (understood in those days as the opposite of 'assimilation'), defined as 'equal opportunity, coupled with cultural diversity, in an atmosphere of mutual tolerance'.

On the basis of this policy, significant political and social institutions have engaged in concerted attempts at positive action to address the needs of those citizens widely referred to as 'ethnic minorities'. Initially, however, religion was only rarely considered in terms of the implications of the new plurality. An early exception to this was an intervention by Bishop John Taylor, in a 1977 Church of England General Synod debate on the hard-hitting British Council of Churches' (1976) Community and Race Relations Unit's report on *The New Black Presence in Britain*. Bishop Taylor (quoted in Wolffe, ed., 1993: 193) argued that 'The existence of religious minorities presents us with both problems and opportunities which are distinct from those that arise in the presence of racial and cultural minorities, and should not be lost sight of or evaded.'

Nonetheless, despite Taylor's prescient identification of these matters, in relation to religious diversity the interplay between law and social policy was, for most of the closing years of the previous century, relatively underdeveloped. However, in the past decade it has come to the forefront in its own right but also, and often controversially so, in relation to some of what are often called the other 'strands' of equality and diversity law and policy (Eberle, 2002). Today, in the opening years of the twenty-first century, in the light of both the demographic changes referred to in chapter 1, and due to the range of matters that lie at the interface between religion and public life highlighted in other chapters of this book, social policy, and issues arising from diversity of religion and beliefs, can indeed no longer either be 'lost sight of' or 'evaded'.

2 Religion and the Law: Policy Context Starting-Points in Race and Ethnicity

Study Activity 17

After reading sections 2 and 3 of the chapter:

(i) *describe* some of the contextual changes that have taken place over the past twenty years in the relationship between religious and ethnic identity

(ii) *discuss* with reference to the analyses in Panel 10 some of the key differences and commonalities between different kinds of discrimination and unfair treatment on the basis of religion

(iii) *evaluate* the usefulness and limitations of law in tackling religious discrimination

Religions and the Legal Systems of the UK

The legal framework for the practice of religion in the UK is clearly of importance to religious groups since it has a bearing on the degree to which religions can operate in accordance with their own traditions (Trigg, 2007). It is also significant for the state and the wider society in relation to the framework for how religions interact with matters of wider public interest (Bradney, 1993; Edge and Harvey, eds, 2000; Edge, 2006). In general terms, the legal system for England and Wales differs from that of Scotland, and these differences could well develop still further in the light of political devolution from Westminster. Northern Ireland, in turn, has many provisions that are different from those that exist in the rest of the UK.

Unlike some other European countries, the UK has no formal list of religions officially recognized by the state, although such a list exists for the purpose of the recognition of religion within the Prison Service. From time to time, although there are no clear criteria, the courts have to decide whether a particular organization or movement is a 'religion' in order, for example, to interpret a legal provision in relation to charity law. In the past, indicators of religious status have been taken to include monotheistic belief, but even this cannot be a firm requirement since, for instance, it is clearly problematic with regard to Buddhism. In a 1999 decision of the Charity Commission for England and Wales, the Church of Scientology was held not to fall within the definition of a religion in charity law, and it is also not recognized as a religion by the Prison Service.

Religion and Free Exercise

Most forms of overt legal religious discrimination have now been ended (although some continuing ones concerned with the monarchy and the succession were noted in chapter 3). However, the degree to which the present law accommodates the diverse practice of a range of religious traditions is being continually tested (Wilson, 1990). For example, Sikhs had to engage in a lengthy struggle before being allowed exemption from a 1972 *Road Traffic Act* requirement for motorcyclists to wear safety helmets. The *Road Traffic Act* 1988, re-enacting the *Motor-Cycle Crash Helmets (Religious Exemption) Act* 1976, now exempts a follower of the Sikh religion 'while he is wearing a turban' from the crash helmet requirements applicable to others. A similar exemption was granted by the *Employment Act* 1989 to allow turbaned Sikhs to work on construction sites without a helmet or hard hat as required by new safety regulations.

Another example has been the exemption for Jewish and Muslim methods of animal slaughter from the general legislation that governs the protection of animals at the time of slaughter (Charlton and Kay, 1985–6; Kay, 1993). A *Statutory Instrument* of 1995, implementing the European Community's Directive on this matter, contains provision to allow Jews and Muslims to follow the requirements of their religious traditions (known, respectively, as *shechita* and *dbah* slaughter) in which the otherwise general requirement for the pre-stunning of animals prior to slaughter has been waived.

Family, marriage and burial law has also been the subject of some legal and social debate involving the religious communities, raising questions about the relationship to religious law and practice of social legislation on matters such as marriage, divorce and inheritance (Pearl, 1986). There has also been debate about the extent to which employers can or should provide time and facilities at work for the performance of obligatory prayers and days off for the observance of religious festivals.

Until recently, the response of the legal system to increased religious diversity has generally proceeded on the basis of the historically distinctive approach found in English law of ad hoc and pragmatic developments rather than seeking to provide generally applicable new frameworks for law. It has therefore often been concerned with defining permissible exceptions to generally applicable laws (Poulter, 1986, 1990a, 1990b). However, from the early 1990s onwards there was intensifying debate about the extent to which the law should protect people against forms of direct discrimination connected with religious identity.

Much of the previously developed legislation and social policy that was designed to deal with social identities based upon race and ethnicity did not sit easily with the rising importance of religion in the self-definition of individuals and groups that occurred throughout the 1990s (Taylor, 1992; Baumann, 1996, 1999; Modood, 1998), partly as a by-product of both domestic and international developments.

Religious Identity: Recognition and Debates About Protection

In the UK, for many years Northern Ireland was the exception in having legal provisions against religious discrimination in employment and for the prosecution of incitement to religious hatred. In the common law tradition of England and Wales, there continued to be some traditional provisions against blasphemy and blasphemous libel. However, as the testing of these provisions in the courts during the controversy over *The Satanic Verses* demonstrated, these laws only give protection to the Christian religion and, sometimes, more particularly only to the doctrines and practices of the Church of England.

In England, Scotland and Wales, since the introduction of race relations legislation there have been provisions against discrimination in relation to a member of an 'ethnic group'. One of the factors that is taken as being indicative of this is that of a long, shared group history of which religion may be a dimension. Jews have therefore been judged to be an 'ethnic group', as also have Sikhs following the case of *Mandla v. Dowell Lee* in 1983. Muslims, however, generally fell outside the scope of the *Race Relations Act*. Being members of a community that (as also with Buddhists and Christians) defines itself in relation to its diversity of ethnic groups, Muslims have not been viewed as having a shared history linked to a shared ethnicity in the same sense as Jewish or Sikh people.

Thus 'indirect' discrimination has been the most that white Muslims, Buddhists or Christians could claim under Race Relations law, by pursuing a case as an Asian or an Arab or as a Yemeni or a Pakistani, relying on a racial or national identity, and complaining that certain practices or procedures may have had a disproportionately adverse effect because they unjustifiably interfere with their religious observance.

As noted in chapter 5, in many ways, *The Satanic Verses* controversy served as both a magnifying glass and a lightning rod for these developments. Reflecting on its broader implications during the early days of the controversy in her book *Letter to Christendom,* the Muslim writer Rana Kabbani (1989: 8) noted that: 'Rushdie's book brought into the open the frustrations of a Muslim minority for whom the much-vaunted multicultural society was a sham. ... Faced by the majority community, still overwhelmingly Christian in law and institutions if not in belief, Muslims felt powerless and unprotected.'

The dangers to wider social cohesion of significant groups of people feeling 'powerless and unprotected' had, in the 1970s, already been recognized with regard to the impact of discrimination on the grounds of 'race' and 'ethnicity'. Thus the 1975 White Paper on *Racial Discrimination* had argued that:

> where unfair discrimination is involved, the necessity of legal remedies is now generally accepted. To fail to provide a remedy against an injustice strikes at the rule of law. To abandon a whole group of people in society without legal redress against unfair discrimination is to leave them with no option but to find their own redress.

What had been argued in that *White Paper* with regard to ethnicity began increasingly to be argued with regard to religion by Muslim groups and organizations. In fact, this very passage was quoted in the UK Action Committee on Islamic Affair's 1993 report, *Muslims and the Law in Multi-Faith Britain: The Need for Reform*, that argued in favour of the need to introduce legislation to address religious discrimination.

Of course, as has been briefly noted in chapter 3, issues of religious discrimination and disadvantage had formed a significant part of public and political debate in the nineteenth century. At that time, in England, this was especially because such discrimination was still, following the restoration of the monarchy and the re-establishment of the Church of England, enshrined in the law in ways that privileged Anglican Christians relative to all other religious and non-religious groups, until the pace of reforms during the nineteenth century eventually led to a position, by the beginning of the twentieth century, in which the major legal, political and social disabilities for non-Anglican Christians had been removed.

That history is in many ways different to the present. However, for engaging with these issues in a contemporary way it is, arguably, also important to take some account of the particular religious, legal, social and political heritage within which the contemporary forms of these issues are located. Neither historical ignorance nor amnesia about the history of religious discrimination is likely to provide a healthy basis upon which to try to tackle the issue of religious discrimination today. Instead, there are things that it might be possible to illuminate by comparison and contrast. Thus, commenting on the historical developments noted above, but perhaps also with relevance to the social dynamics of the late twentieth century re-emergence of a focus on discrimination on the grounds of religion, the legal academic St. John Robilliard (1984: ix) pointed out that:

> The early story of the struggle for religious liberty was one of sects establishing an identity of their own, with their members being freed from the obligation of supporting a faith they did not hold. From the struggle for existence we pass to the struggle for equality, in many important fields, with the Established Church.

However, as Muslims (who in the early 1990s were the main group raising this issue) were to discover, it was far from straightforward to reintroduce the concept of religious discrimination into public discourse and ultimately into law. Nevertheless, some possibilities in this regard had, as early as 1992, been discussed in the Commission for Racial Equality's (1992) *Second Review of the Race Relations Act*. However, the scope of the race relations legislation under which the Commission operated made it difficult for it to develop work in this area. While the case of *Mandla v. Dowell Lee* had established that discrimination against Sikhs came within the purview of the Act on the basis that for Sikhs as well as Jews religion could be seen as a dimension of ethnic belonging, this could not easily be 'stretched', either in terms of the law – or even within Muslim self-understanding – to include Muslims who are not a single religio-ethnic group but include adherents of diverse ethnicity.

3 Religion and Discrimination: The Emerging Evidence Base

The CRE, ICRC and Runnymede Trust

Nevertheless, it was generally recognized that there were issues of discrimination that did need tackling somehow and increasingly strong representations began to be made for the Commission for Racial Equality (CRE) to undertake work on religious discrimination. Therefore, from 1992 onwards the Commission tried to collect case evidence and in 1994 it conducted a survey of 2,047 agencies dealing with complaints of religious discrimination, including Race Equality Councils, solicitors, Law Centres, Citizens' Advice Bureaux, academics and religious organizations.

There was only a low response rate to the survey, with the subsequent *Position Paper on Religious Discrimination* produced by the Commission noting that 'specific information was received about 38 cases of alleged religious discrimination'. However, the Commission also noted with regard to this relatively low reported incidence that, 'This was not surprising given the lack of monitoring by all the agencies surveyed, and also the lack of any direct legislation on the issue.'

In other words, where legal frameworks do not encourage individuals to report issues in terms of religious discrimination, they are not surprisingly likely to couch such issues in other terms – such as those of ethnicity or gender – in the hope of getting matters addressed through another route.

In October 1995, the Commission established a Project Group to further develop work in this area. Towards the end of 1996 it carried out a consultation exercise with religious communities around the UK to explore the scope of the current Race Relations legislation and to debate whether amendment to the law was needed in order to make discrimination on the grounds of religion unlawful. As an outcome of this exercise, the Commission reported that: 'The overwhelming majority of those who participated in the consultation believed there was a need for legislation outlawing religious discrimination.'

Although it would still be some time before such a recognition moved up the political and legislative agenda, signs of a shift with regard to the place of religion within public policy could be observed throughout government and these shifts began to prepare the ground for at least the 'thinkability' of legislation on religious discrimination. Thus, in 1996, the Inner Cities' Religious Council (ICRC) issued a leaflet and booklet entitled *Challenging Religious Discrimination: A Guide for Faith Communities and Their Advisers*. This was followed, in 1997, by the Commission for Racial Equality's leaflet entitled *Religious Discrimination: Your Rights* that outlined, under the terms of the *Race Relations Act*, ways in which unfair treatment on the basis of religion could be addressed as 'indirect racial discrimination'.

In 1997, through both its title and its contents, the report of the Runnymede Trust's Commission on British Muslims and Islamophobia, entitled *Islamophobia: a Challenge for Us All*, introduced into the wider currency of public discourse the notion that, alongside shared dynamics of discriminatory experience there may also be particularities of Muslim experience signalled by the word 'Islamophobia'. At the start of the report (Runnymede Trust, 1997:1) it was explained that 'In recent years a new word has gained currency. ... It was coined in the late 1980s, its first known use in print being in February 1991, in a periodical in the United States.' The periodical concerned was *Insight* (4 February 1991) in which the first use of the word Islamophobia known (as of March 1997) to the compilers of the Oxford English Dictionary appeared, where 'Islamophobia' was cited as a substantial reason for the USSR's reluctance to relinquish its position at the time in Afghanistan. The *Islamophobia* report goes on to say of the word itself that:

> The word is not ideal, but is recognisably similar to 'xenophobia' and 'europhobia', and is a useful shorthand way of referring to dread or hatred of Islam – and therefore to fear or dislike of all or most Muslims. Such dread and dislike have existed in western countries and cultures for

> centuries. In the last twenty years, however, the dislike has become more
> explicit, more extreme and more dangerous. It is an ingredient of all sec-
> tions of our media, and it is prevalent in all sections of our society. Within
> Britain it means that Muslims are frequently excluded from the economic,
> social and public life of the nation ... and are frequently victims of dis-
> crimination and harassment.

But in order for legislative change to occur, it is often necessary not only to
effect a shift in political debate; governments frequently require justificatory
evidence. In 1992, the Commission for Racial Equality's *Second Review of the
Race Relations Act, 1976,* had argued that, 'a law against religious discrimination
should be given serious consideration'. At that time, the former Tory Government
Home Secretary Michael Howard (quoted in the CRE *Position Paper on Religious
Discrimination*) had replied that: 'I have yet to be convinced that legislation
could be justified. So far, there is little hard evidence of discrimination against
individuals on religious rather than racial grounds ...' However, Howard also
went on to say, 'but I can assure you that the Home Office remains ready to look
at any evidence'.

While marshalling some evidence, the Runnymede Trust report on
Islamophobia was the report of a *Commission* rather than of a *research* project,
and although Muslim organizations endeavoured to submit such evidence to
government, no systematic research supported by Government itself had been
undertaken into the possibility of religion being an axis of discrimination in its
own right.

Religious Discrimination in England and Wales: Research

In 1990, however, the Home Office commissioned research on religious discrimination in England and Wales from the University of Derby's Religious Resource
and Research Centre. The project team conducted questionnaire and fieldwork
research into evidence of religious discrimination, both actual and perceived; the
patterns shown by this evidence, including its overall scale; the main victims, the
main perpetrators, and the main ways in which discrimination manifests; and the
extent to which religious discrimination overlaps with racial discrimination.

The aim of this research was to identify the broad range of policy options
available for dealing with religious discrimination. In January 2000, the project
issued *Religious Discrimination in England and Wales: An Interim Report* and, in
February 2001, the Home Office Research, Development and Statistics Directorate
published its Research Study No. 220 on *Religious Discrimination in England and
Wales*.

The project's findings highlighted some of the potentially distinctive aspects
of unfair treatment on these grounds, as when a group of Bahá'ís observed (in

Weller, Feldman and Purdam et al., 2001: 103) that, 'it's not out and out discrimination; not as bad as what ethnic minorities experience, but there's a whole part of your life people don't care about' while a group of Hindus and Jains commented (in Weller, Feldman and Purdam et al., 2001: 103) that:

> Discrimination is difficult to prove. It can always be said that it was an individual's attitude rather than an inadequate or discriminatory policy; as a result, you can't get action taken. People are laughing in your face: discrimination is an experience, the experience of a slap in the face.

Overall, though, the report concluded that ignorance and indifference towards religion were of generally widespread concern amongst research participants from all faith groups. It also found that in institutional settings such ignorance and indifference can contribute towards an environment in which discrimination of all kinds, including institutional discrimination, is able to thrive. Education, employment and the media were the areas most often highlighted as contexts for unfair treatment and for discrimination on the basis of religion.

A consistently higher level of unfair treatment was reported by Muslim organizations than by most other religious groups. Such unfair treatment was also consistently reported to be frequent rather than occasional. Hindu, and especially Sikh, organizations also reported a relatively high level of unfair treatment. Pagans and people from New Religious Movements frequently complained of open hostility and discrimination.

Religious Discrimination: Analysis and Policy Options

In terms of policy options for tackling religious discrimination, research participants generally advocated a comprehensive approach in which education, training and a bigger effort in teaching comparative religion in schools would all play an important part. The strengths and limitations of the law were recognized and many participants thought the law could help if used judiciously and in conjunction with other approaches. The Home Office Research, Development and Statistics Directorate also published a parallel report (Research Study No. 221) from the University of Cambridge's Faculty of Public Law on *Tackling Religious Discrimination: Practical Implications for Policy Makers and Legislators* (Hepple and Coudhary, 2001) that explored the strengths and weaknesses of the various legal options.

The Religious Discrimination in England and Wales Research Project's *Interim Report* (Weller and Purdam, 1990: 7–10) included an attempt to analyse and differentiate the various forms of discrimination on the grounds of religion. This analysis was undertaken on the basis that discrimination and unfair treatment on the basis of religion may manifest itself in distinctive and specific ways as in anti-Semitism or Islamophobia; it might also be helpful to have a framework that could identify any generic phenomena associated with the experience across all religious groups that experience unfair treatment.

At the same time, it was recognized that 'religious discrimination' could only ever be a convenient 'shorthand' umbrella term for a range of types of discrimination experienced and that some differentiation between these types was needed in order to inform the evolution of policy responses that would be appropriate to specific issues (Weller, 2003). The main aspects of what the project identified as dimensions of unfair treatment on the basis of religion are summarized in Panel 10. Thus with regard to prejudicial attitudes relating to religion while law may have a part to play in terms of its symbolic as well as operational effects in marking out the limits of what is acceptable and unacceptable, an educational response may be most appropriate and effective. However, to tackle actual direct discrimination, education alone may not be sufficient. In this, recourse to law and the operational restraints and effects deriving from it may be critically important to any effective response.

Panel 10: Analysis of Types of Discrimination on the Grounds of Religion

1. *'Religious prejudice':* This is attitudinal. While it might not result in discriminatory behaviour, it can certainly wound individuals, and can form a basis for exclusion.

2. *'Religious hatred':* This occurs when 'religious prejudice' becomes solidified into a settled attitude of mind and will, and is then sometimes clothed in a specific ideological justification that can often result in violent behaviour.

3. *'Direct religious discrimination':* This is deliberately unfair and exclusionary action based on religion.

4. *'Indirect religious discrimination':* This is the exclusionary consequence of unexamined practices or procedures that may not be informed either by prejudice or intent directly to discriminate, but which nonetheless result in unfair treatment and exclusion due to their not having taken account of a changed social and religious context.

5. *'Religious disadvantage':* This is experienced by any religious group outside of the privileged alignments that, within a range of European societies, exist between a particular religious group or groups and the state.

6. *'Institutional religionism':* This admittedly somewhat inelegant neologism was coined by analogy with the findings of the report of the commission of inquiry into the Stephen Lawrence affair (which identified 'institutional racism' in the Metropolitan Police) in order to signify the complex and systematic combination of two or more of the above dimensions.

Source: Weller (2006b: 21–2)

Employment, Equality, Religion and Belief

As a response to a European Directive on discrimination in employment that derived from the *Amsterdam Treaty* of the European Union, in 2003 new legal rights were introduced with regard to employment, religion and belief. In line with the provisions of the *European Convention on Human Rights and Fundamental Freedoms*, the Regulations relate to both 'religion' (as generally understood) and 'belief' (meaning any settled philosophical system or orientation) governing an individual's life.

These new rights are set out in the *Employment Equality (Religion or Belief) Regulations*, 2003, which, for the first time in England, Wales and Scotland, made discrimination on these grounds illegal (Cumper, 2003). In the context of employment (including vocational training defined to include staff and students of both further and higher education) the Regulations prohibit direct discrimination on grounds of religion or belief (except for genuine and determining occupational requirements). The regulations also prohibit indirect discrimination (except for objective justification that is both appropriate and necessary). Finally, they prohibit harassment, as well as victimization on the grounds of pursuit of issues relating to discrimination or harassment on the grounds of religion or belief.

In contrast to discrimination on the grounds of race, gender and disability, it was still not illegal to discriminate on the grounds of religion or belief in the provision of goods and services. Nevertheless, the introduction of these Regulations marked a step forward in the evolution of legal frameworks appropriate to a religiously plural and secular society, in a key area of social life that has a central bearing on the life chances of individuals and communities. The Regulations both codified expectations of behaviour and, for the first time outside of Northern Ireland, provide individuals in England, Scotland and Wales with means of redress supported by the possibility of legal proceedings and sanctions.

In Northern Ireland, the *Fair Employment Act* proscribed discrimination on the grounds of religious or political opinion in the area of employment. All public sector employers and all companies with more than ten employees must report each year to the Equality Commission on the religious composition of their workforces, and they must also review their employment practices every three years. Non-compliance can result in criminal penalties and the loss of government contracts. In addition, the 1998 *Northern Ireland Act* stipulates that all public authorities must show due regard for the need to promote equality of opportunity, including on the basis of religious belief and must report their plans to promote equality to the Equality Commission, which reviews such plans every five years.

Beyond the legal requirements within which they must now operate, many organizations are now also positively trying to take religion into account in developing their equal opportunities policies and practice. To assist in this (ACAS) the Arbitration, Conciliation and Advisory Service (2003) has produced a guidance booklet on *Religion or Belief and the Workplace: A Guide for Employers and Employees.*

But although discrimination in employment was one of the main areas of concern identified in the Religious Discrimination in England and Wales Research Project and other work (Yarrow, 1997), and the introduction of the new Regulations therefore represented a significant development, there were still substantial areas of social life within which it remained, in England, Wales and Scotland, not illegal to discriminate on the grounds of religion or belief. The *Equality Act*, 2006, tackled aspects of this, by making it illegal to discriminate on the grounds of 'religion or belief' or lack of it in the provision of goods, facilities and services, education, the use and disposal of property, and the exercise of public functions.

4 Religion, Equalities 'Strands' and Human Rights: New Developments

> ### Study Activity 18
>
> After reading section 4 of the chapter:
>
> (i) *discover* about the remit and agenda of the Commission for Equality and Human Rights (see: http://www.cehr.org.uk)
>
> (ii) *discuss* what clashes might occur between religious rights and other 'strands' of human rights and diversity agendas
>
> (iii) *evaluate* the extent to which it is likely that a single body will be able successfully to deal with all equalities 'strands'

'Bringing Human Rights Back Home': The Human Rights Act, 1988

In parallel to the research on religious discrimination, the implementation, in 2000, of the *Human Rights Act*, 1998, introduced into domestic law the provisions of the *European Convention on Human Rights and Fundamental Freedoms*. Key to the religion provisions of the Convention and the Act are those of Article 9 of the Convention stating that:

> Everyone has the right to freedom of thought, conscience and religion: this right includes freedom to change his belief and freedom, either alone or in community with others and in public or private, to manifest his reli-gion or belief, in worship, teaching, practice and observance. Freedom to

manifest one's religion or beliefs shall be subject only to such limitations as are prescribed by law and are necessary in a democratic society in the interests of public safety, for the protection of public order, health or morals, or for the protection of the rights or freedom of others.

Under the *Human Rights Act*, 1998, government and all bodies acting as 'public authorities' must examine how far their policies, practices and proposals conform with the Convention, since individuals will now be able directly to appeal to its protection within the UK courts (Evans, 1997; Edge, 1998; Poulter, 1998; Evans, 2001). The full implications of this are still subject to interpretation, as the courts build up a body of case law deriving from the Act.

However, one thing that was key to this and other subsequent developments in the field of social policy and law on equality and matters of religion and belief is that, significantly for the 'secular' dimension of the three-dimensional religious landscape of the UK, the provisions of the *Human Rights Act* are concerned not only with religion and the rights of believers, but rather with 'religion and belief', and this became clear in the first piece of law for England, Wales and Scotland that specifically addressed discrimination relating to religion.

Equalities and Human Rights: An Emerging Unified Approach

The 2006 *Equality Act* established the Commission for Equality and Human Rights (CEHR), which was scheduled to become operational from October 2007. The establishment of this new Commission reflects the government's intention to bring together the various so-called 'equalities strands' into a more unified structure. The CEHR will take on the previously separate legal roles of the Equal Opportunity Commission (dealing with sex discrimination), the Commission for Racial Equality (dealing with racial discrimination) and the Disability Rights Commission (dealing with disability discrimination), with regard to equalities legislation in the areas of gender, race and disabilities, while it is also charged with responsibilities with regard to the newer equalities 'strands' concerned with discrimination and equality of opportunity in relation to religion and belief, sexual orientation and age.

The CEHR's remit with regard to Scotland is different, in that there it covers only human rights matters that are reserved to Westminster, while other human rights matters are to be covered by the Scottish Commission for Human Rights, unless the Scottish Commission agrees that the CEHR should deal with such matters. In February 2005, the Department for Trade and Industry and the Cabinet Office announced a Discrimination Law Review and an Equalities Review which has been considering the fundamental principles of discrimination legislation and its underlying concepts. Its intention is to address concerns about inconsistencies in the current anti-discrimination legislative framework and to develop a clearer and more streamlined legislative framework, having due regard to 'better regulation' principles and being more user-friendly.

Tensions Between the 'Strands'

As equality and diversity law and policy developed, questions were increasingly asked about how far pluralist societies can and should go in accommodating difference and to what degree. Such questions are helpfully summarized by Gerald Parsons in the introductory article to the second of his edited volumes on *The Growth of Diversity: Britain From 1945*, which is entitled 'Deciding How Far You Can Go'. In this essay, Parsons (1994: 19) argues that, in the light of the increasingly plural nature of our society we need constantly to ask questions about:

> how far any of us can go in any particular direction without throwing out something vital to the preservation of a viable balance in British society between the interests of a variety of particular religious groups, the interests of dissenting groups and individuals within them, the concerns of those who stand outside and claim the right to criticise all religions, and the well-being, coherence and creative co-existence of the community of communities that is Britain at the end of the twentieth century.

In the context of the diversity of equalities and human rights agendas (Ghanea, Stephens and Walden, eds 2007) in themselves, these tensions can sometimes become quite sharp. The Religious Discrimination in England and Wales Research Project has already highlighted some of the tensions that can emerge in the context of the provision by religious groups of community services. One example recounted in the report (Weller, Feldman and Purdam et al., 2001: 84–5) was that of a multi-purpose, Christian community centre that provides activities and services for elderly people and youth as well as space for other groups. It was reported that the staff of the centre were generally committed to equalities as part of their Christian belief. However, a member of the centre's staff who had been involved in campaigning activities in relation to the provisions of Section 28 of *The Local Government Act* wrote a letter to a newspaper that might be interpreted as being anti-gay and lesbian.

A white, male, staff member of the centre recounted that the centre was then approached by the council asking them *hypothetically* if they would accommodate Qur'an classes and lesbian assertiveness groups on their site (these groups had not actually requested use of the centre). Upon informing the local authority that the centre could not allow these uses of its premises, funding was cut, and many services that had been critical to one of the most disadvantaged communities in the area suffered as a result.

From the perspective of the member of staff concerned, this was felt to reflect a growing secular, and especially anti-Christian, sentiment. It was his opinion that, if the council had taken a similar approach to a Muslim organization or a minority ethnic organization, then this would have been considered racist. In his view the action taken against his own centre actually amounted to what he described as 'discrimination against white Christian organizations under the guise of equal opportunities'. He also expressed scepticism about how many South Asian centres employ non-South Asian staff, and drew attention to what he felt to be a 'selective application' of equal opportunities policies, which he perceived as being to the disadvantage of religious organizations in general and, in this case, specifically to organizations with a Christian basis.

Significantly, this example was connected with issues relating to sexual orientation. This is an area in which there is significant and substantial public debate within some religious groups (for example, the Church of England and other Christian traditions) while for others there is very little sign of public debate. But it is also an area in which controversy has ensued following the further development of an overall approach to equality and diversity enshrined in the law. These debates came to a head especially with the government's consultation on its proposals to extend its Sexual Orientation Regulations beyond the field of employment rights to also cover the receipt of goods and services.

As with the other equalities strands, the aim of these Regulations was stated to be to ensure that individuals are not denied access by virtue of their sexual orientation. However, the religious belief and convictions of a number of religious groups mean that they would wish to avoid being put in a position of having, as they would see it, to promote a gay and lesbian lifestyle, as distinct from not treating somebody equitably purely because of their sexual orientation. However, many gay people, including within religious groups (such as within the Lesbian and Gay Christian Movement) would hold that for gay and lesbian people to be treated in a fair and equitable way it is not possible to separate out their sexual expression from their identity as a whole in order to be 'half accepted'.

Much of the public debate centred on concerns raised by the Roman Catholic Church about whether the regulations would, in effect, mean that Catholic adoption agencies might need to close down, due to withdrawal of public funds if they did not consider the placing of adoptees with gay and lesbian applicants. Although concerns about the legislation were shared by significant groups inside the Church of England, it should be noted that the Church of England Children's Society had for some years already been operating on the basis of the needs of the child being the key criterion for placement rather than the sexual arrangements of the applicants and so it did not itself find the Regulations threatening in relation to its practice which had already, for some years, not ruled out adoptions by gay and lesbian couples.

However, as with the proposals for faith-based schools to accept a proportion of pupils of faiths other than the one on which the ethos of the school was founded, the strong position taken by the Catholic Church hierarchy nationally resulted in ecumenical Christian partners also acting on its behalf in terms of highlighting the issues posed in relation to the religious freedom to hold and practise traditional Catholic doctrine, and thus bringing into focus the tension between two equalities 'strands'.

5 Religious Diversity, Social Cohesion, Terrorism and Security

Study Activity 19

After reading the next sections of the chapter:

(i)   *describe* the context in which policy has moved from an emphasis on 'multiculturalism' to an emphasis on 'cohesion'

(ii) *discuss* how far the shift from 'multiculturalism' to 'cohesion' represents a real change in government policy and how far it is a 'repackaging' of previous policy

(iii) *evaluate* the usefulness and limitations of the models from Irish experience set out in Panels 11 and 12 for understanding and addressing some of the present tensions with regard to perceived separatism, extremism and terrorism

From Diversity to Social Cohesion

Already, in the light of *The Satanic Verses* controversy, an editorial (18 February 1989) in the generally liberal UK newspaper, the *Independent*, under the title 'Limits to mutual tolerance', had noted with regard to the multicultural policy approach originally espoused by Roy Jenkins that,

> Roy Jenkins' philosophy was predicated on the expectation that the minorities would also demonstrate tolerance, and the implicit belief that all manifestations of cultural diversity would be benign. It is becoming disturbingly apparent that this is not the case. The time has therefore come for an examination of how a tolerant, multi-cultural society should handle the intolerant behaviour on the part of a minority.

In fact, it should be noted that in response to *The Satanic Verses* controversy even Roy Jenkins (1989) himself had been recorded as saying, 'In retrospect, we might have been more cautious about allowing the creation in the 1950s of

substantial Muslim communities here.' In connection with *The Satar*
controversy, the writer Fay Weldon (1989: 31) had put it even mo*
claiming that, 'Our attempt at multiculturalism has failed. The Rushdie A*
demonstrates it.'

During the 1990s, questions increasingly began to be raised about the potential
dangers of traditional 'multiculturalism' failing to address new social developments and realities (Alibhai-Brown, 2000). But it was following the summer 2001
disturbances in the northern towns that questions about how 'social cohesion'
can be achieved became very much a part of the agenda of national and local
government. Some of the issues involved were explored in the Denham (2001)
report on *Cohesive Communities* and the Cantle (2001) report on *Community
Cohesion*.

The reference to 'cohesive' and 'cohesion' in the titles of these reports signalled
an important shift in government thinking, influenced also by the shock of the
9/11 attacks in the USA on the World Trade Center and the Pentagon. This
contrasted with the emphasis taken within the overall approach of the earlier,
independent, 'Parekh Report' of the Commission on the Future of Multi-Ethnic
Britain (2000) that had been commissioned by the Runnymede Trust. Instead
of an emphasis on cohesion, this advocated a vision of the UK based on a
'community of communities'.

Bombings, Extremism and Religion

The emphasis on 'cohesion' continued to develop and, furthermore, gathered pace
and intensity following the Madrid train bombing of March 2004 and, most close
to home, the London Transport bombings of 7 July 2005 which resulted in the
deaths of 52 people and the injury of 700 others. These events, followed quickly
by the failed attempts of 21/7, resulted in what might be described as a 'social
policy shock'. Although parts of the UK – especially in Northern Ireland, and at
periods also in London and Birmingham – had previously experienced high levels
of terror violence by the Provisional IRA in pursuit of British withdrawal from the
north of Ireland, there was a widespread sense that these most recent atrocities
were different in nature.

First of all, the bombers acted without regard to their own personal safety and
security. Indeed, from videos later seen that were made by those who took part in
the 7/7 bombings, it was evident that the fact that these bombings brought death
to their perpetrators was something that was not to be avoided, but, rather, to
be embraced by them, being understood as an act of martyrdom. Indeed, these
attacks were the first instance of such 'suicide bombings' to have occurred in
Europe and were later officially claimed by Al-Qaeda. Secondly, they were perpe-
trated not by people coming from outside the country but by young men who had

been brought up in the UK and who were, to all outward appearances, integrated members of British society. On 1 September 2005, a tape featuring Mohammad Sidique Khan, one of the bombers, was broadcast on the Arab satellite TV station, al-Jazeera, in which he explained that,

> I and thousands like me are forsaking everything for what we believe. Our drive and motivation doesn't come from tangible commodities that this world has to offer. Our religion is Islam, obedience to the one true God and following the footsteps of the final prophet messenger.
>
> Your democratically elected governments continuously perpetuate atrocities against my people all over the world. And your support of them makes you directly responsible, just as I am directly responsible for protecting and avenging my Muslim brothers and sisters.
>
> Until we feel security you will be our targets and until you stop the bombing, gassing, imprisonment and torture of my people we will not stop this fight. We are at war and I am a soldier. Now you too will taste the reality of this situation.
>
> (Source: Wikisource at: http://en.wikisource.org/wiki/Tape_of_Mohammad_Sidique_Khan)

Among Muslims, for those with an awareness of the conflicts in the world there can be a strong attraction involved in turning the traditional understanding of the world as divided into *dar al-harb* (referring to territory that lies outside the sway of Islam) and *dar al-Islam* (referring to those lands in which Islam has taken root) into a completely dichotomous approach to the western world, with which an apocalyptic struggle must be waged – as illustrated in the tape of the 7/7 bomber. Therefore, in the wake of the London Transport bombings, the government launched a 'Preventing Extremism Together' initiative and created joint 'Task Forces' together with members of the Muslim communities in order to address these issues within that community.

Resources from Ireland

In the atmosphere of heightened tension consequent upon the impact of foreign and military policy abroad, terror attacks at home, and popular anxiety arising from this for the future of a cohesive society it may be that there is value in learning from dimensions of the historical conflict over Ireland. In their instructive book *Moving Beyond Sectarianism: Religion, Conflict and Reconciliation in Northern Ireland* Joseph Liechty and Cecelia Clegg explain the deep-seated and multi-layered admixture of Protestant and Catholic religion and Loyalist/Unionist and Republican/Nationalist politics that has manifested itself all too often and with such devastating effect in the phenomenon of 'sectarianism' as found in Northern Ireland.

Such an approach to 'the others' can be characterized in ways set out in Panel 11. In addition to these characteristics of 'sectarianism', Liechty and Clegg also identify what they call a 'scale of sectarian danger' through which the conflictual 'temperature' and destructive potential of 'sectarianism' is escalated by words and by actions and which is set out in Panel 12:

Panel 11: Sectarianism, Communalism and Religion

… a system of attitudes, actions, beliefs and structures

- at personal, communal and institutional levels
- that always involves religion, and typically involves a negative mixing of religion and politics

… which arises as a distorted expression of positive human needs especially for belonging, identity, and the free expression of difference

… and is expressed in destructive patterns of relating:

- hardening the boundaries between groups
- overlooking others
- belittling, dehumanizing, or demonizing others
- justifying or collaborating in the domination of others
- physically or verbally intimidating or attacking others

Liechty and Clegg (2001: 102–3)

Panel 12: A 'Scale of Sectarian Danger'

1. We are different, we behave differently

2. We are right

3. We are right and you are wrong

4. You are a less adequate version of what we are

5. You are not what you say you are

6. We are in fact what you say you are

7. What you are doing is evil

8. You are so wrong that you forfeit ordinary rights

9. You are less than human

10. You are evil

11. You are demonic

Liechty and Clegg (2001: 245)

Separatism, Segregation, Visible Difference and Diversity

The change of approach to social policy that accompanied a general sense of alarm following 7/7 was highlighted in a statement released by the Chair of the former Commission for Racial Equality, Trevor Phillips, on 22 September 2005. In this, Phillips (2005) argued that

> the aftermath of 7/7 forces us to assess where we are. And here is where I think we are: we are sleepwalking our way to segregation. We are becoming strangers to each other, and we are leaving communities to be marooned outside the mainstream.

At a government level, following a 2006 Cabinet reshuffle, the emphasis on 'cohesion' led to the establishment of a Race, Cohesion and Faiths Directorate in what was then the newly created Department for Communities and Local Government (DCLG). The new Directorate continues the work initiated by the former Faith Communities Unit in the Home Office, but it connected this with the wider agendas of race and cohesion. It is responsible for tackling racism, extremism and hate, as well as for promoting inter-faith activity in England and Wales. It also engages with faith communities to ensure government policies and services are delivered in appropriate and equitable ways. In 2006, against the background of the developing concerns around 'cohesion', the DCLG set up a Commission on Integration and Cohesion that reported in 2007.

During 2006, many of these general concerns and policy trends were symbolically clustered around a series of statements by high-profile Labour politicians criticizing some forms of head covering worn by some Muslim women. Until then, in the UK – and in contrast with the situation in France – this had generally been a matter that had been handled by relatively low-key negotiations at the local level. What now took place, however, was a series of media statements by leading Labour politicians, which appeared to have all the hallmarks of a co-ordinated use of the media rather than a random collection of unrelated initiatives.

These statements began with Rt. Hon. Jack Straw, Member of Parliament for Blackburn (a constituency with a very high proportion of Muslim residents) and former Labour Government Home Secretary who had, in the past, been quite strongly associated with initiatives to address discrimination and unfair treatment on the basis of religion. In October 2006 Straw suggested to the local newspaper, the *Lancashire Evening Telegraph,* that women wearing a *niqab* can inhibit good community relations. *Niqab* is the term used for a piece of cloth that covers the face and, sometimes, through a transparent part, the eyes also. *Hijab* – which is much more common and refers to the covering of the body except the face and hands – is generally seen by Muslim scholars as obligatory. However, there are differences of view concerning the *niqab*, with only a minority of scholars seeing this as obligatory.

Straw explained that he had asked women visiting his constituency surgeries to consider uncovering their noses and mouths in order, in his opinion, to allow for better communication. He made clear that he did not support a legal ban on the wearing of such coverings, but also stated that he wanted Muslim women to abandon the practice. It is against this background that politicians and some parts of civil society have increasingly engaged in challenging a perceived 'separatism' on the part of Muslims and have emphasized a need for shared values and social cohesion.

From an alternative perspective, in a 20 November 2006 piece on 'Blame it on the Burka' in the online journal *Catalyst: Debating Race, Identity, Culture and Citizenship*, Fareena Alam (2006) wrote, 'Thousands of column inches have been laid at the altar of six square inches of fabric.' Alam also noted that:

> The day Straw issues his pained desire to look at the faces of veiled Muslim women, a Muslim woman was assaulted in East London and had her hijab pulled off. A Liverpool woman's niqab was torn off at a bus stop by an elderly white man, and a young woman wearing a niqab in Straw's Blackburn constituency was verbally abused by three youths. ... Dozens of similar incidents occurred throughout the country.

Towards the Future

The diversities of religion and belief in the UK and the opportunities and issues that arise from this are complex and challenging (Verma, 1990; Parekh, 2000; Weller, 2006a, 2006b). This complexity is intensified by the fact that communities and individuals in the UK do not live in a national vacuum. Rather, they live at the intersection between the global and the local in a world that is both increasingly globalizing and localizing. They are simultaneously part of transnational communities of information and solidarity, while also sharing in the civic society of the state of which they are citizens. In the UK, as elsewhere in the world, religious groups and those motivated by secular visions have great potential to contribute to the common good, but they can also become sources of fragmentation and conflict.

Since in the popular mind post-7/7 and 9/11 Muslims have often become associated with the violence and destructiveness that can be associated with religion, it is perhaps important to close with some words by a Turkish Muslim scholar, Fethullah Gülen. Gülen comes from a context in Turkey that has known severe tension and sometimes outright conflict between ideological secularists who aim to keep religion out of public life, and political Islamists who wish to implement a society ruled by religious norms.

As a traditional Muslim scholar, Gülen has spoken clearly and unambiguously against terrorism in the name of Islam. The movement associated with his teaching has been involved in education and civil society initiatives that have engaged with people of all faiths and none. And Gülen stands against all ways of thinking and acting that may promote the illusion that the uncomfortable plurality of the contemporary world can simply be abolished. Against such illusions Gülen (2004: 249–50) warns that:

> different beliefs, races, customs and traditions will continue to cohabit in this village. Each individual is like a unique realm unto themselves; therefore the desire for all humanity to be similar to one another is nothing more than wishing for the impossible. For this reason, the peace of this (global) village lies in respecting all these differences, considering these differences to be part of our nature and in ensuring that people appreciate these differences. Otherwise, it is unavoidable that the world will devour itself in a web of conflicts, disputes, fights, and the bloodiest of wars, thus preparing the way for its own end.

The challenge facing those of diverse religion and belief and the wider states and societies in which they are set is that of encouraging the common visions and structures necessary for sustaining an integrated but richly diverse community, but avoiding both assimilation or fragmentation. Now, more than ever recognized for much of the twentieth century, it is recognized that societies and states need to respond in positive ways to the challenges and opportunities presented by increasing religious diversity. At the same time, it is also more evident than ever that religious communities themselves will need to develop still further their own responsibilities within the civil societies of which they are a part and, at all levels of their organization and activity, intensify their commitment to the development of positive inter-faith relations and to the furtherance of the common good.

Resources for Further Learning

Alam, F. (2006), 'Blame it on the Burkha'. *Catalyst: Debating Race, Identity, Culture and Citizenship*, 20 November 2006.

Alibhai-Brown, Y. (2000), *After Multiculturalism*. London: Foreign Policy Centre.

Arbitration, Conciliation and Advisory Service (2003), *Religion or Belief and the Workplace: A Guide for Employers and Employees*. London: ACAS.

Bauman, G. (1996), *Contesting Cultures: Discourses of Identity in Multi-Ethnic Britain*. Cambridge: Cambridge University Press.

Bauman, G. (1999), *The Multicultural Riddle: Rethinking National, Ethnic and Religious Identities*. London: Routledge.

Beclett, C. and Macey, M. (2001), 'Race, gender and sexuality: the oppression of multiculturalism'. *Women's Studies International Forum*, 24, 3–4, 309–19.

Bradney, A. (1993), *Religions, Rights and Laws*. Leicester: Leicester University Press.

British Council of Churches (1976), *The New Black Presence in Britain: A Christian Scrutiny*. London: British Council of Churches.

Cantle, T. (2001), *Building Cohesive Communities: A Report of the Ministerial Group Chaired by John Denham*. London: The Home Office.

Charlton, R. and Kay, R. (1985–6), 'The politics of religious slaughter: an ethno-religious case study'. *New Community*, 12, 3, 409–503.

Cohn-Sherbok, D. ed. (1990), *The Canterbury Papers: Essays on Religion and Society*. London: Bellew Publishing.

Commission for Racial Equality (1990), *Britain a Plural Society: Report of a Seminar*. London: Commission for Racial Equality.

Commission for Racial Equality (1997), *Religious Discrimination: Your Rights*. London: Commission for Racial Equality.

Commission on the Future of Multi-Ethnic Britain (2000), *The Future of Multi-Ethnic Britain*. London: Profile Books.

Commission on British Muslims and Islamophobia (2001), *Addressing the Challenge of Islamophobia*. London: Commission on British Muslims and Islamophobia.

Cumper, P. (2003), 'Religious discrimination in Britain: new opportunities and fresh challenges within employment', in N. Ghanea, ed., *The Challenge of Religious Discrimination at the Dawn of the New Millennium*. Leiden: Martinus Nijhoff Publishers, pp. 157–84.

Denham, J. (2001), *Community Cohesion: Report of the Independent Review Team Chaired by Ted Cantle*. London: The Home Office.

Dusche, M. (2005), 'Multiculturalism, communitarianism and liberal pluralism', in J. Malik and H. Reifeld, eds, *Religious Pluralism in South Asia and Europe*. New Delhi: Oxford University Press, pp. 120–44.

Eberle, C. (2002), *Religious Conviction in Liberal Politics*. Cambridge: Cambridge University Press.

Edge, P. (1998), 'The European Court of Human Rights and religious beliefs'. *International Comparative Law Quarterly*, 47, 680–7.

Edge, P. (2006), *Religion and Law: An Introduction*. Aldershot: Ashgate.

Edge, P. and Harvey, G., eds (2000), *Law and Religion in Contemporary Society: Communities, Individualism and the State*. Aldershot: Ashgate.

Evans, C. (2001), *Freedom of Religion Under the European Convention on Human Rights*. London: Oxford University Press.

Evans, M. (1997), *Religious Liberty and International Law in Europe*. Cambridge: Cambridge University Press.

Ghanea, N., ed. (2006), *The Challenge of Religious Discrimination at the Dawn of the New Millennium*. Leiden: Martinus Nijhoff Publishers.

Ghanea, N., Stephens, A. and Walden, R., eds (2007), *Does God Believe in Human Rights?: Essays on Religion and Human Rights*. Leiden: Martinus Nijhoff Publishers.

Gülen, F. (2004), *Towards a Global Civilization of Love and Tolerance*. New Jersey: The Light.

Hepple, B. and Choudhary, T. (2001), *Tackling Religious Discrimination: Practical Implications for Policy Makers and Legislators*. (Home Office Research Study 221). London: Research, Development and Statistics Directorate, The Home Office.

Husband, C. (1994), 'The political context of Muslim communities' participation in British society', in B. Lewis and D. Schnapper, eds, *Muslims in Europe*. London: Pinter, pp. 79–97.

Inner Cities Religious Council (1996), *Challenging Religious Discrimination: A Guide for Faith Communities and their Advisers*. London: Inner Cities Religious Council.

Jenkins, R. (1967), *Essays and Speeches*. London: Collins.

Kabbani, R. (1989), *Letter to Christendom*. London: Virago.

Kaye, R. (1993), 'The politics of religious slaughter of animals: strategies for ethno-religious political action'. *New Community*, 19, 2, 235–50.

Liechty, J. and Clegg, C. (2001), *Moving Beyond Sectarianism: Religion, Conflict and Reconciliation in Northern Ireland*. Dublin: The Colomba Press.

Malik, J. and Reifeld, H., eds (2005), *Religious Pluralism in South Asia and Europe*. New Delhi: Oxford University Press.

Modood, T. (1998), 'Anti-essentialism, multiculturalism and the "recognition" of religious groups'. *Journal of Political Philosophy*, 4, 4, 378–99.

Modood, T. and Werbner, P., eds (1997), *The Politics of Multiculturalism in the New Europe: Racism, Identity and Community*. London: Zed Books.

Modood, T. and Werbner, P., eds (1997), *Debating Cultural Hybridity: Multi-Cultural Identities and the Politics of Anti-Racism*. London: Zed Books.

Parekh, B. (1990), 'Britain and the social logic of pluralism', in Commission for Racial Equality, *Britain a Plural Society: Report of a Seminar*. London: Commission for Racial Equality, pp. 58–78.

Parekh, B. (2000), *Rethinking Multiculturalism: Cultural Diversity and Political Theory*. Basingstoke: Macmillan Press.

Parsons, G. (1994), 'Introduction: Deciding how far you can go', in G. Parsons, ed., *The Growth of Religious Diversity in Britain from 1945. Volume II. Issues*. London: Routledge, pp. 5–21.

Pearl, D. (1986), *Family Law and the Immigrant Communities*. London: Jordan's.

Phillips, T. (2005), 'After 7/7: sleepwalking to segregation'. *Commission for Racial Equality*. 22 September 2005.

Poulter, S. (1986), *English Law and Ethnic Minority Customs*. London: Butterworth's.

Poulter, S. (1990), *Asian Traditions and English Law: A Handbook*. Stoke-on-Trent: Trentham Books.

Poulter, S. (1990), 'Cultural pluralism and its limits: a legal perspective', in Commission for Racial Equality, *Britain a Plural Society: Report of a Seminar*. London: Commission for Racial Equality, pp. 3–28.

Poulter, S. (1998), *Ethnicity, Law and Human Rights: The English Experience*. Oxford: Clarendon Press.

Rex, J. (1985), *The Concept of a Multi-Cultural Society*. Coventry: University of Warwick Centre for Research in Ethnic Relations.

Rex, J. (1996), *Ethnic Minorities in the Modern Nation State: Working Papers in the Theory of Multi-Culturalism and Political Integration*. Basingstoke: Macmillan Press.

Robilliard, St. John (1984), *Religion and the Law: Religious Liberty in Modern English Law*. Manchester: Manchester University Press.

Runnymede Trust, The (1997), *Islamophobia: A Challenge for Us All*. London: Runnymede Trust.

Saghal, G. and Yuval-Davis, N., eds (1992), *Refusing Holy Orders: Women and Fundamentalism in Britain*. London: Virago Press.

Taylor, C. (1992), *Multiculturalism and the Politics of Recognition*. Princeton: Princeton University Press.

Trigg, R. (2007), *Religion in Public Life: Must Faith be Privatized?*. Oxford: Oxford University Press.

UK Committee on Islamic Affairs (1993), *Muslims and the Law in Multi-Faith Britain: The Need for Reform*. London: UK Committee on Islamic Affairs.

Verma, G. (1990), 'Pluralism: some theoretical and practical considerations', in Commission for Racial Equality, *Britain a Plural Society: Report of a Seminar*. London: Commission for Racial Equality, pp. 44–57.

Weldon, F. (1989), *Sacred Cows: A Portrait of Britain, Post-Rushdie, Pre-Utopia*. London: Chatto and Windus.

Weller, P. (2003), 'The dimensions and dynamics of religious discrimination: findings and analysis from the UK', in N. Ghanea, ed., *The Challenge of Religious Discrimination at the Dawn of the New Millennium*. Leiden: Martinus Nijhoff Publishers, pp. 57–81.

Weller, P. (2006a), '"Human rights", "religion" and the "secular": variant configurations of religion(s), state(s) and society(ies)'. *Religion and Human Rights: An International Journal*, 1,1, 17–39.

Weller, P. (2006b), 'Addressing religious discrimination and Islamophobia: Muslims and liberal democracies. The case of the United Kingdom'. *Journal of Islamic Studies*. September, 17: 295–325.

Weller, P. (2007), '"Human rights", "religion" and the "secular": variant configurations of religion(s), state(s) and society(ies)", in N. Ghanea, A. Stephens and R. Walden, eds, *Does God Believe in Human Rights?: Essays on Religion and Human Rights*. Leiden: Martinus Nijhoff Publishers, pp. 147–79.

Weller, P. and Purdam, K., et al. (2000), *Religious Discrimination in England and Wales: Executive Summary of an Interim Report*. Derby: University of Derby.

Weller, P., Feldman, A. and Purdam, K., et al. (2001), *Religious Discrimination in England and Wales*. (Home Office Research Study 220). London: Research, Development and Statistics Directorate, The Home Office.

Wilson, B. (1990), 'Old laws and new religions', in D. Cohn-Sherbok, ed., *The Canterbury Papers: Essays on Religion and Society*. London: Bellew Publishing, pp. 210–24.

Wolffe, J., ed. (1993), *The Growth of Religious Diversity: Britain From 1945. A Reader*. Sevenoaks: Hodder and Stoughton.

Yarrow, S. (1997), *Religious and Political Discrimination in the Workplace*. London: Policy Studies Institute.

Yuval-Davis, N. (1992), 'Fundamentalism, multiculturalism and women in Britain', in J. Donald and A. Rattansi, eds, *'Race' Culture and Difference*. London: Sage, pp. 278–91.

Index

Religions in the UK:
2007-2010 Directory
ISBN 978 0 901437 30 3

Over 300 pages, plus CD-ROM with organizational entries

Religions in the UK has become the standard work of reference on the United Kingdom's faith communities, their organizations and places of worship.

Previous editions were widely welcomed for their unique and comprehensive coverage.

The directory is a one-stop-shop for organizations looking for accessible reference material and information about the nine world religious traditions with substantial communities in the UK.

Edited by Paul Weller, Professor of Inter-Religious Relations at the University of Derby.

To purchase your copy today please contact:

The Multi-Faith Centre
University of Derby
Kedleston Road, Derby, DE22 1GB
Tel: 01332 591285
Email: mfc@derby.ac.uk

A joint project between the Multi-Faith Centre at the University of Derby and The University of Derby.